Cycling the Rhine Route

Cycling the Rhine Route

**Bicycle Touring Along the Historic Rhine River
From the North Sea to Switzerland**

John Powell

Photographs and maps by the author

Cycling Resources
books are published by
Van der Plas Publications / Cycle Publishing, San Francisco

Published by
Van der Plas Publications
1282 7th Avenue
San Francisco, CA, 94122
U.S.A.

Distributed or represented to the book trade by:
U.S.A.:	Seven Hills Book Distributing, Cincinnati, OH
U.K.:	Chris Lloyd Sales and Marketing, Poole, Dorset
Canada:	Hushion House Publishing, Toronto, ONT
Australia:	Tower Books, Frenchs Forest, NSW

Publisher's Disclaimer
We acknowledge that wearing a helmet while cycling can significantly reduce the risk in case of accident, collision, or fall. Any cyclists depicted in this book riding without a helmet are doing so strictly as a matter of personal choice and does not imply the publisher's endorsement.

Publisher's Cataloging in Publication Data
Powell, Frederic John Winchcombe, 1946–
Cycling the Rhine Route: Bicycle Touring Along the Historic Rhine River from the North Sea to Switzerland /John Powell. San Francisco, CA: Van der Plas Publications., 2000.
p. ill., maps;   21.6 cm.   Includes index and bibliography
Summary: Gives background information and route descriptions, with route maps, for bicycle tour from the Netherlands to Switzerland, via Germany and France, following the Rhine River.
ISBN: 1-892495-23-6
LCCN: 99-71323
1. Bicycle touring - Europe - Directories 2. Bicycle trails - Europe - Guidebooks
3. Europe - Bicycle touring - Guidebooks. I. Powell, John II. Title

Dedicated to the memory of my good friends
Vincent Imbrailo,
Paul de Beer,
Tony Wray,
who took the shortcut.

Acknowledgments

Multiple thanks are due to:

Caroline for support, belief, sympathy, and when needed, a good kick.

For assistance, information and co-operation, especially the German National Tourist Board (DZT) in London; Virgin Atlantic Airways Ltd., of Crawley; KLM Royal Dutch Airlines and their partners, Northwest Airlines.

For support and humor, to Richard and Jane (Jindapon) Bell of Broadstairs and Margate (England) Youth Hostels, and for much assistance, especially photo printing and top advice, Ed and Jan Yorath of Ramsgate. Thanks too, to Friederike and Dave of Margate, for space.

About the Author

John Powell was born in Pietermaritzburg, South Africa and educated at St. Charles' College in that city. He worked in the telecommunications engineering sector in South Africa for some years before leaving to travel and work in Europe.

On his return to Africa he worked and traveled widely in what was then Rhodesia (and is now Zimbabwe), Mozambique, and Botswana, as well as in South Africa.

His curiosity about almost everything led him into many different fields, from ship-chandling to the dairy industry, and he continued to travel extensively in Southern Africa.

After a spell of working in youth hostels in England, he returned to Africa and was involved in managing Backpacker hostels.

A holiday cruise on the Rhine persuaded him to explore the entire river by bicycle, and this book is the result of a number of these journeys between the Netherlands and Switzerland. He lives in East Kent, England.

Table of Contents

Introduction

The Rhine river is the most important waterway in Europe. Not only does the Rhine provide direct access to the very heart of the continent, but this route offers the fascination of over two thousand years of recorded and visible history.

From the North Sea to Switzerland, you can cycle a great deal of the route within sight and sound of the river. Ancient towpaths, country roads and dike-top tracks, provide largely motor-traffic free zones. Even in the cities encountered along the way, the bike paths often hug the river banks, passing through parks, woodlands and gardens.

Air quality in industrialized areas has improved dramatically since the 1970s. The advice previously given to cyclists to avoid the Ruhr region of the Rhine valley because of air pollution, is even more oridiculous today than it was twenty years ago.

Rhine water quality has shown dramatic improvement. Between 1971 and 1990, for instance, the concentration of mercury and cadmium in the waters of the Lower Rhine decreased by 90%. Oxygen content increased by 50%.

Fishes have been re-introduced to the Rhine where it had once become impossible for them to live and the river is on the way to becoming the living artery of nature it once was.

The Rhine is navigable to sea-going ships up to Mannheim, 600 kilometers upstream, and to Basel in Switzerland by river boats. Mannheim, once the largest inland port in Europe, has now been displaced by Duisburg. Most of the Rhine ships are built at Duisburg, which is strategically situated at the confluence of the Ruhr and Rhine rivers. Strasbourg, the major French city on the Rhine, is the fourth biggest port in France.

The route described in this guide begins at the mouth of the "Old" Rhine at Katwijk aan Zee, on the North Sea coast of the Netherlands. Since the Great Flood of AD 839, when the course of the Rhine was changed, the main flow of the river has been down the Lek and the Waal rivers. Nowadays only about 0.2% of the Rhine's waters reach the sea lock at Katwijk. There is no longer a natural Rhine mouth, the water passing into the North Sea through many outlets, including the artificial "mouth" created at Hoek van Holland.

This route passes through Dutch countryside, into ancient towns and cities, then across the German border. It meanders on across the Rhine plain, through the narrow gorge to the Rhine

Rift Valley. Here the river becomes the boundary between France and Germany. On the French side of the river lies Alsace, in essence French, in character, German. At the meeting-point of Germany, France and Switzerland, this journey ends — at the city of Basel.

To reach your destination, you will travel between tilled fields, through riverine forest glades, past hills and valleys adorned with grape vines, under lowering castle-topped cliffs and brooding mountains, into cities vibrant with living culture; seagoing ships and barges carrying passengers and cargo on the waterways add to the magical movement and life of the Rhinelands.

The most loved myths and legends of Germanic peoples have originated in the Rhinelands. The Knight of the Swan, Lohengrin, son of Parsifal, guardian of the Holy Grail, came to Kleve to rescue Elsa of Brabant from the tyrant Frederick of Telramund. The greatest Rhine legend, the Nibelungenlied, unfolds along the river from the Netherlands to the Burgundian city of Worms. Virtually every twist and turn of the Rhine will bring you into the domain of yet another tale.

For those who don't have the time or inclination to cycle the entire route, there are abundant opportunities to ride the trail. You can begin anywhere from Basel to the coast, cycling selected parts of the route, taking the train or motoring in between.

Whatever choice you make, you can be sure that the people you meet along the way will be friendly and helpful, and the Rhine route will de-

In the Delta Region of Holland, most of the waters of the Rhine flow through various distributaries. The original course of the river, followed by our route, is now the small stream called the Old Rhine, shown here at the river lock near Harmelen.

liver every type of mood and magic you could wish for.

How Difficult Will It Be ? Who Can Do It ?

In general terms, the cycling is mostly pretty easy. Of course, it all depends on your overall fitness, your preparation, physical, mental, and logistical. For an average cyclist, the degree of difficulty can technically be described as easy to moderate. This book was written with cyclists of all abilities in mind, so whatever route you choose, you can adapt the information to your specific needs.

The Rhine, on its journey from Basel to the sea, drops a mere 245 meters (800 feet) in the 850 kilometers (530 miles) of its course, on average, in the reverse direction, a rise of one meter every three and a half kilometers (3 feet every 2 miles). There are some steep sections, usually on deviations from the river bank, but few are long. Of course, there is no sin in stopping to admire a view, or pushing your bike up a slope to stretch your legs. If you have any doubts about your fitness, check with your doctor. You'll probably find that you'll be encouraged to get some exercise. It's always a good idea to have a physical check-up before doing a trip such as this.

Away from the river banks, a broad selection of circular routes and suggestions presents opportunities for more robust cycling activity, or equally, gentle riding. The waters of the tributaries of the Rhine come hurtling forcefully down from the mountains as often as they meekly join the mainstream with hardly a ripple. In the valleys and gorges of these streams and rivers, you can usually find quiet roads and ancient villages to explore. There are so

Alsatian riverside scene, south of the Ottenheim barrage, Germany.

many options that you will easily find those that suit your needs and limitations.

Pacing yourself is an important factor in cycle touring. It's supposed to be fun, remember, neither painful nor a chore. There are many books about how to cycle, cycling diets, how to choose a bicycle and touring equipment, and every other aspect of two-wheel (or three-wheel), self-propelled activity. Every book I've read on the subject has contributed in one way or another to the pleasure I get from cycle touring; you can never know too much, only too little.

How Much Time Is Needed ?

If you're very fit and you only want to collect miles, you could cycle from the North Sea to Basel in 6 days.

If you want to enjoy the scenery and the sights, it'll take as long as you want. You could easily spend an active and interesting six months along the way. Most people don't have the opportunity to spend more than a few weeks at a time on such a trip, so detailed planning is a prerequisite.

If you're an average cyclist and you spend about four hours a day in the saddle, you'll probably travel at most, around 64 kilometers (40 miles). Any more time spent cycling will reduce your opportunities to explore and to enjoy your surroundings.

It's also a good idea to plan rest days, to let your body recover. This all depends on your age, physical condition, the way you cycle and other factors, but rest days are a must.

You can decide to cycle specific sections of the route, motoring, taking the train or even traveling by boat in between. There are areas where you could go hiking or enjoy activities other than cycling. Whatever you decide, your holiday in the Rhine valley will be full of unforgettable moments.

2
Suitability for Cycle Touring

The region covered by the Rhine route is a wonderful area for touring by bike, although it varies from country to country. Each country has its own tradition of bicycle use.

There is a healthy cycling culture in the Netherlands. In this country of 15 million people, there are about 12 million bicycles and 10,000 kilometers (6,200 miles) of bike paths.

Dutch motorists who, broadly speaking, are also cyclists at times, are mostly respectful of cyclists. There are heavy penalties for those who exhibit anti-cyclist (anti-social) tendencies.

Germany, like the Netherlands, has a vibrant cycling culture. Thanks to the effective political clout of the Green Party, and the nature of the people, there are facilities for cycling that rival those in the Netherlands.

Being a large country with diverse geographical features, there are far more physical barriers to movement than you find in the Netherlands. Then again, there are more opportunities to cycle.

Alongside the river there are no hills to negotiate; sometimes you may have to ride through a dip to avoid a lock or a slipway area. At times the cycle track is drawn away from the river bank to skirt factories or harbors. On the river banks sometimes there are quarries (where gravel and sand is dredged from the riverbed) to bypass.

German motorists display a healthy respect for cyclists, more, I have been told, out of fear of damaging their beloved vehicles than consideration for their fellow road users. But whatever the reason, I have never found it too disagreeable to cycle (willing or not) on a busy German roadway.

Where I have had to share a bike path with moped (Motorfahrrad or "Mofa") riders, I have never had anything but consideration from the motorized brigade, so I presume that is the general trend. You may also encounter motorcycle policemen patrolling bike paths, which is a very comforting sight in a foreign country.

The French are exceptionally keen cyclists; they can boast the greatest cycle road race in the world, the Tour de France. There are cycle-friendly towns and cities in Alsace and there are dedicated bike paths as well.

The upper Rhine valley was canalized to improve navigation and, more importantly, to control flooding. As the canals were built on French soil, access to the Rhine river b90ank from that side is cut off to a certain degree.

French motorists, particularly truckers are, in general, considerate of cyclists. However, it's always a good idea to be prepared to observe the rule of "give way to traffic approaching from the right," even at minor intersections, especially in country areas and villages.

The Swiss city of Basel (Basle or Bâle) hosted the International Velo-City Conference in 1995. Participants agreed that it is definitely a cycle-friendly city. Cars have largely been excluded from the city center by the introduction of pedestrian areas and the use of tram systems which extend out of town and even out of the country. City bike paths and the rule allowing cyclists to travel contrary to the motor traffic flow along one-way streets, make Basel a pleasure to cycle around.

In Switzerland there are some bike paths outside the cities and where they exist, you are obliged to use them. Footpaths are forbidden to cyclists however, and only designated bike paths may be used. In the Basel area there is a network of about 80 kilometers of bike paths.

When to Go

My favorite time of year for cycling on the Rhine is April to June. Nearer the coast, the temperatures can get quite low at night, but generally the daytime temperatures are comfortable. Inland, April temperatures are relatively high for that far north, as evidenced by the early blooming fruit trees in the Rheingau. Late summer (September through October) is similar, though usually warmer.

July and August can produce extremely hot days, or week-long rainfall. Also, in summer, one needs to book well ahead for accommodation and stick with arrangements, thereby taking some spontaneity from the trip,

which is one of the cyclists' major freedoms.

Either side of summer, cycle routes tend to be less crowded. In early spring, a disadvantage may be that the riverside tracks are still suffering the effects of winter floods; damage is usually repaired very quickly by maintenance crews, but they have to wait until the river and the weather allow access.

Sunny days bring cyclists of all descriptions out onto the roads and bike paths, especially on weekends and festival holidays. During summertime, many cycle routes become exceptionally busy.

If you start your tour at Basel, you will find that there is little difference in April–May (or September–October) weather compared with the North Sea coast. However, the campsites in the south may be a bit later opening than the north, some by a month or more.

There is sometimes a winter season (November through March) when it is reasonably pleasant to cycle the Rhine route. Some of the best (and wildest) festivals are held at this time of year, especially the pre-Lenten carnivals and Easter time celebrations. I have cycled the Rhine route to Switzerland during a January when temperatures reached 14 degrees C and it rained only one day in three weeks.

The Netherlands:
Springtime and late summer are the best times to travel in the Netherlands. Although it is still relatively cool in April and May, there is less rain than during summer months and the fall. You will seldom have more than a few consecutive days when it won't rain at all. Spring rain normally comes in short sharp showers.

In April, most of the campsites are closed and will only begin opening for the season around the beginning of May.

The flowers, for which the Netherlands are traditionally famous, are blooming in April and May and give the countryside additional appeal. This does bring a lot of visitors though — sometimes as many as in July–August.

June can bring great cycling weather, with long hot sunny days. It can also rain for extended periods. September is another good month to cycle in the Netherlands, with temperatures between those of May and June but generally wetter.

July and August are holiday months and you might find great difficulty getting accommodation, unless you plan and book well in advance. If you have a small tent, you can usually find a campsite manager who will squeeze you into a corner of the camp. Facilities are mostly geared towards maximum occupation, so you shouldn't have to queue for a shower. At this time you'll also get the greatest amount of rain and the highest temperatures. The days are inordinately long, giving lots of daylight time for outdoor activity.

Germany:

My favorite time of year on the German section of the Rhine is May–June. It is a bit cooler than summer, but sometimes can get very hot. The campsites have just opened for the season and aren't as crowded as in July–August. The days are pleasantly long, too, with the longest day coming on June 21. Nights can be quite cold. Some years produce long June downpours, however. September–October is also a good time to cycle the route, when the main holiday season is done and the rains are less frequent.

France:

The Alsatian flower-bedecked towns and the wine route on the lower slopes of the Vosges mountains are an indication of the relative mildness of the climate. However, it can get extremely cold in winter. April to October is the best time for cycling here, though it may rain more often and for longer periods, from June to August.

Switzerland:

April and May are the best times for visiting the Basel area by bicycle, although nights can be very cold. September is another good month to cycle here, as it's still warm and there is less rain than in June–August.

The Weather

We'll look at the typical weather patterns for each of the countries we pass through along the Rhine.

The Netherlands:

The Netherlands has a maritime climate, which is subject to extreme changes in short spaces of time. The summers are warm but can become very hot. Rainfall varies from short showers to week-long downpours. Winters can be harsh. Springtime, though a bit cool, is relatively dry and my favorite time for cycling here.

Along the coast the normal onshore and offshore winds blow at varying strengths; the best way to avoid them is to get an early start and to take a break in the late afternoon. There are no true prevailing winds as such, but what passes for them, away from the

Temperature information for major cities along the route

Max. temp C/F (top line) Min. temp C/F (btm. line)	March	April	May	June	July	August	Sept.	Oct.
Utrecht (Netherlands)	10/49	13/55	18/64	21/70	22/72	22/72	19/67	14/57
	1/34	4/40	8/46	11/51	13/55	13/55	10/50	7/44
Düsseldorf (Germany)	10/49	15/58	18/65	22/72	24/75	23/73	20/68	15/58
	2/36	4/40	8/46	11/51	13/55	13/55	10/50	6/44
Cologne (Germany)	11/51	16/60	20/68	23/73	25/77	24/75	21/70	14/57
	2/36	5/41	8/46	12/53	14/57	14/57	11/51	7/44
Frankfurt (Germany)	11/51	16/60	20/68	23/73	25/77	24/75	21/70	14/57
	2/36	6/43	9/48	13/55	15/58	14/57	11/51	7/44
Strasbourg (France)	9/48	14/57	16/60	23/73	24/75	26/79	21/70	15/58
Basel (Switzerland)	9/48	13/55	18/64	21/70	23/73	23/73	19/66	13/55

coast, generally blow from the west and south-west.

Germany:
The Rhine route from Germany to Switzerland can be divided into three climatic areas. From the Dutch border to the Rhine Gorge (the lower Rhine plain), the climate is temperate, with cold winters and warm summers. There is a maritime influence, making it changeable and cooler than further inland.

The Rhine Gorge area tends to be warmer than the lower Rhine flood plain, as it is sheltered and the ground retains solar heat well. The continental influence makes the weather more stable and predictable.

Average sunshine hours per month

	March	April	May	June	July	August	Sept.	Oct.
Netherlands	128	157	214	218	210	205	148	102
Düsseldorf	124	180	217	180	186	155	150	93
Cologne	124	150	186	210	186	155	150	124
Frankfurt	155	180	248	210	210	186	150	93
Basel	140	163	195	214	232	209	160	109

Average rainfall in mm and inches

Rainfall in mm/ inch	March	April	May	June	July	August	Sept.	Oct.
Utrecht	N/A	49/1.9	52/2.1	58/2.3	77/3.0	87/3.4	72/2.8	72/2.8
Basel	N/A	60/2.4	78/3.1	89/3.5	84/3.3	89/3.5	74/2.9	60/2.4

France (Alsace):

The southernmost section of the Rhine route (especially on the Alsace plain) can become very hot in summer, with heavy and long falls of rain. However, this is also the driest region in France. Winters can be very cold, especially under the influence of the nearby Alps, but are generally quite short in duration for this latitude. Strasbourg is only 138 meters (456 feet) above sea level.

Switzerland:

Switzerland is relatively far south in Europe. Being in the center of the continent, it has a stable climate. In Basel (277 meters/908 feet above sea level) the summers are warm to hot, and the winters extremely cold but with low humidity. Winters however, are generally shorter than on the high ground.

For local weather forecasts:

The Netherlands: phone (06) 8003
Germany: phone (069) 80620
France: phone (05) 36680267 (Bas Rhin),
                phone (05) 36680268 (Haut Rhin)
Switzerland: phone 162
                Road and pass information is available from phone no. 163

3
How to Get There

In this chapter, you will be given the information necessary for getting to and from your route. This includes information regarding airlines' and railways' policies on transporting bikes and other travel tips.

Many Americans, Canadians, Australians, New Zealanders, and South Africans begin their European holidays in the UK, because it's the country with the most familiar language, and a natural springboard to the Continent by ferry, train, automobile or airplane.

From the USA:
From the USA, you can fly directly to a number of United Kingdom (UK) airports from a wide choice of US airports. The major British carrier is British Airways. Virgin Atlantic Airways fly to Europe from New York, Boston, Washington DC, Miami, San Francisco, Los Angeles, and other airports.

The Dutch air carrier KLM has regular flights from the USA (in partnership with Northwest Airlines) to the Netherlands. KLM offers a non-stop service to Amsterdam (Schiphol) from Atlanta, Boston, Chicago, Detroit, Los Angeles, Houston, New York, Orlando, Minneapolis, San Francisco, and Washington (Dulles).

Many airlines regularly fly to Germany from the USA. In partnership with United Airlines and other carriers, the German national airline Lufthansa (Deutsche Lufthansa AG) has a network world-wide. German international airports near the Rhine are Frankfurt am Main (the busiest and best connected), Köln-Bonn, and Düsseldorf. At Frankfurt am Main airport terminal, there is an InterCity train station linking passengers to the whole of Germany and the rest of Europe.

Strasbourg airport is linked to all major airports in Europe, through Air France, Lufthansa, Crossair, Air UK and other carriers.

Flights from the USA to Euro-Airport at St Louis (Basel-Mulhouse airport) are generally via hub airports such as London, Schiphol, and Frankfurt am Main, but there are direct flights as well.

From Canada:
There are direct flights to the Netherlands with KLM from Calgary, Halifax, Montreal, Toronto and Vancouver. Air Canada and other carriers also operate on the Canada–Amsterdam route.

Lufthansa has a scheduled service to Frankfurt am Main from major Canadian airports. Air France and

Swissair fly from Canadian airports to EuroAirport (Saint Louis to Basel–Mulhouse), as well as to Zurich.

From Australasia and Africa:
Australians, New Zealanders and South Africans can fly direct from major airports in their home countries to Amsterdam Schiphol airport, to Frankfurt am Main and to Zurich on regular scheduled services.

From the UK:
Regular daily flights operate from around the UK to Germany; from London Heathrow, Manchester, London City, and Glasgow to Frankfurt am Main, Köln-Bonn and Düsseldorf. You can fly directly to Basel with Crossair and British Airways, from London Heathrow, Manchester, and Birmingham airports. From London City Airport there are regular scheduled flights to Frankfurt am Main.

From Eire:
There are daily flights from Dublin to Frankfurt am Main. You can fly directly to Zurich with Crossair and Aer Lingus.

If you're under 26 years old, you'll find good travel deals offered by various organizations in your country. Many universities have travel departments (e.g. Campus Travel).

Transporting Bicycles by Air

Shop around when buying tickests to get the best price both for yourself and for the bike. Many carriers on long-haul routes to Europe will carry bicycles. Some will only carry single-seaters (i.e. no tandems). Most require that the bike be boxed and will supply boxes for about US $20 each. They nor-mally carry limited stocks of boxes so it's a good idea to order one in advance. Many airports have bicycle boxes for sale, as do bike shops. Your local bike shop probably can give you a box in which bicycles are delivered. Bike box dimensions are typically (as per KLM-Royal Dutch Airlines) length 177 x width 23 x height 102 centimeters (70 x 9 x 40 inches).

Where bikes are taken unboxed, pedals must be removed, handlebars fixed sideways and outstretched parts covered. Unboxed bikes are given lower priority and might not be accepted on your flight. Some airlines don't accept bikes as part of your luggage allowance and will charge them at either excess piece or weight rates. Certain types of aircraft will not accept bikes as luggage, so check this if you have connecting flights. Some aircraft will only carry limited numbers of bicycles, sometimes as few as one.

Excess piece or weight charges are standardized by agreements amongst airlines worldwide, so you gain little in shopping around.

Virgin Atlantic Airways policy is that bicycles must be boxed, with the handlebars fixed sideways. For packing purposes it would be advisable to remove the pedals. Only single seat touring or racing bikes (including fold-ups) are accepted as luggage. Tandems, recliners and trikes are treated as freight.

As the baggage allowance on Virgin Atlantic is two pieces, your boxed bike is treated as one piece of luggage. Any excess baggage is charged at between US $85 and US $110 per piece, depending on routing, at current rates. The Virgin Africa and Australasia routes accept bikes as part of your 20 kilogram baggage allowance, with excess charges being expressed as a percentage (typically 1 to 1.5%) of a specified fare. Flights within Europe with Virgin Atlantic have the same restrictions.

Lufthansa and United airlines carry bicycles on international and internal flights. Bicycles are treated as special excess baggage and there is a charge for this. Bikes cannot be included in your free baggage allowance. Lufthansa requires that pedals be removed, handlebars turned sideways (parallel with the crossbar) and fixed in position. You may be asked to let the air out of the tires. On United Airlines, your bike must be in a bag or box. If you want to take more than one bike, the second and subsequent bikes will be charged as items or will incur excess weight charges.

The current charge for bike transport on Lufthansa is DM 100 (US $50) per bike, per one-way journey outside the IATA-Europe zone, DM 50 (US $25) in the IATA-Europe area. You must make a special request, well in advance, for this service. Often there are restrictions on numbers of bikes carried (usually 4 maximum), depending on the type of aircraft. Tandems and recliners are treated as bulk cargo and the cost of transporting them depends on both weight and dimensions.

Unpacked bikes cannot be carried on Lufthansa airport buses or airport Intercity train connections, but if boxed must be allowed as accompanied luggage.

KLM does not accept tandems, but carries single seater bikes. Northwest Airlines do take tandems (operations reference #NWGBAG BIKE).

Checking in and Collecting Bikes at Airports

You must check in your packed bike as any other piece of luggage. It's best to get to the check-in desk early, so you don't have any last minute hitches to iron out immediately before you leave.

Collecting your bike is the same procedure as for getting your bags in the arrivals hall of the airport. If you send your bike as freight or unaccompanied luggage, you'll have to do a bit more running around. Your airline or shipping agent will tell you what to do.

Warning

Food and Agricultural agencies work with Customs departments to prevent diseases and unwanted foreign plants being imported into their countries. If you are bringing used camping equipment or bikes with you, or taking them home, you will have to declare this to the Customs people at entry and departure points. Failure to do so may lead to these goods being confiscated. Importantly, ensure that everything is spotlessly clean, as dirty equipment will be seen to pose the greatest risk.

If you're bringing, or returning with, any clothes or equipment that have been used around animals or in a farm environment, those items need to be perfectly clean as well. Foodstuffs are also restricted, so check with your local representative of the Food and Agriculture agency before importing or exporting anything. Be particularly careful with fruit, meat, eggs, and dairy products.

Rail and Bicycle

If you make a train reservation and you are taking your bike along as accompanied luggage, you must make a separate reservation for your bicycle. If you do not do this, there may not be space in the bike carriage for your bicycle.

If you are traveling from the UK to start your train journey in Ostend (Belgium), you must buy your bicycle ticket at Ostend railway station, from the luggage clerk. However, you must still have an advance booking for your bicycle. Make sure you have time to get the ticket before the train leaves. A bike ticket from Ostend to Germany costs about BF 400.

Rail passes valid in the Netherlands, Germany, France ,and Switzerland at discounted or cheaper prices cannot all be purchased in those countries. Many must be bought in your home country. The same applies to UK or Eurail passes, which have to be purchased outside the areas they will be used. There are some passes which can be bought in the country of travel, by foreigners, on production of a passport. This also applies to metro and tram passes.

Some night train journeys are cheaper. Discounts are usually given to groups, seniors (over 65), people under 26, members of certain organizations and so on.

United Kingdom:

The Channel Tunnel express train service, Eurostar, leaves from London Waterloo International station and from Ashford (Kent) International station. At Brussels and Paris, you can transfer to trains traveling to the Netherlands, Germany, France, and Switzerland. Bicycles are carried on Eurostar only if they are disassembled and in a proper bicycle bag. Folding bikes, which can be carried aboard as ordinary luggage, must also be in a bike bag.

The Channel Tunnel Shuttle service (le Shuttle) leaves from Folkestone (Kent) terminal and terminates at Calais, France. Bicycle transport is a coach with a bike trailer. Book at least a few days before you travel, longer in summer. At the Calais terminal, you can connect with trains to the Netherlands, Germany, or Switzerland, or join the French freeway system. The undersea tunnel trip takes 30 minutes.

Netherlands:

Most trains carry bicycles but not between 06h00 and 09h00 and from 16h30 to 18h00, Monday through Friday. But on public holidays, weekends or during July–August, they'll carry your bike at any hour, subject to available space. This means you should book ahead.

You can travel with your bike any ime on boat trains from Hoek van Holland. Many trains have limited cycle space, a few can take 40+. Only unloaded, accompanied bikes are accepted. You must load and unload your bike from the train yourself. There is a fixed charge for bike tickets, but it's higher on Mondays and Fridays in July and August. Buy your ticket for the trip and your bike ticket at the ticket office. If the ticket office is closed, you must buy your seat tickets from a coin machine and bike tickets from the train conductor.

The carriage for bikes has a bicycle pictogram on it. Open the automatic doors by pressing the button alongside. If there is no space for your bike in the cycle carriage, you must wait for the next train. There is a leaflet available from the Netherlands Railways, titled "Fiets en Trein" (Bike and Train). Tandems are carried as normal bikes. Folding bikes are free of charge. Bike rental is available at numerous stations, including tandems, child seats and panniers. Prices vary according to area and season.

Germany:

Unloaded, accompanied bikes can be transported on D trains and most RE and RB trains. InterRegio (IR) trains must be booked at least 1 day ahead to guarantee space. There is a flat rate fee for bike tickets on IR trains, irrespective of distance traveled. Bike tickets (Fahrradkarte) must be bought at the ticket office. Bicycles are generally excluded from trains during the weekday commuter rush hours, as in the Netherlands. Bikes are not carried on InterCity Express (ICE) trains. Some EuroCity (EC) and InterCity (IC) trains carry bikes as accompanied luggage. Book in advance; there is a fee, currently DM 3.00 (US $1.50).

On trains where your bicycle is kept in a goods compartment separate from the passenger areas, it must be unpacked. In this case you may have to walk (or run) half-way along the train to or from your coach. Trains do not stop for long at intermediate stops, so make sure the Guard understands exactly where you and your bike are getting off. Where you can board trains with your bike and sit in the same coach, usually on regional and local train services, it isn't necessary to unpack your bike. However, as many intermediate stations have low-level platforms, make sure you'll be able to lift your loaded bike up or down about a meter, through train doorways.

You can buy International Bicycle Tickets for trains coming from countries neighboring Germany (except Poland) at a fixed price. Groups of 6 cyclists or more must book at least one week in advance.

Bikes as unaccompanied luggage are handled by EMS. You need a passenger ticket and must contact EMS a few days before traveling. They collect, pack and deliver to the destination of your choice. Contact them through your travel agent or rail booking office.

About 300 train stations rent out bikes ("Fahrradverleih") between Easter and the end of October, some all year. The rental fee includes insurance. Discounts are given to rail ticket purchasers, usually half-price rental, if the value of their rail ticket exceeds a specified amount. Bicycles must be returned to where they are rented, but sometimes can be returned to other stations.

In Germany there are some good train ticket concessions available, especially for younger people (under 26 years) and groups. Some are not advertised widely, but be aware especially of the weekend family group (maximum 5 people; typically two adults and up to three children) concession which allows unlimited travel anywhere in the country on non-express trains for about US $20 in total, from Friday to Sunday. Bicycle tickets must still be bought separately. Ask locally.

France:

Many French railway stations have bikes for rent. In general, information about the German railway system applies to France. The French rail system is exceptionally efficient and inexpensive.

Switzerland:

You can rent bicycles at Swiss rail stations. Prices depend on the type of bike rented as well as the duration of the rent period. Prices are about three to five times that of rent prices in the Netherlands. You can return the bike to a different station from which you rented it, for an additional charge. You should book a rent bike in advance to ensure one will be available. Groups must book a week in advance.

At the rail station you can check your bike in as luggage for a small fee, if you have a train ticket. Without a ticket, you'll be charged four times the standard check-in price. It's best to check in your bike and any luggage 24 hours before departure. You're allowed 3 pieces of luggage. However, you may check your bike in as late as 30 minutes before departure. The bike must be unladen and have a railway label attached.

Rail stations often have safe storage facilities for bikes, as do many hotels and restaurants. There are rail-air luggage facilities, but not for USA flights.

Switzerland does not offer discounted rail fares to students. Groups of 10 or more passengers can get reduced rates.

Swiss Rail publishes an excellent booklet about traveling by train with a bicycle. It includes prices, timetables, maps and how and where to rent, store, park and transport bikes. Services outside Switzerland are equally well detailed.

Ferry services from UK to Continental Europe:

Ferries cross between the UK and continental Europe from a large number of seaports, many on a daily basis. Some ferries operate a number of times per day, others sail a few days per week. Prices are seasonal and fluctuate according to demand and competition. Services may be changed at short notice, so check bookings before traveling.

Bus (Coach) Services from UK to Europe:

The European Bike Express operates a route from the UK through France to Strasbourg and Basel. The coach and trailer are specifically built for transporting cyclists and their equipment. The bike trailer can carry 53 cycles of

From UK	To	Line	Bike	Time
Dover (Kent)	Ostend (Belgium)	Hoverspeed	Y	2h00
Dover (Kent)	Calais (France)	P&O/Stena	Y	1h15
Dover (Kent)	Calais (France)	(Superferry)	Y	0h45
Dover (Kent)	Calais (France)	Hoverspeed	N	0h35
Dover (Kent)	Calais (France)	Sea France	Y	1h30
Felixstowe (Suffolk)	Zeebrugge (Belgium)	P & O (day)	Y	5h45
Felixstowe (Suffolk)	Zeebrugge (Belgium)	P & O (night)	Y	8h00
Harwich	Hoek van Holland (NL)	Stena Sealink	Y	3h40
Hull	Rotterdam (NL)	P&O North Sea	Y	12h30
Hull	Zeebrugge (Belgium)	P&O North Sea	Y	14h30
Newcastle (Tyneside)	IJmuiden (Netherlands) (for Amsterdam)	Scandinavian Seaways	Y	14h00
Ramsgate (Kent)	Ostend (Belgium)	under review		

all types, including tandems and trikes. The coach is air-conditioned, there is plenty of leg room, a courier is aboard to look after you and there are snacks and drinks available. CTC members qualify for a discount. Ticket prices vary according to the number of stages you travel, with Basel being the limit of stage 1 fares. The current time-table finds the bus arriving at Basel at 03h00, but budget hotel bookings can be made through the EBE office. On the return trip to the UK, the coach reaches Basel at 23h45. From early May to mid-September, this weekly service leaves England on Saturdays, returning on Sundays.

The Eurolines buses (coaches) depart from London, and Dover, with connections throughout the UK and Eire. The Amsterdam service travels via Rotterdam, Den Haag, and Utrecht. Tickets are valid for up to 6 months and can be open-ended. Round trip tickets, special passes and reduced prices for young people as well as older travelers are offered. Smoking/non-smoking and daytime/overnight journeys are offered to over 750 destinations throughout Europe. Bicycles are generally not carried due to space restraints, but it's worth checking, as the coach may be running empty enough for them to relax the rules. Bikes in bike bags obviously have a better chance of being transported as luggage. Hosteling International members are entitled to a discount on tickets.

Europabus, the bus (coach) service provided by a number of European rail operators, has a London to Köln (Cologne) link which operates throughout the year, with more coaches operating during summer. The journey takes about twelve hours. They do not nor-mally carry bicycles, but see (Eurolines) above.

Going by Barge or Ship With Bike:

You can travel from Amsterdam and Rotterdam to Basel, and points between, on board one of the many luxury ships which ply the Rhine. There are also regular sailings between cities and landing points by passenger ships of various shipping lines. You can obtain the pertinent information at local tourist offices and travel agents.

Passport and Visa Requirements

These guidelines apply to citizens of USA, Canada, Eire, UK, Australia, New Zealand, and South Africa.

As a general rule, ensure that your passport has more than a full year's validity when you travel anywhere in the world. Some countries will not allow you entry otherwise.

USA and Canadian citizens need a valid passport to enter the Netherlands, Germany, France, and Switzerland. Children's details must be recorded on their parents' passports unless they have their own passports. No visa is required for visits up to three months. Immunization certificates are not necessary. Residents returning to the USA and Canada do not require certificates of vaccination.

EEC citizens must be in possession of a full passport or an identity card (picture-ID) issued by their government, to travel in other EEC member states. Children's details must be recorded on their parents' passports unless they have their own passports. If children have ID cards, children over ten years of age must have photo-ID.

Australians and New Zealanders require no visas for the Netherlands, Germany, France, and Switzerland for visits of up to three months. South Africans should check locally, as the rules may change from time to time; currently visas are required to enter France, but see next paragraph. Full passports valid for the relevant period are required. Normally, more than a year's validity on non-European passports is demanded.

Technically, there are no borders between countries in the "Schengen" area of Europe (Germany, Spain, Netherlands, Belgium, France, Luxembourg, and Portugal), so if you can get into one without a visa, you should be able to get into them all.

Travel Tip:
Always carry some form of identification with you; it's a peculiar form of arrogance, and not very smart either, to be unable to produce a passport or identity document in a foreign country, when you are legally obliged to identify yourself to officials in your home country.

Customs and Immigration Procedures at Entry

Wherever you arrive in Europe, if you are not a citizen you must complete a document about your origins, intentions and finances. This completed form, with your passport will allow you entry, or not, to the country you intend visiting, so fill it in with care.

Borders between EU countries with common frontiers are now "open."

However, when officials deem it necessary, you may be stopped and your papers checked. Border controls may also be temporarily reinstated when it is considered necessary. The United Kingdom does not subscribe to the open border policy and all persons arriving in the UK are subject to immigration and customs controls, even when coming from an EEC member state.

Bicycles and travel requisites can be imported tax free into any EEC country, on condition they are re-exported. No import license is required.

Vaccination/Inoculation Regulations:
At the date of writing, none are required. However, check with your local embassy or travel agent, to ensure this ruling still applies.

Switzerland is not an EU member, so everybody, including EU nationals, has to undergo frontier checks. Personal belongings required for a holiday stay are not subject to tax. Tobacco and alcohol duty-free allowances are available only to persons over 17 years of age. You can import foodstuffs only as required by one person for one day. Medicines must be for your personal use only. Meat products are dealt with separately, so it would be wise to check the current regulations beforehand if you intend bringing any form of meat, raw or processed, to Switzerland. My advice is, don't!

Currently (1999), no persons from the USA, Canada, EU countries, Australia, New Zealand, or South Africa require inoculation or vaccination to enter Switzerland.

4
Touring Matters

This chapter will deal with important general information concerning each of the countries you'll be traveling through.

Local Taxes

Different taxation methods and rates apply for different types of goods and services in the various countries, as listed here.

Netherlands:
Value added tax (VAT) and service charges are always included in room rates. Local and tourist taxes may apply and vary according to region.

Germany and France:
Tourist and local taxes apply in some areas. VAT is always included

Power Supply

Electricity supply in Europe is 220/240 Volts, 50 Hz (cycles per second). As the standard North American supply is 110 Volts, 60 Hz, you need a transformer to run any mains electric equipment you bring from there. Plugs/sockets are also of a different pattern and you need an adaptor (available at all travel stores, airports etc.). If you have dual voltage equipment, you must move the switch to the appropriate position.

Accommodation

For accommodation booking services, see Appendix B.

To reserve hotel accommodation, most hotels want you to communicate by E-mail rather than fax because it's free and convenient.

Hotels

Netherlands:
Most hotels in the Netherlands are smaller than American tourist hotels, with far fewer rooms. They are graded on a star system, from one star at the bottom end of the facility and price ladder, to five stars at the top. Graded hotels conform to a basic standard and you will find them spotlessly clean and scrupulously well-maintained.

Room prices usually include breakfast.

The Netherlands Reservation Centre (NRC) is a booking service for hotels, campsites and cabins.Germany:

You will find a high standard of hygiene, facilities, and service in German hotels, of whatever grade or price.

The majority of hotels provide buffet breakfasts inclusive in the price, which vary broadly, but are always filling. Usually bread and bread rolls, cheese and sliced meat are basic to the meal, as are tea or coffee. You may find breakfast cereals, fruit juices, jams, boiled or scrambled eggs, bacon, fresh fruit, and herbal tea provided.

In the tourist and holiday areas of the country it's imperative to book hotel rooms well in advance, especially for the summer season. Brochures and booklets, available from the German Tourist Board (DZT) in your country, detail graded and price-bracketed hotel accommodation in specific areas. Local tourist offices, usually found in the town hall (Rathaus), provide information about local accommodation. You may also find Info-boards with hotel information along your route.

Hotels expect faxed or written confirmations of booking. Short notice cancellations incur cancellation fees.

Most hotels have restaurant facilities. On rest days (Ruhetag; normally smaller hotels) hotels take guests, but except for breakfast, the restaurant is closed.

France:

French hotels are graded on a star system, with four stars "L" (luxury) at the top, to one star for plain, fairly comfortable establishments. A "T" grade indicates a simple hotel, with basic comforts. Some hotels are still being graded (EC), others are not registered ("NH") within the government regulated grading system. Most hotels in Alsace (over 400) are two star graded, indicating that they are good hotels with average facilities. This means you get what you see and you'll have a comfortable stay. Restaurants are also graded according to this system, including those in hotels.

Prices are posted outside hotels and they generally conform with the rates charged by similar establishments in Germany. Room prices don't include breakfast. Half board (demi-pension) includes room with either dinner or luncheon, but not breakfast. Alsace is noted for its hospitality and your Alsatian hosts will go out of their way to make you comfortable. Almost every hotel has bicycle storage facilities.

Farm Inns (Fermes-Auberges) are mostly found in hiking areas, often high in the hills. They offer traditional cooking and rooms or dormitories.

Switzerland:

Swiss hotels are uniformly good, clean and comfortable. Despite its reputation to the contrary, Switzerland has some excellent inexpensive hotels and Basel has its fair share. The Swiss Hotel Association publishes an annual guide to over 3,000 hotels and pensions. This book is available from the Swiss Tourist Office and also comes on CD-ROM.

Because of the long season and the many fairs and exhibitions held in Basel, it's best to make reservations well in advance of your visit. However, local tourist agencies will generally find you a bed if you arrive without booking, though you may then pay more than you anticipated. Reservations can be made at agencies situated at airports and main rail stations.

Onward Luggage Transfer

In the Netherlands, the VVV (Regional Tourist Information Offices) operate a system of onward luggage transfers for cyclists. You can arrange with them to collect your luggage at your hotel and deliver it to your next destination on a daily basis. Get details from travel agents or a Netherlands Board of Tourism office.

Bed and Breakfast

The Netherlands:

Often the VVV will be the only place you can arrange accommodation in private homes. However, there is a club of cycling and hiking enthusiasts who arrange low-cost B&B accommodation for strictly only cyclists and walkers. You need to be a member (fee about US $8) and accommodation varies from place to place, costing upwards of US $13. See Appendix B.

Germany:

The German Tourist Board produces a booklet of bed and breakfast establishments. Local Tourist Information offices also have details.
Accommodation is always good, sometimes exceptional and prices vary over a broad range to reflect this. Budget travelers will find accommodation to suit their pockets quite easily in most areas. Garni hotels provide bed and breakfast at reasonable prices, with a wide choice of facilities. Payments should be made in cash, in German currency. Checks, credit cards and other forms of payment are not generally acceptable. You shouldn't expect your hosts to speak much, if any, English and should prepare accordingly. Cyclists are widely catered for.
If you have time, look for "Zimmer Frei" notices in house windows, where Bed and Breakfast accommodation is on offer in private houses.

Value is always good, but be prepared with some stock phrases (and expected answers) in German. Always indicate you're English-speaking and if your host cannot understand English, or your attempts at German, sometimes a neighbor will be rustled up to do the honors, or somebody will be telephoned to translate.

France:

"Chambre d'hôte" accommodation offers sleeping facilities with breakfast in a private house. Normally you would have a wash basin in your room, sometimes a private shower. Chambres d'hôte are graded by way of one to four "blades of wheat" symbols, according to comfort, as well as the surroundings. There are 1,820 chambres d'hôte and gîtes de France in Alsace.
"Gîtes de France" are fully equipped and furnished apartments, houses or cottages in country villages or on farms, sometimes wine estates. They are graded according to setting and comfort level, indicated by one to four blades of wheat symbols. They're designed to accommodate couples as well as large families. Rental periods are generally longer than one night, typically for a holiday period, but some can be rented for a weekend.
You can also rent villas, apartments or studios (open plan self-contained units), usually for a week or more, though some can be had for shorter stays.

Youth Hostels

Hostels of the International Youth Hostels Federation belong to the umbrella body, Hosteling International (HI). Membership of your home organization automatically allows you the use of any of the 5,000 hostels in 60 member countries. You can join the association at any hostel, but it's cheaper to buy membership in your own country. It's best to book ahead for European hostels through the International Booking Network, from any major hostel, anywhere in the world. HI issue an annually updated handbook for Europe and the Mediterranean, and national associations also issue handbooks with opening times, price guides, and facilities at each hostel.

Netherlands:

There are 38 youth hostels in the Netherlands, affiliated to Hosteling International. Some hostels open for only part of the year, but most close around Christmas and New Year.

Germany:

The youth hostel movement was started in Germany and continues to operate there with strong support. There are youth hostels all along the Rhine route, some in the most amazing and interesting buildings.

International hostels (Jugendgästehaus) offer later closing and 2 or 4 bed rooms. Breakfast is always included in all hostel prices. At some hostels a local tax is levied on foreigners.

France:

French youth hostels (Auberges de Jeunesse) are open to all members of Hosteling International, irrespective of age. There are ten FUAJ hostels in Alsace, of which the two at Strasbourg and one each at Colmar and Mulhouse are near the Rhine route. French youth hostels are excellent value for money, though the sheet hire charge is very steep, so take your own if you're hosteling.

Some hostels allow camping. Campers must have any one of a number of camping insurance cards, one of which is the International Camping Carnet. Mulhouse and Strasbourg (René Cassin) hostels have camp sites, and Mulhouse offers cycle hire.

There are a number of other hosteling organizations in France, among them the League Française Auberge de Jeunesse (LFAJ). You may also come across a number of private hostels, some called youth or student hostels or even backpacker hostels. As there is no set standard for these establishments, ask to see the facilities before you commit yourself to staying. Some of these alternative hostels are excellent value, with outstanding facilities.

Switzerland:

If you are 25 years old or younger, you'll be welcome at a Swiss youth hostel. Older hostelers will be admitted if there is space. Family groups with young members, however, are exempt from the age barrier. There is a youth hostel in Basel, near the Rhine river south (left) bank, close to the St. Alban ferry.

Friends of Nature Sites

This is an organization which promotes a love of nature. It is non-aligned, non-sectarian and non-political. The international headquarters are in Vienna. If you join the organization, you will be allowed to use their extensive (and inexpensive) camping and accommodation facilities throughout Europe. Prior booking is advisable.

Camping

The International Camping Carnet provides you and the camp management with a certain degree of insured protection. Without the carnet you'll need to give your passport as security, which is never a good idea.

Leisure Centers

In Germany, these "Freizeitzentren" establishments are usually very large camping sites which offer every conceivable type of self-contained accommodation, from chalets to plain tent sites. The accent is on activity and variety. You will find that water sports typically dominate near the Rhine. There are on-site shops and bars, as well as indoor entertainment. Facilities for cooking, laundry and washing are usually outstanding.

Camping Sites

Netherlands:
Camping sites cater mainly for caravanners and often have permanent cabins on site. They also have tent sites, charging for the site, plus a charge per person and for vehicles, including bicycles. Some are obliged to charge a tourist or local tax.

In the holiday areas, larger camp sites have shops where you can buy foodstuffs, and a bar and activity center. Showers and cooking rings are usually metered and use tokens bought from the reception office.

Very few campsites operate throughout the year, normally opening for the season in early May and closing down in October. Some open at Easter, then close again until the summer season begins. A few campsites, however, are open for most of the year, though they will generally not allow tent camping during the coldest months.

Many sites have two or more hikers cabins, which are provided by the national hiking organization. They uniformly have four bunks with mattresses, basic furniture, and cooking and washing facilities. There is a single standard price for the hire of the cabins and heating usually costs extra. For one person it is quite expensive, but very cheap for four, and it means you don't need to haul a tent along, either. Hikers, of course, get priority and booking is usually necessary.

Germany:
There are campsites along the entire length of the Rhine. These vary in size and quality of facilities to an enormous degree. There is a grading system for participants in schemes operated by the two main German camping organizations. They issue booklets with details of their campsites, updated every year. Even at their busiest time, the larger campsites will be able to squeeze in an extra tent, but groups should book ahead during the summer season. You may come across permanent camps, where people live year round and non-residents are excluded.

Hot showers and, where provided, cooking facilities, are often (but not always) metered. It's most likely that the meter requires a token for operation, so always ask at the reception. Some smaller and more remote campsites tend to lock the showers and kitchens at night, so check the times they're available.

Check out time is normally midday, but some campsites require that you leave earlier. Out of season most are rather relaxed, but in season the pressure of demand on the sites requires that you leave on time, or face having to pay for an extra day.

France:

While there are quite a few camping sites registered with the local tourist boards, you will always find others which are not. Often the unregistered sites have equally good facilities for camping, but are not always geared towards holiday activities such as swimming, tennis and golf. At the same time, this doesn't mean that one would necessarily be cheaper than the other, so if there is another campsite nearby and you're budget conscious, compare prices before deciding.

Camp sites are classed firstly according to whether they cater more for short (T = tourisme) or long (L = loisirs) term visitors and secondly according to their physical position and the facilities offered. You will find camp sites geared towards families and long stay campers, with sporting and social activities on site and nearby. Besides tent and caravan sites, they have bungalows, chalets and mobile trailer homes, some of which can usually be rented. There are also camp sites in natural surroundings (aires naturelles) and countryside camp sites (camping rural), which tend to be less expensive.

Camping areas are usually open from Easter or the beginning of May until the end of October. Not all have hot water on tap, nor in the showers. Some shut and lock the showers at specified times, normally 22h00 to 06h00. Lavatories (toilets) are always accessible, though. Some sites include hot showers in the price, others will ask extra to use them and issue you with a token to place in the meter. Some camps have coin-metered hot water and gas, but not many. Check with the receptionist the time the hot water or cooking gas will run per token or coin.

You are charged for the tent site and also per person. Always say you are traveling by bicycle or you will have to pay for an automobile (car) as well. You will generally have to pay in advance for your stay, on arrival.

A guide to camping in Alsace is available from your local French Tourist office, from regional tourist authorities in Alsace, or from tourist and information offices all over Alsace. Most maps also show positions of camp sites, but not all sites shown may still exist.

Switzerland:

There are about 400 camp and caravan sites in Switzerland. There is a campsite to the east of Basel, though it is far out of the way for cyclists.

Mini-Camping

In the Netherlands, small camping sites tend to exist in the most popular holiday areas. There is a broad range of pricing, but I have always found them to be expensive as tent sites. They are geared towards caravanners and rent out full sites at the same price, irrespective of space actually used. This is fair enough, but tough on one person's pocket. It's also a good idea to ask to see the facilities and determine the extra costs for using them. Most showers are metered, some costing a small fortune to feed before the hot water appears. Also ask if the showers and toilets are closed at any time, particularly at night.

Camping on the Farm

In the Netherlands it's called-"Camping bij de Boer." You'll come across farm camping sites, often indicated by rough hand painted signs offering "camping." Facilities vary, but normally you'll get a hot shower, toilet facilities and clean drinking water at a comparatively low price. Don't confuse these sites with the mini-camping sites which cost considerably more. In Germany it's referred to as "auf dem Bauernhof." There are some campsites on working farms and these are usually officially sanctioned, evidenced by the official camping sign leading you to them. They provide basic facilities of showers, washrooms and clean water.

In France it's called "camping à la ferme." Registered farm camping sites are restricted to six sites for twenty persons, allowing 150 square meters per site. Drinking water, electricity, trash cans, picnic table and seating and full washing facilities, wash basin and toilets are provided. Expect to pay extra for hot water showers, but the overall prices are the budget traveler's dream.

Wild Camping

As the Netherlands is the most densely populated country on earth, it's unlikely that you'll be able to camp wild without being disturbed. It's quite common for farmers to offer camping sites with basic facilities at very reasonable prices, so it's hardly worth the trouble to camp wild. You should always get permission to camp from a landowner or occupier.

In Germany, wild camping, once quite common in parts of Germany, though frowned upon, has been officially outlawed, to protect fragile areas.

In Switzerland the advice is simple: Don't even contemplate it.

5
Money, Weights, and Measures

Signatories to the European common currency agreement changed their national currencies for a single common unit, the Euro (symbol), on 1 January 1999. The Netherlands, Germany and France committed to this system simultaneously. Switzerland is not a member of the European Economic Community and not involved in these changes.

The change-over to the Euro initially affects only inter-bank transactions. National currencies continue to be used for normal transactions. National hard currencies will be replaced by Euros between January and June 2001.

The advantage for the traveler is that currencies in the Euro pool are fixed at a pre-determined rate against one another and prices are quoted in Euros as well as local currencies. This allows for easy comparison of prices throughout the common currency area. Also, travelers' checks are available in Euros, so it is possible to move throughout the common currency area, without having to purchase pre-determined amounts of the various currencies in advance.

In recent years, ATM's (cash dispensers) have become the cheapest and easiest way to obtain local money in while abroad. You can use either your bank debit card or your credit card. The advantage is that your money will be exchanged at the bank rate, which is much more favorable than the tourist rate you'd be getting at the change counter in a bank or exchange office.

Monetary Systems and Local Names of Coins

The Netherlands:
The unit of currency is the Guilder ("gulden"), divided into 100 cents. There are 5 cent ("stuiver"), 10 cent ("dubbeltje"), 25 cent ("kwartje"), 1 Guilder, 2,5 Guilder ("Rijksdaalder"), and 5 Guilder coins.

Guilder is written as "f." You may also see guilder abbreviated as Dfl, Hfl, Gld, or NLG. Banknotes used are fl 10, fl 25, fl 50, fl 100, fl 250, and fl 1,000.

There are no restrictions for the import or export of currencies.

You can cash travelers' checks and Eurocheques, draw money against all major credit cards and exchange foreign currency at Post Offices, banks and exchange bureaux. GWK exchange bureaux are found at major rail stations, at border crossing points as well as at Schiphol airport. Before you begin any currency dealings, you should determine the rate of exchange and, especially, commissions payable. Commissions vary considerably between agencies and you could pay far more than you expect.

Banking hours are 09h30 to 16h00, Monday through Friday in most large towns. Some banks open Saturday mornings, but it is not common practice. In smaller towns, bank opening hours may be shorter.

Post Offices open Mondays through Fridays, 08h30 to 17h00. In some places, they open Saturdays, from 08h30 to midday.

Major credit cards are accepted by many hotels, restaurants, shops, airlines and car rental companies.

Germany:

The Deutsche Mark (DM) is the German unit of currency, divided into 100 Pfennig (Pf). Coins are 1 Pf, 2 Pf, 5 Pf, 10 Pf, and 50 Pf, with 1 DM, 2 DM and 5 DM coins as well. Prices are written DM 27,49. Banknotes are 10 DM, 20 DM, 50 DM, 100DM, 200 DM, 500 DM, and 1,000D M.

Paying by credit card is not as common as in the USA. They are generally taken at hotels, larger department stores and gas stations. If you have Eurocheques, they will be accepted in many restaurants and shops which don't accept credit cards. The red and blue EC symbol marks places which accept Eurocheques.

Travelers' checks in Deutschmarks and Euros are accepted at face value by shops, hotels, restaurants and many other places. Checks in foreign denominations are exchanged by banks and bureaux de change.

No restrictions exist on the amount of foreign or local currency, or any payment media, imported into or exported from Germany.

Banks are closed Saturdays and Sundays. Normally they open weekdays from 08h30 to 13h00 and 14h30 to 16h00, but often open until 17h30 on Thursdays. In cities, banks usually stay open during lunchtime. Bureaux de change at airports and border crossing points, normally open 06h00 to 22h00 daily. Major railway station bureaux cater for all international trains.

France:

The French franc (Ff or F) is the unit of currency in France, divided into 100 centimes (c). Prices are usually written in the form 23 F 55 (twenty-three francs and fifty-five centimes). Coins are 5 c, 10 c, ½ F, 1 F, 2 F, 5 F, and 10 F. The 10 F coin is made of two different colored metals and is quite distinctive. Banknotes in use are 20 F, 50 F, 100 F, 200 F, 500 F, and 1,000 F.

Banks open weekdays only, 09h30 until 16h30, but many close for an hour (sometimes 90 minutes) for lunch.

You can import and export unlimited amounts of foreign currency, but if you intend re-exporting more than 50,000 francs of banknotes, you must declare the amount you bring into the country.

Major credit cards are widely accepted in shops, hotels, restaurants and many hypermarkets for amounts over 100 francs (about US $ 17). Always check receipts as no decimal point will be shown between francs and centimes. Cards without a "smart-card" microchip and which still operate with a magnetic band are not always easily read by French machines and may be rejected. Get your bank to code your card for use in Europe if possible. Your credit card company should have a free-phone number to assist you. Cash dispensers, or ATMs, connected to the appropriate network can give money against certain credit cards.

Most banks in France no longer accept Eurocheques.

Switzerland:

The Swiss franc (Sfr, also CHF) is the unit of currency, divided into 100 centimes. Coins are 5 c, 1 0c, 20 c, ½ Sfr, 1 Sfr, 2 Sfr, and 5 Sfr. Banknotes in current use are Sfr 10, Sfr 20, Sfr 50, Sfr 100, Sfr 500, and Sfr 1,000. In German speaking areas of Switzerland, centimes are commonly called "Rappen."

Swiss franc travelers' checks are cashed at face value in hotels, restaurants and shops. Foreign currency traveler's checks are exchanged only at banks and by official exchange offices at airports and main railway stations. Eurocheques, backed by check guarantee cards, are widely accepted and can be cashed as well. Credit cards are also widely accepted. Banks open 08h30 to 16h30, weekdays only.

There are no restrictions on the import or export of foreign currency.

Weights and Measures

Europe uses the metric (SI: meter, gram, second) system of measurement.

In continental Europe, the decimal point is indicated by a comma (,) and the division between numerical thousands is indicated by a space or a period. However, in this book we'll adhere to the English convention, using the decimal point and reserving the comma (or a space) as a separator between thousands.

1 000 000 or 1,000,000 = one million

1 000 000 000 or 1,000,000,000 = one milliard (USA = one billion)

1 000 000 000 000 or 1,000,000,000,000 = one billion (USA = trillion)

Multiples:

kilo	=	x 1 000
deci	=	x 1\10
hecto	=	x 100
centi	=	x 1\100
deca	=	x 10
milli	=	x 1\1 000

Abbreviations:

cm	=	centimeter
m	=	meter
km	=	kilometer
g	=	gram
kg	=	kilogram
t	=	tonne (1,000 kg)
l	=	liter
ha	=	hectare

Conversion Factors

Distance

1 inch	=	2.54 centimeters
1 meter	=	approximately 39 inches (39.3701)
1 kilometer	=	0.62 miles (0.62138)
1 mile	=	1.6 kilometers (1,6093 m)

To convert miles to kilometers, multiply miles by 8 and divide by 5.
To convert kilometers to miles, multiply kilometers by 5 and divide by 8.

Area:

1 hectare =	2.471 acres
1 acre =	0.4047 hectare

Velocity:

10 miles per hour = 16 kilometer per hour

10 kilometers per hour = 6.2 miles per hour

Mass and weight:

1 kilogram =	approximately 2.2 pounds (2.20458)
1 pound =	approximately 0.45 kilogram (0.4536)
1 ounce =	approx. 28.35 gram

In the Netherlands, Germany, and France, the use of pounds weight in speech is common, especially when buying food. Nowadays these terms relate to metric measures.

English	Dutch	German	French	Meaning
pound	pond	Pfund	Livre	0.5 kg
half pound	half pond	halbes Pfund	demi-livre	0.25 kg
quarter pound	kwart pond	Viertel-pfund	N/A	0.25 kg
ounce	ons	N/A	N/A	100 g

Volume:

1 US gallon =	3.785 liters
1 Imp. gallon =	4.546 liters

Temperature:
The standard system of temperature measurement in Europe is the Celsius (Centigrade) scale (C). Freezing point is at 0°C and boiling point at 100°C.

Human body temperature (blood heat) is normal at 37°C.

Conversion from Fahrenheit to Celsius:

°C = (°F − 32) x 5/9

Conversion from Celsius to Fahrenheit:

°F = (°C x 9/5) + 32

°C	−5	0	5	10	15	20	25	30	37	100
°F	23	32	41	50	59	68	77	86	98	212

Time:
The 24-hour clock is widely used. Correctly, the format is two numbers representing the hour, two numbers representing the minutes, separated by a lower-case "h" (e.g. 09h53). However, you will see a variety of formats in use: 0953, 09:53, 09.53 are the most common. In the Netherlands, you may see the "h" separator replaced by a "u" (09u53).

00h00	=	midnight
01h00	=	one A.M.
09h30	=	nine-thirty (half-past nine) A.M.
12h00	=	midday (noon)
13h00	=	one P.M.

21h30 = nine-thirty (half-past nine) P.M.

23h59 = one minute before midnight

Note:
What is half (an hour) past the hour to English-speakers, means half (an hour) before the following hour to Dutch- and German-speakers. For example:

English	Dutch	German

half past one	half twee (half two)	halb zwei (half two)
ten thirty	half elf (half eleven)	halb elf (half eleven)

Central European Time (CET):
All countries on the Rhine route observe CET, which is one hour ahead of Greenwich Mean Time (GMT), i.e. at noon in London, it is 1 P.M. in continental Europe.

Summertime daylight saving:
In Spring, clocks on the Continent are moved forward one hour, returning to Standard time in autumn. Since 1998, the UK has conformed with the Continent, changing time on the same days in March and October.

Calendar dates:
The convention for writing numerical dates differs from that used in North America. The "Day/Month/Year" system is preferred. For example, 12 May 2001 is written 12-05-01 (also 12/5/01), rather than 5-12-01.

6 Touring Equipment

This chapter deals with the following subjects: Bicycle touring and camping equipment, packing the bike and related special tips, availability, renting versus buying, and suitability of equipment for the area.

You have a number of options in terms of equipment and cycles. You can bring your own bike and equipment with you, buy new or used in Europe, or rent bikes along the route.

If you have your own bicycle and touring equipment, it makes sense to bring it with you. Bring your bicycle seat (saddle), if nothing else; it takes time to wear in a new seat. If you buy a bicycle in Europe, ask the dealer to deduct the cost of the seat.

Bicycles

You could cycle the Rhine route on virtually any bicycle. For energy-saving and comfort, use a bicycle with at least five gears. For off-road riding you'll mostly need fifteen gears.

Britain is reasonably good for buying used bicycles and cycle-touring equipment. English-speakers will find it easier to deal with the complexities of choosing and buying goods in their native language. If you're going directly to the Netherlands, Germany, France, or Switzerland, you need to be reasonably familiar with the relevant language. Otherwise find an English-speaking cycle salesman. Compare prices with other shops, to ensure you get a good deal.

You need something strong enough to last your trip and hopefully a lot longer. If you can't spare the time to shop around for specific types and brands of equipment, there's enough adequate off-the-peg gear to get you on the road in a day's shopping. General cycle dealers on the continent mostly have a fair range of bikes, so you should find the type you want and the fit your need. Recent (1998) price comparisons between English bike shops and Continental (and USA) dealers indicate that new goods tend to be 30% more expensive in the UK.

If you intend cycling short distances and you aren't looking for a 24-speed tourer or similar, used (secondhand) 3 or 5-speed cycles are sold cheaply every day. Look through the advertisement columns of local newspapers. Check if the frame is true and the front forks and cranks aren't bent. You can also rent bicycles en route, from many railway stations and bike shops. They are more likely to be suitable for short treks and day trips.

There are a number of schools of thought concerning touring bikes and equipment. Read as much as you can about cycle-touring before you buy, and try out various types of bikes and equipment first. Load and wind are factors to consider and having ten, fifteen or twenty-one gears on your bike gives you more flexibility and range.

My personal choice is a hybrid (city bike cum mountain bike) with 24 indexed derailleur gears (effectively 17 gears). Cantilever brakes produce the stopping power needed for a loaded bike. The tires are mountain bike tires, but I use slick (smooth) treads for better speed. In winter I use narrower tires with roadster treads. The bike frame has the necessary fastenings for front and rear pannier racks (carriers) and water bottles. The wheels have strong rims. I use standard parallel cage pedals, which have no quills, clips or straps. With a loaded bike, I like to keep my feet free for better control and safety.

The straight or upright handlebars with bar ends allow me to sit in an upright position to observe everything around me and I can change to any number of hand positions to prevent cramping. My bicycle seat has a broad base, is filled with soft gel and is also sprung. I'm quite happy to sacrifice a little crank efficiency for a contented rear end. I use twist-grip gear shifters, for excellent gear and steer control.

Bicycles can be rented from almost anywhere in the Netherlands. Besides rental firms, dealers, repair shops and many railway stations rent out bikes. You must produce picture identification and pay a deposit. Sometimes you can leave your passport instead of deposits, but it's not advisable to travel through a foreign country without identification. I don't like leaving my passport as security — it is illegal to do so with a British passport (and many other national passports).

Prices depend on the quality and features of the bicycle rented, as well as the rent period. Normally you can rent a bike for a day or a week. The bike must be returned to the point of rental. If you have a valid train or rover ticket, you can get a voucher from the ticket office at a station with rental facilities and exchange it for a bike at the depot. Daily rates are about 20% less than average prices elsewhere.

There are bicycle safe parking facilities at about 100 train stations around the Netherlands.

On the Rhine Route through the Netherlands, you can rent bikes at Leiden, Alphen, Woerden, Utrecht, and Arnhem railway stations.

VVV (local tourist agencies) offices have lists of bicycle and equipment rental places.

When buying a bicycle in the Netherlands it's a good idea to shop around. Many bike shops have touring equipment and some have camping gear as well. If your budget doesn't stretch to Dutch prices, you should be able to root out some good used (secondhand) equipment in larger towns. If you're unsure of the seller, don't deal, as stolen bikes constitute a large part of the informal market.

In Germany there are numerous cycle rental businesses and bikes can be rented at most holiday resorts as well. Local Tourist offices will tell you where they can be found.

The German Railways (DB) rent out bikes at some 370 stations (Fahrrad am Bahnhof). Rental charges at stations are considerably lower (about half price) for adult passengers arriving by train who can produce a ticket valued at DM 16 (note: subject to change) and children with tickets costing half that amount. Cycles rented from the DB are mostly suitable for day use. Sometimes you can leave the bike at another station, but expect to pay extra.

The French Railways has a similar bike rent scheme.

The Swiss railways also have a rent scheme. They offer a wide range of bikes, though mountain bikes are rapidly gaining ascendancy.

Cycle Touring Equipment

You can get advice from cycling organizations such as the CTC (Cyclists' Touring Club of Great Britain). You must be a CTC member or a member of affiliated organizations like the AIT. It's worthwhile joining, as you get inclusive insurance coverage, the opportunity to buy the indispensable camping carnet and free travel and touring advice. The paperwork can take a month, especially during holiday periods.

I use front and rear panniers, strapping my sleeping bag, tent poles and sleeping mat on the rear carrier. I attach baggage on my carrier in a lengthwise position, which cuts down wind resistance and reduces the chances of soaking. Sideways loaded carriers are less aerodynamic, besides destabilizing the bicycle. In the Netherlands and Germany, many cyclists use saddle-bag type panniers; the section which crosses over the carrier and holds the two side bags together, forms a third bag. If you rent panniers, you will generally get this type.

Panniers

Rear panniers should be angled away on the pedal side, so your heels aren't impeded when you're pedaling. The hooks or clips attaching the panniers to the rack (carrier) should be very strong and strongly attached to the pannier. Rear facing pockets are useful. Your rear panniers will doubtless carry some heavy loads and come in for a good bashing, so buy the best you can, not necessarily the most expensive. For extra waterproofing, use trash (bin) bags to line panniers.

Front panniers should ideally hang low on the rack and have a clean profile. I prefer mine to have about half the carrying volume of rear panniers. If you pack them evenly, balancing weights, you'll seldom find any negative differences in the handling qualities of your bicycle; you'll often find an improvement. Splash covers are necessary for front panniers and good sets come equipped with effective covers. The trend nowadays is to load forward where possible, which makes sense as it reduces the load on your rear wheel, which carries the bulk of your body weight. However, consider the effects of forward weight on steering and braking.

Pannier racks are available at larger bike dealerships on the Continent. There is little sense in spending vast amounts of money on equipment you may never use again, but you should at least ensure you get equipment that does the job.

Backpacks

I've seen cyclists carrying full-sized backpacks (rucksacks) on their backs. Not only does a backpack put an additional strain on the spine and back muscles, but it transfers the center of gravity to the highest point possible creating stability and control problems. It also prevents you from effectively looking back, an essential survival action. For short trips and mountain biking, a small day pack is reasonable, as long as the minimum weight is carried, perhaps a lightweight jacket, first aid kit and some tools. But it never makes sense to cycle with a loaded backpack on your back at any time.

Stretch (bungee) straps are not favored by many experts, in case they work loose and head directly for the spokes of your wheel. For the larger baggage I use flat nylon straps with end clamps. But I do use bungees for small items like my windcheater or my lunch bought along the way. Bungees are very strongly built and equally useful for suspending your bike from a tree to create a makeshift repair station.

Fenders (mudguards)
In the Netherlands, the law requires that, if you have fenders, the rear one must be colored white or yellow over a height of at least 30 centimeters (12 inches), with a red rear light with reflector attached either to the fender or elsewhere. Clip-on flexible plastic fenders do the job, but not as well as full length fenders, attached by means of V-shaped wire struts. There are clips which allow these fenders to break away from their mountings in case they get jammed against a wheel.

Lamps (lights) and reflectors
For night cycling you need front and rear cycle lamps. These must conform to a certain pattern, but just about any front light will do if it gives off a white light and you can see and be seen. I use a battery powered headlamp with a halogen lamp (bulb, globe) which fits onto a hotshoe mounted on my han-

dlebars. This also doubles as a flashlight (torch).

Rear lights must be red and highly visible. LED type lights haven't earned approval, but may be used to supplement rear lights, as long as they emit a steady light.

White front and red rear flat reflectors are required. They must be of a pattern prescribed by law. You can buy them just about anywhere. Spoke reflectors are compulsory for both wheels. Your bike must definitely have reflecting pedals, though you may be told otherwise.

Bells
Wherever you cycle on the Rhine route, you're obliged to have a bell on your bicycle. You are also obliged to give fair warning to other cyclists and pedestrians before you overtake them.

Rear-view mirrors
The best alternative to having eyes in the back of your head, but can never really replace a safe glance over the shoulder. Various types are available, from the standard handlebar fitted mirror to those which fit to the crossbar and give you a view to the rear, either side of the seat post. The arguments about the time required to focus your eyes and inattention to the road ahead are rather specious, given that motorists can do exactly the same at much higher speeds.

Tools and Spare Parts

You will need some tools, if only to save yourself the cost of visiting a bicycle repair shop for even minor problems. Labor costs are fair, but for an hour of a bike mechanic's time (often the minimal charge), I can camp for up to four nights.

Basic tools

- [ ] Bicycle pump with connector which fits your bike valve, Schrader (car-type) or Presta
- [ ] Puncture repair kit
- [ ] Folding universal bike tool; Allen keys, straight screwdriver, star (Phillips) screwdriver
- [ ] Spoke key (spanner)
- [ ] Chain link remover
- [ ] Small pliers with cutting edge
- [ ] Universal bike wrench — get good quality steel, not soft iron or cast metal, otherwise they strip or break
- [ ] Adjustable wrench (shifting spanner) to fit the largest nut you feel competent to deal with

Special tools

Freewheel removers are essential to replace broken spokes on the gear side of rear wheel hubs. If you have a very heavily loaded bike, you could save a lot of labor costs by knowing how to use one and how to true your wheels. But note that there are different types and sizes and if you have to buy another freewheel unit, you may require a different tool than the one you have. Bike shops are reluctant to sell these tools, the excuse being that they are workshop tools and require special skills and training. I think it's a way of forcing cyclists to pay even more for the poor quality spokes for which they have already been ripped off. In two lessons anybody can learn how to

change a spoke and true a wheel while up to their backsides in crocodiles.

Spares:

- [ ] Insulation tape
- [ ] Spokes
- [ ] Inner tube; useful until it also gets punctured, but tubes can become irreparable
- [ ] Longest cable insert; can be cut to fit any brake or derailleur, but make sure the diameter of the cable matches those on your bike
- [ ] Short section of chain, or chain links and pins

If you're not an everyday cycle repairer, I suggest you get the excellent booklet *Roadside Bicycle Repair* by Rob van der Plas, published by Bicycle Books. It's also helpful as a point and communicate tool, due to the clear pictures and illustrations. You might save yourself a lot of trouble if you practice on a bike before you leave home.

Camping Equipment

No you don't have to camp out when touring by bike. But if you do, here are some suggestions for the equipment needed. Ideally, a tent should be lightweight, double-skinned (inner tent and full separate flysheet). The inner and groundsheet should be joined together as one piece, with the groundsheet forming part of the inner walls as well. The tent should be well ventilated, with insect-screened sealable vents front and rear. Your body gives off moisture in its recovery process when you're sleeping, so you need decent ventilation through your tent.

Stability in wind is important. The ubiquitous dome-type tents are least stable, with low, tapered tube or pup tents being most stable.

If you can collapse the tent inner inside the erected fly, dry it and pack it away, that's a great advantage when you want to leave the campsite on a rainy day. I use a small viscose towel which soaks away moisture immediately, leaving my tent dry enough to pack. There should be a section (usually at the entrance) where you can cook under cover during bad weather and store your extra luggage while you're sleeping. But be exceptionally careful when cooking near a tent. Most are made of synthetic materials which can go up in flames in seconds; if you're inside, you're toast.

Sleeping bags and mats

A good three-season sleeping bag with staggered seams is necessary for proper warmth. Temperatures can plummet anytime and it is never fun to spend a cold, sleepless night. After a day's cycling, your body needs rest and recovery time. Down bags, though warmest, lightest and packing very small, are utterly useless when wet. Bags stuffed with a mix of down and fiber are little better. Buy a bag that is longer than your body, as your body stretches out when recumbent and you need a little space to move.

Sleeping mats insulate you from the cold ground rather than providing comfort, though they'll do both to degrees reflected by their price. Some campers prefer three-quarter length mats, to reduce the load. Most mats are so light it hardly makes a difference. The thicker mats roll up into bulky

Camping out at Driebergen-Rijsenberg in the Netherlands.

packages and are awkward as baggage. I use a self-inflating, non-slip, full-length mattress which weighs in at 850 grams (1.875 lbs.) but is worth every extra ounce carried and every extra penny spent. It rolls into a tiny neat parcel and packs away easily. New products come onto the market constantly and self-inflating mattresses now come as light as 350 grams — less than a pound in weight.

In continental Europe, you'll find various items of camping equipment at hardware stores. There are specialist camping shops as well, usually in bigger centers. Some campsites sell gas canisters.

If you have problems getting gas for your stove, look for the nearest gas company depot, usually at the easily identified gas works with its high-rise metal structure. They often stock less common items.

Camp cookers (stoves) and cooking equipment

You can't take any kind of fuel and often not cookers either, on an airplane. Plan on buying what you need when you start your journey on the ground. You'll have a wide choice and you can be certain of getting equipment that uses widely available fuel.

What you will be cooking determines your equipment needs. Consider the fuels that are available. Factor in the weight of the cooking equipment, stove and supply of fuel. Don't be tempted to carry liquid fuel, as a spillage could cause severe problems.

Other useful bits and pieces

Towels made of super absorbent viscose are great for drying wet tents, bike seats and even sopping wet heads. Can also be used as lightweight bath towels.

Towels made of (synthetic) chamois provide a lightweight substitute for a bath towel. Should be washed after use to prevent odors, and kept damp.

Containers: your friendly neighborhood pharmacist (chemist) has plastic containers of all sizes in which bulk orders are supplied. These are tough and seal well, just the thing to carry your supplies of food, tools, or anything else. Wash them thoroughly before use. They could double as mugs.

Duct tape (Cloth tape backed with strong gum) is useful for repairing everything from pannier rips to tears in rainwear. Wrap a meter or so around a tubular container.

Rope: carry a section of nylon rope, about 4 meters (13 feet) long. Use for extra support for your tent, replacing broken tent guys, staking out your bike in an upright position and countless other things.

Dress

There is massive choice in cycling clothing available everywhere nowadays. Comfort, safety and hygiene are of prime importance, whatever you choose to wear.

When you use energy, your body heats up and then does its darndest to cool down. The end result is sweat, too often in greater volume than your skin can trade. Unless you dispose of the excess moisture, you're going to become uncomfortable. Garments with wicking properties, like viscose and polyester or poly-cotton mixes, are ideal next to your skin. At the opposite end of the scale are nylon and lycra.

Layer dressing is a great idea because for the same weight of clothing, you get greater choice and comfort.

Wicking only works properly if all your layers of clothing have wicking properties, maintaining the movement of moisture away from your skin.

Wash and wear fabrics make sense, too.

Loose, flapping garments around steering and drive mechanisms can cause dangerous control problems. Avoid clothing that catches the wind, as this makes you waste energy. Your garments should fit you well, neither too restricting when you're cycling, nor too loose. Shoelaces can catch in pedals and chain gears. As with equipment, pack and dress according to the dictum that if anything can get into the moving parts of your bicycle, it will.

All shirts, jackets and other clothing worn on your upper body, should be long enough to cover you effectively when you're cycling. Short garments will expose and cool your kidneys and reduce your ideal body temperature to an uncomfortable level.

Seat side
Padded cycle shorts are a great idea for preserving your goodwill towards your seat. They are also designed to soak up moisture and prevent chafing. You can buy the padding separately, which can be attached to the inside of shorts. Padded undershorts are also available. Whatever you decide to wear, avoid clothes which place a thick seam between you and the saddle (like many jeans do), as well as materials such as nylon that make you sweat in that region. This also very much applies to underwear. I wear poly-cotton shorts and cotton underpants and in colder weather, I pull on a pair of jogging longs with elasticized anklets and waistband.

This area (buttocks/groin) is where you're most likely to have prob-

lems if you don't take adequate care. Hygiene is of the utmost importance if you don't want saddle sores and the like. Wash yourself carefully every day and put on a clean change of clothing next to your skin as well.

Rain Gear
In the rain a cheap lightweight rainsuit will do, though it will probably get very wet (from body moisture) inside as well. If you're going to cycle longer distances, get a rainsuit which 'breathes', allowing your body moisture to escape, while keeping the rain out. These materials are more expensive, but with care can last a long time. Look for inside pockets with easy access. Outside pockets must seal properly, with a covered zip or velcro fastening. Outer pockets, however, are never really effective, most tending to either collect moisture, or be only usable when it's no longer raining. Rain ponchos are useless in wind, which usually accompanies rain, as they work as sails and can be blown about, causing all sorts of problems.

Helmets
At the date of writing (1999) it is not compulsory to wear a bicycle helmet in the Netherlands, Germany, France, or Switzerland, though this may change. Because there is proof that healmet wearers survive accidents that they wouldn't survive without, it makes sense to use one. If you damage the helmet, you must replace it, as it is only effective once.

Gloves:
Cycling gloves protect the palms of your hands if you fall, provide more padding against jarring, soak away sweat from your palms and improve your grip on the handlebars.

Glasses (spectacles):

You can keep your glasses in place in different ways, usually involving some kind of sweat-band. My band slides onto the two arms up to the lenses and is adjusted by sliding a toggle behind my head. It's lightweight, comfortable, effective and washable. I also use flip-up, clip-on sunshades. The flip-up feature is especially useful as you can ride through dark areas without having to remove the shades.

Going Out on the Town

Most nightclubs, concert halls and other entertainment areas prefer to see their customers dressed for the occasion. Smart-casual dress is fine for most occasions, with sneakers, jeans, tee-shirts, shorts and sandals being least acceptable. Casinos have dress rules which include jacket and tie for entry to salons. In the Netherlands, the better restaurants and clubs expect men to wear jackets, but ties are not always required. A small clip-on bow tie weighs very little and can be the difference between entry and embarrassment. Formal occasions always call for formal wear, which means suits for men and smart dresses (at last a chance to wear that little black number which every travel book will tell you to bring along) for women.

7
Safety Issues

This chapter deals with all issues relating to your security, both while riding your bike and when staying overnight or sightseeing.

Dealing with Traffic

General traffic rules and road safety (for RH/LH users):
Common traffic laws apply in the Netherlands, Germany, France, and Switzerland, with few exceptions. International highway signs are used throughout these countries.

If you're used to traveling on the left hand side of the road, it takes a short time to adapt to cycling on the right. Soon it becomes second nature, but you should be ultra-cautious until you're used to it. Most importantly, look left for nearside oncoming traffic, and not right as you're accustomed to doing. Also, look back over your left shoulder for maximum effect, not over your right shoulder.

Take time to work out the traffic flow before committing yourself to action. If in doubt, don't follow the herd, but wait until you're comfortable with your decision. You can be a pedestrian and push your bike to where you want to be. Use bike and pedestrian lights to your advantage every opportunity you get. Don't take chances.

Traffic travels on the right hand side of the road.

Overtake to the left of a vehicle or object. If the vehicle you want to pass is stationary and unlikely to move, you may overtake on the right. My advice is to play safe and always overtake on the left, when safe to do so.

Always be aware that you will be overtaken on the left. Don't automatically (if you normally travel on the left hand side of the road) move left to give way to a vehicle approaching from behind. They are not going to expect such a move.

In the Netherlands, cyclists never have right of way as a matter of course; you must give way to all other traffic, unless a traffic sign indicates otherwise. The rules are quite clear. Cyclists must give way to all traffic approaching from the right, including other bicycle traffic. Cyclists must also give way to all motorized traffic approaching from the left, unless signs clearly indicate otherwise. This applies to roads of all classes, so even if you are on a major road, you must give way to traffic approaching along a minor road.

Cyclists must give clear and timely hand signals, to indicate their intentions. You must come to a complete stop at "Stop" signs. Your speed must be adapted to road and traffic conditions.

Cyclists must give clear and timely audible (bell) warnings. You must have a bell and you must use it. There is no question of being rude or aggressive, it's as much for your own safety as that of pedestrians and other road users.

Where provided, bike paths must be used, however much better or more level the adjacent road surface may be. If the bike path provided is part of the motor roadway and is indicated by paint markings on the road surface, only that section of the road may be used by cyclists.

You will find some bike paths are unidirectional, others allow traffic in both directions. Many are shared with small motorcycles and motor scooters, as well as pedestrians.

At traffic circles (roundabouts), traffic circulates in an anti- (counter-) clockwise direction. Traffic entering the circle from the right sometimes has right of way over traffic already circulating, but most often traffic in the circle has right of way over traffic entering. Look for traffic signs well in advance and act accordingly. You will either see "Give Way" signs (inverted triangle) or "Right-of-Way" (yellow diamond with white border) signs. Usually, but not always, bicycle lanes are demarcated around the outer circumference of traffic circles, with signs indicating whether, and where, cyclists should give way. Where there are no signs, or no marked bike path, give way to the right as a matter of course. However, you are best advised to keep to the outer perimeter of the roadway and very carefully watch for vehicles which may cut you off to effect an exit,

or vehicles disregarding you on entry to the roundabout. Most of all, keep your head, be ultra-cautious, and don't get angry when a motorist does something stupid — they're probably having a nervous breakdown negotiating the roundabout, anyway.

You may only cycle two (and no more) abreast where you cause no hindrance to other traffic. Large groups of cyclists have the right to travel in bunches in some areas, but they usually have motor escorts with warning lights. In the interests of your own safety, cycle in single file, irrespective of how many are in your group.

You are obliged to use front and rear lights after dark. This is usually half an hour after official sundown, but use lights as soon as dusk falls, as well as in rain or mist, to ensure you are seen. You must have a visible white front reflector and a red rear reflector in fixed positions on your bicycle. The rear (red) reflector must be fitted to a fender (mudguard) at least 30 centimeters (12 inches) long and colored white or yellow in the Netherlands. Reflecting pedals are mandatory and spoke-mounted side reflectors or reflective tire sidewalls are also required.

Bicycles must be in good repair, roadworthy and safe to ride. Tires must be good, without excessive wear and brakes must be effective. Safe and adequate handlebars are mandatory.

Freeways are forbidden to cyclists, as are certain other roads, usually clearly marked. There are two signs indicating this. A blue circle with a pictogram of the rear end of an automobile (motor car) means that only motor vehicles are allowed past that point. The other sign is round with a red border and a bicycle silhouetted against a white background. Often you will see local language equivalents of

"No Bicycles" painted on an oblong sign below. On many cycling maps the bicycle-excluded roads are marked.

You have right of way when you see, immediately before an intersection, a yellow diamond- (lozenge) shaped sign with a white border. This normally relates only to the intersection immediately following the sign and does not give you the right of way thereafter. Keep an eye on the traffic, however, and be prepared to take evasive action.

Often at signaled intersections, you will see a smaller set of lights mounted lower down than normal traffic lights, usually at eye level and within arm's reach of a cyclist. These are for cyclists' use. The signals are usually displayed as red or green bicycles if on bike paths, or the normal red, amber and green if on a roadway. Many signaled intersections have control buttons mounted at the stop line. Use these to change the lights in your favor. Lights change sequentially through amber to green as well as red.

If you carry passengers on your bicycle, children under ten years of age must be seated in a child seat. These can be bought or hired at most bicycle shops.

The best rule is to watch the traffic very carefully and be prepared to give way at all times, especially inside roundabouts and at unsignaled intersections. It's not a matter of being intimidated, but purely of common sense. You can have a great holiday, or be a hospital case. Cycle assertively, but not aggressively. A bicycle is a legitimate vehicle and has the right to be on the road.

All distances in Europe are given in kilometers.

In the Netherlands you'll find an almost confusing array of bike route signs. They are well maintained, however, and once you know which sign relates to your particular journey, you can depend on them completely.

Standard road signs for cyclists are round and painted blue, sometimes white, with a pictogram in the middle. Routes shared by mopeds and cyclists have a white bicycle pictogram in the center of the sign. Bike paths shared with pedestrians have a vertical dividing line with an adult and child depicted on one side and a bicycle on the other. Two way traffic is shown with two arrows pointing in opposite directions.

Where mopeds are forbidden use of the bike path the traffic sign will appear as a small black on white oblong, with either "fietspad" or "rijwielpad" written on it. In Germany the sign reads "Keine Mofas" and pictograms show the black outline of a motorcycle, sometimes an automobile as well, on a white background, struck through diagonally with a line.

On motor roadways, bike paths are demarcated by either continuous or broken white lines, with pictograms of bicycles at intervals, painted on the road surface. In Switzerland a broken yellow line is painted on the roadway.

Signs for special routes have logos or codes and appear in a variety of colors. For instance the LF1 long distance route signs are prefixed either LF 1a or LF 1b, depending on whether you are traveling northwards or southwards, and they are painted green and white.

Signs specifically indicating bike paths and quiet country roads are shaped like the bottom half of a pyramid and mounted on a short post, about a foot high. You will find them at intersections. They're called "paddestoelen" (toadstools) and they indicate distance as well as direction on all four sides. On top is a number which can be cross-referenced with maps and guides.

City guide maps are usually found at the entrance of large towns. Smaller villages sometimes have the map in the shopping area, or outside the town hall, near the information office.

Personal security and safety of effects

Outside major cities there is little more than petty crime, but you won't consider the loss of your bicycle to be unimportant. I always lock my bike as a matter of course, no insult intended to the locals, but I have everything to lose by being over-sensitive.

A sturdy U-lock is best, but a long, thick cable lock combination makes it easier to lock the bike to something permanent. If you thread the cable through your bike wheels, frame and luggage and attach that to an immovable object, like a lamp-post, you are less likely to find anything missing on your return. It's no good locking only your bike frame to a post, for you may lose your wheels, seat or anything that comes off easily. This is the downside of quick-release hubs and seat-post clamps. Ensure that your bike can't be lifted off the post.

Larger towns in the Netherlands have bicycle lockers or guarded parking areas. In Basel (Switzerland) there are safe storage facilities at rail stations, as there are safe storage places around other cities, including at hotels, restaurants and parking areas. Bike storage facilities are usually indicated by a pictogram of a bicycle under a peaked, sloping roof, much like a flattened caret (^). Sometimes the caret is replaced with an elongated, inverted "L."

Europe has its share of con-artists, ever on the lookout for an easy mark, usually a gullible foreigner, but you can still be open and friendly whilst taking care. Most people are genuine, friendly and hospitable, without any thought of dishonesty.

Hotels, and often hostels and campsites, have safes in which you can deposit your valuables. Don't leave money, checks, credit cards, passports and other valuable items lying around. In big city hostels and in camp sites, I sleep with my money belt, keys and documents inside my sleeping bag or sheet bag. Under your pillow is not safe, it's a favorite with thieves.

Maximum blood-alcohol level permitted is 80mg/100ml. This equates roughly to half a liter of beer, but bear in mind that beers are of different strengths and every person reacts differently to alcohol.

Health Precautions

Be sure to read the section in Chapter 6 that deals with your choice of clothing and the health reasons for choosing garments made of the correct materials. The value of good personal hygiene cannot be overstated.

If you are on medication, or may require medication during your trip, make sure you take enough with you. Also, have your prescription available to present to customs officers and to doctors you might see for treatment.

The Netherlands has one of the highest health care standards in the world. Life expectancy is higher than the USA average. Doctors and nurses understand English as many medical textbooks are available only in English.

If you are not an EEC citizen, you need to be covered by health insurance to qualify for medical treatment. EEC citizens need only produce the E111 form available from any Post Office in the UK and Eire.

In the Netherlands, for assistance with rules and regulations, call the Health Service's Foreign Affairs Department in Utrecht, during office hours, at (030) 618881.

Water can safely be drunk from domestic supplies, but never from fountains, streams, rivers and springs, throughout the Rhine countries. If in doubt, ask, otherwise boil water before using. Where water is not safe to drink, you will normally find a picture sign indicating this. The words "non-potable" or "Kein Trinkwasser" means that you should not drink the water. Bottled water, carbonated (gaz) and plain (sin gaz), is available everywhere.

Smoking is a common habit, and Dutch tobacco products are highly es-teemed by smokers around the world. If you are a non-smoker and anti-smoking, you should carefully choose your train carriage or restaurant seat. Non-smoking areas are normally clearly marked.

Foodstuffs are produced and supplied to the most stringent health standards. Use the same criteria for buying food as you do at home.

Remember that not all the organisms you will come into contact with are the same as those your body is used to, so ease yourself into adventurous eating and drinking. Whatever you do though, don't miss out on the local dishes and drinks.

German and French medical services are equally as good as those in the Netherlands. Doctors and nurses will generally understand English.

Switzerland has no state medical service and is not a member of the EEC. You should take out health and

Bicycles-only facility and windmill at Oud-Ade, the Netherlands.

accident insurance for your stay, as you must pay the full cost of medical treatment.

The problem of exhaustion ("the bonk," or "rider's knock") is discussed in many bike books, but bears repetition. It's easy to get carried away with sight-seeing or the enjoyment of cycling along, forgetting to eat and drink to refuel your body. When your body is burning energy at a high rate, it needs a reservoir of slow-release fuel to keep it going. Eating carbohydrates such as bread or bananas at regular intervals, is good practice. Don't miss breakfast or lunch under any circumstances. Some cyclists carry chocolate bars to refuel in emergencies, but that energy won't last long and will worsen the problem after a while. Power Bars and similar energy foods are more suitable. The answer is to adopt a routine of regular eating habits.

Dehydration is another concern. In cool weather or if a cool breeze is blowing, you may not feel the need to drink. However, as you cycle your body is continuously sweating and you need to replace that liquid. Here again, adopting a routine is the answer. You can, for instance, decide that every hour, on the hour, you will drink a mouthful of water, whether you feel thirsty or not. You know you're dehydrated when you don't urinate, by which time it's too late. Fast relief from dehydration can be had by drinking a solution of salt and sugar, or a mix of milk and regular cola. Medical help should be sought however, to ensure there is no lasting damage.

Even in the far north latitudes of the Rhine regions, the sun can burn skin. Sunburn can occur even when there is complete cloud cover. Make sure all exposed parts of your body, especially the more angular parts, such as your ears and nose, are protected with sun screen. Commonly forgotten parts are elbows, necks and the backs of knees, until bath-time. Sunstroke can be extremely dangerous, so covering your head and neck is recommended.

To avoid cramping, you should do some muscle stretching exercises when you stop and again before you start off again. Stretching exercises are a good idea at the beginning and at the end of your day, as well as at the intermediate stop

The only problem bugs I've encountered in the Rhine region are the midges (gnats, miggies) which seem to congregate in dense swarms at specific points along the water's edge at certain times of the day. They do not bite or sting so don't panic if you encounter them.

There are bees and wasps around, of course, but I've never been troubled by any. If you're allergic to the stings, you should bring the anti-histamines you normally use. The oft repeated warning against singing or whistling as you cycle along is here repeated. A bug in the windpipe is not a pleasant thing.

You should always be aware of the dangers of sexually transmitted diseases and take the necessary precautions.

How Far to Ride

This question is a matter of simple arithmetic: speed, saddle time, distance, routing, point to point, etc.

To get the most from your journey, plan your itinerary bearing in mind your capabilities as well as your intentions.

If you are an average cyclist and haven't done a lot of long-distance cycling or are not used to carrying extra weight on your bicycle, use the following ball-park figures to help you decide how far to cycle every day.

Average speed

You will probably average about 14 to 16 kilometers per hour (8.75 to 10 miles per hour). This takes into account only the time you spend in the saddle. Road surfaces will be a factor, as hard surfaces are easier (and faster) to cycle on than softer ones. Hardened gravel or sand roads are measurably slower than asphalt or brick-paved tracks. Bumpy and worn surfaces are slower again. Wet weather will slow you down, as well as head and cross-winds. Factor in as much as a 30% lower average speed if you expect adverse conditions. On very hot days you may want to take a break through the hottest period.

Saddle time

The time you spend cycling will be time you do not spend sight-seeing, eating, shopping, photographing and so on. Daylight varies from about 7 hours in mid-winter, to nearly 18 hours in mid-summer. Also, you may need to arrive at, or leave from, your accommodation at a specified time.

In order to maximize your time, energy and enjoyment, set an achievable target destination. If you decide to leave your lodgings at 09h00 and expect to reach your destination at 20h00, that gives you 11 hours to travel, with all the sight-seeing and exploring you

want to do along the way. In general, an average cyclist should have enough energy to cycle a good 4 to 5 hours in a day, provided they are in good health, well-rested and using appropriate equipment. That saddle time would give you a minimum range of 56 (14 km/h x 4 hrs) kilometers and a maximum of 80 (16 km/h x 5 hrs) kilometers (35 to 50 miles).

If you have over-estimated your energy or fitness levels, don't spoil your holiday by "toughing it out." Completing your journey by train can be a refreshing experience. If you're not sure of your abilities, it makes sense to choose a route that keeps you within easy reach of a train network.

Nuclear Reactors

Along the Rhine route you will pass a few nuclear reactors used for electric power generation. These plants are maintained to the strictest safety standards. A number of agencies, some independent and without restrictions, monitor the plants constantly. According to the German Federal Environment Ministry, the "average radiation exposure" in Germany "amounts to 2.4 millisievert (mSv) a year" (1992).

Operational reactors along the Rhine route that I know about, are near Kalkar, Mülheim-Kärlich (northwest of Koblenz) and at Biblis (northeast of Worms) in Germany; in the Netherlands the only plant I know that is near the route is one on the Waal river due south of Wageningen.

8 The Countries

In this chapter, we'll briefly introduce each of the countries you will be traveling through — The Netherlands, Germany, France, and Switzerland.

The Netherlands

The Netherlands is situated in northwest Europe, bounded by Germany in the east and north, France in the southeast, and Belgium in the south. The west and north-west lies on the North Sea which is part of the northern Atlantic Ocean. The entire country lies within an alluvial coastal plain which once stretched from French Flanders to Denmark. Much of the country is below sea level, protected from encroaching waters by systems of dikes, sea walls and drains.

A large proportion of the Netherlands has been reclaimed from the sea and the flood plains of rivers, notably the Rhine and Maas. The sea flooded parts of the country during great storms through the ages. Modern engineering tamed the elements sufficiently to allow the reclamation program to continue. However, seasonal river floods, especially in the upper Rhine area, still pose problems. Also, while sea levels continue to rise, land areas are sinking.

Due to flood control measures, many major water courses don't allow for riverside cycling, but you'll never be far from water anywhere in the Netherlands, especially in the south. The route described, however, follows the original course of the Rhine (in its more modern passage to the sea) and will keep you constantly in touch with the river.

The capital city of the Netherlands is Amsterdam, with the seat of government, diplomatic center and Royal residence as well as the International Court of Justice located at Den Haag (The Hague). The modern state began life in Utrecht in 1579 when seven Dutch provinces signed a treaty binding themselves to political union.

The Dutch are divided about one third Catholics, one third Protestants, and one third non-denominational. Since the Reformation, the Dutch have been known for their religious tolerance and they harbored many people who fled their homelands due to religious persecution. However, there are still deep divisions between Catholics and Protestants within the country. Amongst the most famous of the religious refugees were the English group who later went to America and became known as the Pilgrim Fathers.

The official language in the Netherlands is Nederlands (Dutch). Standard Dutch is the formal language taught in schools. Most Dutch people speak a second and often a third language. English is reasonably widely spoken, more so in cities than rural areas.

In the Netherlands you will find great cultural diversity, the result of a colonial past and status as a great seafaring nation. This is reflected in the variety of culinary tastes. Fine coffees, spicy Indonesian foods and traditional Dutch cooking, high quality beer, spirits, and tobacco have been the pride of Holland for centuries.

Dutch beers are exported or brewed in beer drinking countries around the world. Dutch liqueurs are varied and interesting. Genever, a type of gin typically made of juniper berries, is a liquor peculiar to the Netherlands, usually drunk before meals as an aperitif.

Breakfasts ("ontbijt") are not the hasty meals you may be used to. They are strongly biased towards energy foods like a choice of breads and cheeses. You'll get thinly sliced meats, various jams and butter. Black tea, or sometimes fruit tea or herbal tea, is more usually offered than coffee.

Along the road you'll find other opportunities to keep up your energy level. If I come across a pancake ("pannekoek") or waffle vendor, I invariably stop for a bite. Roadside truck stops, restaurants, and bars offer the chance to have an "uitsmijter," which is sliced bread topped with fried eggs on cheese and ham or roast beef slices. You may come to a village or town on market day and the numerous stalls with raw or cooked food will be worthwhile exploring. Bread rolls (broodje) with delicious toppings are standard lunch-time fare.

Dutch sea foods include raw herring (haring) and smoked eel as delicacies. The former Dutch colonies in the East Indies have contributed much to their table, including the enormously varied "rijsttafel" (rice with a wide variety of spiced sauces and foodstuffs).

Dutch cheeses, such as Edam, Gouda, and Leiden, are an essential part of the national cuisine. Yogurt, buttermilk and milk are extremely popular foods as well. Another milk product is vla, a kind of custard pudding.

Local dishes at budget prices can be enjoyed at restaurants with "Nederlands Dis" signs. "Tourist menus" are excellent value as well.

The famous and popular Dutch coffees come in many flavors and strengths. Filter coffee is most commonly drunk, often black.

In the Netherlands, there are sects and communities whose preference for different lifestyles is evident in the way they dress and go about their business. It may seem quaint, curious or even strange to a visitor from another culture, but these people, living in their own country are entitled to their lifestyle without interference. If you want to photograph them, you should only do so with their permission. Some sects do not permit themselves to be photographed and you should respect their decision without argument. Others don't mind if asked. You may also come across Dutch people dressed in national costume, some for carnivals and fairs, others as added attraction at a tourist venue.

The Dutch language has a polite form, but straight-talking is encouraged by the structure of the language, which has no time for vagaries and innuendo.

As many Dutch people speak some English, you will generally find somebody who will understand your questions. However, you can never completely rely on this, so it's a good idea to practice some essential phrases and to attune your ear to the most likely responses.

Dutch Questions

Excuse me please	pardon
Sir	mijnheer
Madam	mevrouw
Please speak slowly	langzaam praten
	alstublieft
Could you direct me to...	kunt U mij de
	weg wijzen naar...
Could you tell me...	kunt U mij zeggen...
where is/are	waar is/zijn
how do I get to	hoe kom ik bij
the nearest	de nabijste
washroom/toilet	het toilet
police station	het politiebureau
hospital	het ziekenhuis
pharmacy/chemist	apotheek
bicycle repair shop	fietsenswinkel
Post Office	de Post
Is it far?	Is het ver?
What was that (you said)?	Wablief?

Expected replies

directly along	vooruit
that way	die richting
turn left	linksaf
right	rechts
directly opposite	tegenover
on the left-hand side	aan de linkerkant
on the right-hand side	aan de rechterkant
go back/return	draai om/keer om
around the corner	om de hoek
at the traffic lights	bij het verkeerslicht
along this road	langs deze weg
crossroads	de kruising
first	eerste
second	tweede
third	derde
fourth	vierde
across	over
under	onder
from...to	van...tot
on top	boven
the bridge	de brug
the canal	het kanaal
the motorway	de autoweg
the road/street	de weg/de straat
the bike path	het fietspad

1. *Fielding's Holland* 1994, H. Constance Hill, Fielding Worldwide Inc., USA ,1994.

2. *The Dutch: How they Live and Work.* Ann Hoffmann, David & Charles (Holdings) Limited, Newton Abbot, UK, 1973.

3. *The Netherlands.* Nina Nelson, BT Batsford Ltd, London, 1987.

Germany

In Germany, you'll be traveling through the "Länder" (states) Nordrhein-Westfalen, Rheinland-Pfalz, Hessen, and Baden-Württemberg.

Germany is situated in north central Europe. In 1990, West and East Germany were re-united, after partition following World War II. To the north lies Denmark and the Baltic sea. The east borders on Poland and the Czech Republic, with Austria to the south-east and south. Switzerland lies along the southern boundary. To the west are France, Luxembourg, Belgium, and the Netherlands. On the northwest corner, is the North Sea.

North Germany is flat, with broad, slow-moving rivers, lakes and marshes. The center east (Bavaria) is mountainous with much afforestation.

Central regions are hilly, with forests in the higher regions. In the Saar area of Germany, once the major coal-mining region, the Hunsrück mountains rise away from the Rhine and Mosel valleys. North of the Mosel valley, the Eifel mountains create another physical barrier. In the south east, the Black Forest covers a considerable part of the country, rising to almost 1,400 meters (4,550 feet) above sea level in parts.

German union was given impetus by the Prussians in the 1840s when most of present-day Germany was owned and ruled by any number of princes, arch-dukes, dukes and other noblemen, many of whom owed allegiance to foreign potentates. It was not an easy road to unification and Germany's neighbors can attest to that. In its history of barely 120 years, the modern German state has not only suffered the turmoil of nationhood, but has acquired and lost colonies, caused the two greatest conflicts the world has known and excited every emotion known to mankind. Today Germany stands as a recently re-united state, central to the peace and prosperity of the European continent.

The Germans are evenly divided between Protestantism and Catholicism. Generally speaking, the southern "Länder" (states) are more Catholic and the northern, more Protestant. The Rhineland is famous for many religious leaders having been born, lived or worked there. From St. Willibrord (the Irish/Englishman) who lived at Wesel, then converted the Danes to Christianity, to Martin Luther, the great reformer whose trial at Worms split the German nation, to the persecution of the Jews, the Rhine has seen it all. Today, with a broad disparity of religious thought, and the lessons of the horror of the Holocaust, Germany guarantees religious freedom in its constitution and vigorously applies the principle.

Standard High German ("Hochdeutsch") is taught in all German schools and is the common language. Many dialects co-exist with High German and regional accents enrich the language, simultaneously creating problems of broader communication. Many Germans speak English, especially the younger generations, though this is not universally true. In cities you are most likely to find the majority of English speakers.

Throughout the Rhine region, the local food and drink has found favor amongst epicures, gourmands and gourmets around the world. Fortunately for the rest of us, local dishes are eaten by the common people and remain affordable, as do the fine wines, beers, and liqueurs. This is not to say that your favorite burger bar will not be represented in towns and cities along the way.

Because of the broad representation of many cultures, religions and communities through the Rhine countries, you will be able to find specialist restaurants which cater to your specific needs, especially in the larger towns and cities. Vegetarians and vegans, or others with certain dietary or religious restrictions should have no trouble fulfilling their needs. Local information offices, or tourist agencies in your own country, have relevant information to hand. Equally, facilities for the physically impaired are generally provided as a matter of course. Check with your agent or one of the national tourist offices.

Supermarkets display a wide variety of foods and delicacies. For the budget traveler, inexpensive food markets like Aldi, Lidl, and Penny-Markt are full of quality low-priced foods and toiletries.

Although the Rhine is famous for its wines, beer is also a favored drink amongst Germans. Drunk driving laws are very strict and cyclists are not excepted. Cyclists have come up with a compromise and the "Radler" takes its name from them. It is essentially a beer shandy — a mix of beer and lemonade, also known as "Alsterwasser."

Germans favor their own regional beers and will always recommend them above others. There is a great variety of beers to choose from, made from various grains, bottom or top brewed, dark and light, ales, lagers and pilseners, high-alcohol, low-alcohol and non-alcoholic. The Irish pubs found in every city serve typical Irish beers as well as the German beers.

German food found the length of the Rhine varies enormously in its regional specialties, but a standard diet resembles that of the Dutch. Along the route, especially in the main tourist areas, you will find roadside "Imbiss" stalls selling snacks, ice-cream, and soft drinks.

German menus always contain a good choice of meat dishes, especially pork. Beef steaks are popular and surprisingly inexpensive for Europe. Argentinian steak is often offered. Pasta is also commonly available, the Swabian "Spätzle," being a particular favorite.

Eating places include the traditional "Gasthaus," "Gasthof," and "Gaststätte" where you can enjoy local dishes and specialities, usually for a reasonable price. The "Rathaus-Keller" (Ratskeller) in any town will provide great food and drink, but can sometimes be quite pricey. Restaurants display menus and prices outside the premises, so you can always see what's on special. Most towns will have a choice of restaurants, offering a wide variety of food from many countries.

Germans set great store by the formalizing of relationships in a proper way. Younger people who have traveled, and there are a great number of them, are more relaxed and easily approachable. A display of good manners and not too much familiarity to begin with, will score you enough points to break down the Germans' naturally understandable reserve. The Germans are a remarkably generous and hospitable people, with a great love of the good life.

Women should be addressed as "Frau," men as "Herr." The term "Fräulein," meaning Miss, should not be used as it will cause offence. Rather call all women "Frau," whether married or not.

When meeting people, and before leaving, it is customary to shake hands with everybody, even children. When entering a shop, it's normal to say "Guten Tag," meaning Good day. When leaving, say "Auf Wiedersehen," Goodbye. If you share a table with others for meals, wish them "Guten Appetit" and your reply to the same should be "Danke, gleichfalls," Thank you, likewise.

If you have been invited to somebody's home, it is usual to take a small gift to your hostess, normally chocolates or flowers. Usually you can get these at rail station shops, but remember that most shops are closed on Sundays and you'll probably have better luck at gas stations.

German Questions

Excuse me please · · · · · · Entschuldigen Sie bitte

Sir · Herr

Madam · · · · · · · · · · · · · · · · · · Frau
Please speak slowly · · Sprechen Sie langsam bitte
Could you direct me to... · Können Sie mir den Weg
· · · · · · · · · · · · · · · · · nach ... zeigen
Could you tell me... · · · · · Können Sie mir sagen...
where is/are · · · · · · · · · · · · · · · wo ist/sind
how do I get to · · · · · · · · · wie komme ich nach
the nearest · · · · · · · · · · die /der /das nächste
washroom/toilet · · · · · · · · · · · · · die Toiletten
police station · · · · · · · · · · · die Polizeiwache
hospital · · · · · · · · · · · · · das Krankenhaus
pharmacy/chemist · · · · · · · · · · · die Apotheke
bicycle repair shop · · · · · · das Fahrrad-geschäft
Post Office · · · · · · · · · · die Post/das Postamt
Is it far? · · · · · · · · · · · · · · · · Ist es weit?
What was that (you said)? · · · · · · · · Wie, bitte?
Expected replies
directly along · · · · · · · · · · · · · · geradeaus
that way · · · · · · · · · · · · · · · · da entlang
turn left · · · · · · · · Biegen Sie (nach) links (ab)
right · rechts
directly opposite · · · · · · · · · · · gegenüber
on the left-hand side · · · · · · · · · · · · links
on the right-hand side · · · · · · · · · · · rechts
go back/return · · · · · · · · · · · · zurückkehren
around the corner · · · · · · · · · · · um die Ecke
at the traffic lights · · · · · bei der (Verkehrs)ampel
along this road · · · · · · · · · auf dieser Strasse
crossroads · · · · · · · · · · · · · die Kreuzung
first · erste
second · · · · · · · · · · · · · · · · · · zweite
third · · · · · · · · · · · · · · · · · · · dritte
fourth · · · · · · · · · · · · · · · · · · · vierte
across · · · · · · · · · · · · · · · · · · · über
under · · · · · · · · · · · · · · · · · · · unter
from...to · · · · · · · · · · · · · · · · von...bis
on top · · · · · · · · · · · · · · · · · · · auf
the bridge · · · · · · · · · · · · · · die Brücke
the canal · · · · · · · · · · · · · · · der Kanal
the motorway · · · · · · · · · · · · die Autobahn
the road/street · · · · der Weg/die Strasse/der Pfad
the bike path · · · · · · · · · · · · der Rradweg

1. *Insight Guides, The Rhine.* Ed. Kristiane Müller, APA Publications, Hong Kong, 1991.

2. *Blue Book Germany.* James Bentley, A&C Black, London, 1987. (later printings available)

3. *Myths and Legends of Germany.* Lewis Spence, Studio Editions Ltd., London, 1993.

France

In France, you'll be traveling in the Alsace region, comprising the departments Haut Rhin, and Bas Rhin (Upper and Lower Rhine, respectively)

Alsace is bounded on the east by Germany, the border being the center of the river Rhine. To the south lies Switzerland, to the north, the German state of Rheinland-Pfalz. To the west is the rest of France.

Although France is predominantly Catholic in outlook, Alsace is equally Protestant as it is Catholic. The major religious difference between this region and anywhere else in Europe, is that churches are shared by both denominations.

The Alsatian wine route clings to the edge of the Rhine valley along the slopes of the Vosges mountains, from Obernai to Thann and produces some of the best wines in Europe. Nearly half the wine drunk in France itself comes from Alsace, a perfect clue as to its quality, value and variety. The fertile soil of the upper Rhine plain also encourages the growing of fruit, from which a wide selection of liqueurs are produced.

Alsace is also famous for its beers. Not surprisingly, all these drinks are matched with food and the Alsatian table is packed with novelty, imagination and excellence. Onions are a favorite food and the onion tart a speciality. Cooking methods and foodstuffs from both Germany and France, and sometimes even further afield, are used to produce the uniquely Alsatian dishes.

The eating experience in Alsace is a carefree, sociable activity, with ample time to savor every mouthful of food or drink. You could spend a whole afternoon enjoying lunch or an entire evening over dinner. Fresh-water fish (carp, zander, perch, pike, trout. eel) dishes are other specialities of the region, as are the fruit tarts (tartes flambées), sauerkraut (choucroute), Münster cheese and the wonderful lamb-beef-pork stew called le bäeckoffa.

By law, French restaurants must display their menus and prices outside the door. Most dishes are served with vegetables.

As midday lunch (le déjeuner) is the largest and most important meal of the day, you will find in smaller towns and villages that the streets are virtually deserted between noon and 14h00.

Although some Alsatians speak Hochdeutsch, many speak the Elsass dialect, which is a soft and lovely language. They all speak French, so communicate in that language if you can. Alsatians are proudly French, so never presume that although their outward appearance may impress you as being German, they are not really French at all. Old-fashioned manners are as important here as they are anywhere along the Rhine.

Young people in Alsace are more likely to speak English than their elders. Older citizens are often fluent in German and French. Policemen are usually sent from other parts of France and some speak very good English and French, but usually no German.

French Questions

Excuse me please · · · Excusez-moi, s'il vous plaît

Sir · · · · · · · · · · · · · · · · · · Monsieur
Madam · · · · · · · · · · · · · · · · · Madame
Please speak slowly Parlez-vous lentement, s'il vous plaît
Could you direct me to... Pouvez-vous m'indiquer le
· chemin de...
Could you tell me... · · · · · Pouvez-vous me dire...
where is/are · · · · · · · · · · · · · où est/sont
how do I get to · · · · · · · · · · · · pour aller à
the nearest · · · · · · · · · · · · · le plus proche
washroom/toilet · · · · · · · · · · · les toilettes
police station · · · · · · · · · · le poste de police
hospital· · · · · · · · · · · · · · · · · l'hôpital
pharmacy/chemist · · · · · · · · · · la pharmacie
bicycle repair shop · · un atelier de reparations des
· vélos
Post Office · · · · · · · · · · · · · · la Poste
Is it far? · · · · · · · · · · · · · · · c'est loin?
What was that (you said)? · · · · · · · Comment?
Expected replies
directly along · · · · · · · · · · · · allez tout droit
that way · · · · · · · · · · · · · · · par là
turn left · · · · · · · · · · · · tournez à gauche
right · · · · · · · · · · · · · · · · · à droite
directly opposite · · · · · · · · · · · · en face
on the left-hand side· · · · · · · · · sur la gauche
on the right-hand side · · · · · · · · · sur la droite
go back/return· · · · allez-vous en arrière/retournez
around the corner · · · · · · · · · · après le coin
at the traffic lights · · · · · · · · · aux feux rouge
along this road · · · · · · · · · suivez cette route
crossroads · · · · · · · · · · · · · · le carrefour
first · · · · · · · · · · · · · · · · · · première
second · · · · · · · · · · · · · · · · deuxième
third· · · · · · · · · · · · · · · · · · troisième
fourth · · · · · · · · · · · · · · · · quatrième
across · · · · · · · · · · · · · · · en face (de)
under · · · · · · · · · · · · · · · · · · sous
from...to · · · · · · · · · · · · · · · de...à/en/au
on top · · · · · · · · · · · · · · · · · · sur
the bridge · · · · · · · · · · · · · · · le pont
the canal· · · · · · · · · · · · · · · · le canal
the freeway · · · · · · · · · · · · · · l'autoroute
the road/street· · · · · · · · · · · · la route/la rue
the bike path · · · · · · · · · · chemin des vélos

1. *Alsace*. James Bentley, Aurum Press Ltd, London, 19882.

2   *Baedeker's France*. James Hogarth (transl.), Jarrold & Sons Ltd., Norwich, 1984. (newer printings available)

Switzerland

Switzerland lies in the center of Europe. To the north lies Germany, to the east, Austria and to the south, Italy. The west borders France. In the northeast, sandwiched against Austria, is the tiny principality of Liechtenstein, the third smallest sovereign state in the world.

About half of Switzerland's land area is taken up by the spectacular Alps mountain range. The St Gotthard glaciers give rise to two of Europe's most important rivers, the Rhine and the Rhône. From the lower Alps, the Swiss plain sweeps northwards to the Rhine valley.

The constitution of 1848 guarantees religious freedom throughout Switzerland, the result of religious wars and conflicts since the sixteenth century. There is no state religion as such. The Christian religions are dominant, with an equal division between Catholicism and Protestantism. Basel is predominantly Protestant.

Switzerland is a multilingual country, with German, French, Italian, and Romansch as official languages. In the Basel cantons, German and French are equally important. The Swiss are generally competent English speakers. In Basel, the commonly spoken form of German is the regional variation of Schwyzerdütsch (Swiss German — a derivation of the ancient Alemannic language), called Baslerdütsch.

The Swiss are well-known for their excellent cuisine. Basel has strong French and German influences, especially those from nearby Alsace and Swabia.

Switzerland is a highly militarized country. Discipline is extremely important to the Swiss and you will be expected to obey all rules without argument, or you will be put firmly in your place. They keep their promises and expect nothing less from others. They are generally reserved and rather insular, with a strong dislike of fanaticism coupled with intense patriotism.

Despite their sobriety, the Swiss participate in an inordinate number of festivals, fairs, carnivals and costume processions. Swiss-style wrestling and flag throwing are old customs continued to this day.

In Basel, the major annual festival is the Fastnacht which takes place on the first Monday following Ash Wednesday. For 72 hours, beginning at 4 A.M. on the Monday, costumed musicians wander the old town, while floats glide through the city streets.

Earlier in the year, Basel celebrates the Vogel Gryff ceremony on the Rhine. Easter, Spring (May day), Swiss national day (August 1), and other memorable days of the year bring out the revelers as well.

1. *Culture Shock! Switzerland*. Shirley Eu-Wong, Kuperard (London) Ltd, London, 1996.

2. *Visitor's Guide Switzerland*. John Marshall, Hunter Publishing Inc, New Jersey, USA, 1995.

General Tourist Information

In this chapter, we'll deal with the more prosaic issues of your trip: useful information, presented here with as few words as possible. First, below is a list of useful telephone numbers.

Health Services

Netherlands:

❑ Doctors ("Arts"):
Weekdays only. Consulting hours vary. Emergencies phone 112.

❑ Dentists ("Tandarts"):
As for doctors

❑ Pharmacies/Chemists ("Apotheek"):

Services Phone Numbers

	Netherlands	Germany	France	Switzerland
Police (emergency)	112	110	17	117
Police (non-urgent)	0900-8844			
Ambulance	112	110	15	114 or 177
Fire brigade	112	112	18	118
Doctor (emergency)	112			2611515
Pharmacy (Chemist)				2611515
Tourist Info	varies	varies	03988250166	120
Weather	06-8003	069-80620	0136680267	162
Local operator	090-8418	010	13	111
International operator	0800-890031	0010	0033 + intl country code	114
Directory enquiries (local)	0900-8008	1188 or 01188	12	111
Directory enquiries (intern'l.)	0900-8008	00118		114
Info in English (pay)	0900-8008			1575014

Monday–Friday, 08h00 to 17h30. Some open evenings, at night and through weekends. All pharmacies (chemists) have a sign on the door indicating where the nearest emergency pharmacy is.

Germany:

❏ Doctors ("Artz"):
From 10h00 to midday and 16h00 to 18h00, except Wednesdays, Saturdays and Sundays. Cities and larger towns have emergency numbers for doctors and dentists on call. Look in the phone book, or ask the local operator for "Ärtzlicher Notfalldienst." Otherwise ask the local police.

❏ Dentists ("Zahnartz"):
As for Doctors, but ask operator for "Zahnärtzlicher Notfalldienst."

❏ Pharmacies (Chemists) ("Apotheke"):
Normal business hours (see *Shops* in following section). A notice gives details of night-time and weekend services.

France:

❏ Doctors ("Médicin"):
Local police have details.

❏ Dentists ("Dentiste"):
In emergencies, call the local operator, otherwise enquire at the info center ("Syndicat d'initiative").

❏ Pharmacies/Chemists ("Pharmacie"):
Local police have details. Local newspapers also print details of emergency pharmacies.

Switzerland:

❏ Doctors (as French/German):
Monday to Friday, 08h00–18h00, closed weekends. For information in English, call the "Anglo-Phone" number, 157 5014.

❏ Dentists: as for doctors.

❏ Pharmacies/Chemists:
Monday to Friday, 08h00–18h00 and Saturdays 08h00–16h00. After hours, call the Anglo-Phone number for information.

Telephone Services

First a word of warning: Calls made from hotels are liable to a surcharge which can be high — sometimes as much as five times normal cost. Some hotel operators can't connect you to long distance servers. International operators can help to access your phone card.

❏ Cell (mobile) phones:
Check with your service provider if your system is compatible with the continental European systems and arrange for "rover" connection.

Netherlands:

❏ Pay phones:
Instructions are printed in English. International calls can be made only from pay phones displaying national flags. Coin pay phones are no longer used.

❏ Phone cards:
Cards valued at ƒ 5, ƒ 10 and ƒ 25 are available from tobacconists, railway stations, post offices, and other outlets. A display shows

you the amount remaining while you talk. Rates are cheaper in off-peak hours, in the evenings and weekends. Chip-Knip cards are rechargeable by credit card and can be bought from banks.

❏ Collect calls from pay phones: Dial 0800-0101. Some pay phones have a button (collect) for calling the operator.

❏ Call home facility: USA direct and similar facilities are available at some pay phones.

❏ Credit card calls: All major cards accepted.

Germany:
You'll find public telephones at post offices, at train stations, in public buildings, inside some stores and restaurants and on the street.

Pay phones for international calls have instructions in English. These are marked "Ausland" or "International."

Pay phones take phone cards or coins (10 Pf, DM 1 and DM 5), also Dutch PTT phone cards. Some take credit cards. Larger Post Offices have phone booths where calls can be made and paid for at the counter. You must leave a deposit before making your call.

Lower call rates apply from 18h00 to 06h00, Monday through Friday and Saturday and Sunday, but only for internal calls.

Phone home services are available. Make sure you have the access codes.

❏ Collect calls: Collect calls are only available to the USA. The number of the operator is often 0010, but may vary by region. Check the

telephone book under "Sonderdienste," for "R-Gespräch."

❏ Note: dialing tone is a continuous high pitched signal, not the buzzing tone you may be used to. Ringing tone is an intermittent long signal of the same pitch. Busy signal is a series of short tones.

❏ Toll free (free-phone) numbers begin with 130. If calling from a payphone, don't insert coins.

France:
Most pay phones accept phone cards ("télécarte"). Buy them from Post Offices, newsagents, tobacconists and wherever they are advertised in telephone booths. Where you see a blue bell sign on a phone booth, you can receive calls, but on other phone booths incoming calls are barred.

Switzerland:
Phone cards: This is called a "Taxcard" and costs Sfr 5, Sfr 10 or Sfr 20. Buy at Post Offices, newsagents and railway stations. Anglo-Phone (1575014) is a 24 hour pay information line in English.

Mail services

Netherlands:
Post Offices ("Postkantoor") open Monday–Friday, 08h30 to 17h00. In larger centers they open Saturdays, 08h30 to midday. Postage stamps are called "postzegels."

Germany:
Post Offices ("Postamt") open 08h00 to 18h00, Mondays through Fridays and Saturdays, 08h00 to noon. In cities,

they may open longer hours, some all night. Stamps ("Briefmarken") are sold in Post Offices, and from vending machines (Briefmarkenautomat) outside. Mailing boxes are painted bright yellow.

France:
Weekdays 08h00–18h00, Saturday 08h00–12h00. In small towns closed for lunch 12h30–14h00 and Saturdays. Some Post Offices open at 09h00 and others may not open every day. Postage stamps are called " timbres."

Switzerland:
Post Offices in large towns open 07h30 to midday and 13h45 to 18h30 weekdays and 07h30 to 11h00 on Saturdays. City main Post Offices may close later.

Poste Restante (Mail holding)

You can have mail sent to any Post Office and collect it there by proving your identity with your passport only. In Holland and France, the item should be clearly marked "Poste Restante," with your name and the name of the Post Office as well. In Germany and Switzerland, your mail should be addressed to you "c/o Hauptpostlagernd." If a specific Post Office is not named, where there is more than one Post Office (as in a city), your mail will be kept at the main Post Office for the area. There is a limit to the time your mail will be held, usually 30 days, so have a return address written on the item(s).

Shops and Stores

Europe Tax-Free Shopping: If you buy goods from shops with "Tax Free"

signs, and you're returning to a country outside the EEC, ask for a Tax Free check. Sometimes there is a minimum value limit. When you leave the country, get the Customs officer to stamp the check and you'll be entitled to a tax refund. All main border crossing points, airports, ferry harbors and international train stations have payment offices which can cash your check. You must carry goods purchased in your personal luggage and you may be asked to show them to the customs officer.

Netherlands:
Legally, shops may open for business from 06h00 to 18h00, with late closing allowed on one weekday. They are limited to 55 hours per week's trading. In many areas, especially away from resorts and main tourist areas, Sunday closing is strictly observed. Shops close on public holidays (see following section).

Germany:
There are no set business hours in Germany and they vary from state to state. In general, all shops close Sundays, and statutory holidays. Do all necessary shopping to take account of this. The law allows shops to open between 07h00 and 18h30, and on Thursdays to open until 20h30.

Shops usually open from 09h00 to 18h30 on weekdays and close at 14h00 on Saturdays. Some open until 18h00 on the first Saturday of each month. Specialist shops, such as bakeries or delicatessen, open early and close early. On Sundays and public holidays they remain closed.

In smaller towns and villages (and even some cities), shops may close for a day or an afternoon during the week, also regional public holi days, especially in the more southern regions. Most close for lunch, usually 13h00 to 14h30.

Gas (petrol) stations often have shops which open long hours, sometimes 24 hours, including Sundays and holidays. They usually sell a range of pre-cooked or uncooked foods, as well as maps, drinks and even bicycle parts.

Bicycle shops and repair shops ("Fahrradgeschäft") are open during normal shopping hours.

France:
The law limits shop opening hours to between 09h00 and 21h30. Many shops close one weekday, often Mondays. Lunch breaks are usually 12h30 to 14h00.

Switzerland:
Shop hours are weekdays 08h00 to midday and 13h30 to 18h30, Saturdays 08h00 to 16h00. Many shops close Monday mornings. Gas (petrol) stations usually have shops and open daily, 08h00 to 22h00.

Public Holidays

Expect all the countries along the Rhine route to be closed for business on public holidays and feast days. Be aware of this and plan ahead. Buy food supplies in advance; holiday weekends can last four days. Banks and post offices will be closed. Some holidays are celebrated on fixed dates, others, especially religious holidays, are movable. Regional holidays affect only certain areas and local feast days are celebrated in cities, towns and villages. First, here is a list of the fixed-date public holidays in the various countries.

Movable feast days: the calculations

❑ Good Friday:
Decided in the church calendar by phases of the moon

❑ Easter Monday:
The Monday following Good Friday

	Netherlands	Germany	France	Switzerland
January 1	X	X	X	X
30 April	X		X	
1 May		X	X	
8 May			X	
14 July			X	
1 August				X
15 August		X	X	
3 October		X		
1 November		X	X	
11 November			X	
25 Dec.	X	X	X	X
26 Dec.	X	X	X	X

	Netherlands	Germany	France	Switzerland
Good Friday	X	X	X	X
Easter Suday	X	X	X	X
Easter Monday	X	X	X	X
Ascention Day	X	X	X	X
Whit Sunday	X			
Whit Monday	X	X	X	
Corpus Christi		X		

❑ Ascension Day:
40 days after Easter Sunday, on a Thursday

❑ Whit-Sunday:
The seventh Sunday after Easter Sunday

❑ Whit-Monday (Pentecost)
The day following Whit-Sunday

❑ Corpus Christi:
The eleventh day after Whit-Sunday, a Thursday

Museums

❑ Netherlands:
Closed Sundays. Normally open Monday to Saturday, 09h00–17h00.

❑ Germany:
Most close Mondays. Normal hours 09h00 to 18h00, Tuesdays to Sundays. Some close for lunch.

❑ France:
Closed Tuesdays. Hours differ depending on size or importance of the town. Enquire locally.

❑ Switzerland:
Closed Mondays. Open Tuesday to Sunday, 10h00–17h00.

Travel Agencies

❑ Netherlands:
Monday to Friday, 09h30-17h30 and Saturday 10h00–16h00.

❑ Germany:
Monday to Friday, 09h00 to 18h00, Saturdays 09h00 to midday. Closed Sundays and statutory holidays.

❑ France:
Weekdays 09h00–17h00. Some open Saturdays.

❑ Switzerland:
Monday to Friday, 09h00–18h00 and Saturday 09h00–16h00.

Tourist Information

The Netherlands:
Offices of the VVV (Regional Tourist Bureaux) are found all over the Netherlands, some even in Germany. The triangular VVV emblem (inverted blue triangle with a letter V in each corner) as well as the international "I" (information) sign identifies them. Offices usually open Monday to Friday, 09h00 to 17h00 and Saturdays 10h00 to midday. In summer, some larger offices open for a few hours on Sundays. Some information and services are charged for.

Germany:

Bureaux are called "Verkehrsamt" or "Verkehrsverein." Many are found at the town hall ("Rathaus"). Don't always expect to find English-speaking staff. See appendix B for some phone numbers. Major train stations have information centers.

France:

Syndicat d'Initiative/Bureau de Tourisme offices are identified by the international "I" (information) sign. They are generally found at town halls ("Mairie" or "Hôtel de Ville"). Some only open a few hours per week, usually extending their hours during the main tourist season or festivals and special events. At the barrages of the Grand Canal d'Alsace you'll also find information offices.

Switzerland:

Information offices are at the various railway stations and around the city where you see the international "I" sign. Opening times are Monday to Friday, 08h30–18h00 and Saturday 10h00–16h00. The Basel Tourism office is on the west bank of the Rhine between the Mittlere Brücke and the Klingental ferry. See Appendix B for details.

St. Joseph's gate through the medieval city walls at Rhens, Germany. Note the flood level markers, showing that the Rhine does occasionally flood the surrounding countryside.

10
Cycle Touring for the Disabled

There is little reason why disabled cyclists cannot cycle the Rhine route. Forward planning is of vital importance if you will need assistance during your trip. It would not be a good idea to plan to travel alone. Find out as much as possible about the area through which you will be traveling, consider the time of year you will be there and the chances of encountering extremes of weather. You can be as independent as possible, just by putting a lot of thought into your proposed journey and knowing everything you can glean from every possible source.

From leaving home, to starting points along the Rhine route and on the route itself, there are facilities to accommodate disabled travelers. The information contained in this section is not as complete a guide as I would wish to give, but hopefully it will assist you to get sufficient information to cycle this route.

Very occasionally, there are barriers along this route which prevent access to non-standard bicycles. For instance, the lock bridge near the Millingen am Rhein ferry service in Route 5a (Chapter 16), is not only just wide enough to allow a standard bike to cross, but requires one to turn very sharply. This would prevent a tricycle, or both in-line and side-by-side tandems from crossing, unless the cyclists carried their bikes across the bridge. However, this section can easily be bypassed.

Camping is possible for disabled persons at many sites in the Netherlands, Germany, France, and Switzerland. See below for the address of the organization Camping for the Disabled.

Parking concessions are available to disabled motorists in all European countries. Check with your national motoring organization how to qualify for these.

Language specific to your needs is very useful to have to hand in foreign countries. *The Disabled Travelers' Phrasebook*, Book 1, Western European languages, has been written to give you greater peace of mind when traveling. Book 1 contains, besides English, Dutch, French, German, Italian, Portuguese, Spanish, and Swedish. In Switzerland, English is widely spoken, and French, German and Italian are official languages. This book is available from the Disabled Drivers' Association, address below.

There are Europe-wide hotel groups which have rooms and facilities suitable for use by disabled persons. You can make reservations directly through them in your home country or via your travel agent. Some of the hotel groups are Holiday Inn, Sofitel, Novotel, and Campanile. Naming of these hotels does not imply that I have used them or that I specifically recommend them, merely that they are available to travelers. The same applies to the travel agents listed below.

Your local Netherlands Board of Tourism should be able to supply you with a pamphlet called "Holland, The Handicapped" and other national tourist boards should have similar publications available.

USA:

❏ The American Automobile Association
  Address: 1000 AAA Drive, Heathrow, FL 32746-5063

❏ Mobility International USA (US branch of a Belgian Association with affiliates in 30 countries for travel information) Address: Box 10767, Eugene, OR 97440
  Phone: (541) 343 1284
  Fax: (541) 343 6812

The Netherlands:

❏ The Royal Dutch Touring Club (ANWB)
  Address: Wassenaarseweg 220, PO Box 93200, 2509 BA The Hague.
  Phone: int+31-70-3146430 (Information for the Disabled)

❏ Stichting Dienstverlening Gehandicapten
  Address: PO Box 222, 3500 AE Utrecht
  Phone: int+31-30-2769970
  Fax: int+31-30-2712892

Germany:

❏ Bundesarbeitsgemeinschaft der Clubs Behinderter und ihrer Freunde (Association of Clubs of the Handicapped and their Friends)
  Address: Eupener Str 5, 55131 Mainz
  Phone: int+49-6131-225514 or 225778
  Fax: int+49-6131-238834

❏ Bundesverband Selbsthilfe Körperbehinderter (Association for the Independent Physically Disabled)
  Address: Altkrautheimerstr. 17, 74238 Krautheim
  Phone: int+49-6294-68110
  Fax: int+49-6294-95383

France:

❏ Comité National Français de Liaison pour la Réadaptation des Handicapés (National Committee for the Rehabilitation of the Handicapped). Address: 38 Boulevard Raspai, 75007 Paris
  Phone: int+33-1-45489013

Switzerland:

❏ Mobility International Schweiz. Address: Hard 4, 8408 Winterthur
  Phone: int+41-52-2226825
  Fax: int+41-52-2226838.

❏ Swiss Invalid Association. Address: Froburgstrasse 4, 4601 Olten
  Phone: int+41-62-321260
  Fax: int+41-62-323105

United Kingdom:

❏ Camping for the Disabled. A membership organization (you

pay a small fee) and information service for disabled campers. Can provide lists of suitable camp-sites in mainland Europe, some on the Rhine route.
Address: 20 Burton Close, Dawley, Telford, Shropshire TF4 2BX.
Phone: int+44-1743-761889 and int+44-1952-507653

❑ Disabled Drivers Association. For information regarding ferry and other cost concessions, advice about holidays abroad, etc. Also foreign language phrase books.
Address: Ashwellthorpe, Norwich, Norfolk NR16 1EX
Phone: int+44-1508-489449
Fax: int+44-1508-488173

❑ Access Travel (Lancs) Ltd. Holidays for disabled persons, accessible accommodation, etc.
Address: 16 Haweswater Avenue, Astley, Lancs M29 7BL
Phone: int+44-1942-888844.

❑ Grooms Holidays Hotels. Self-catering, UK and foreign holidays for disabled people, their families and friends
Address: 10 Gloucester Drive, London N4 2LP
Phone : int+44-181-8008695
Fax: int+44-181-8008696

❑ Youth Hostels Association. Some Youth Hostels have a high standard of facilities for disabled people. For details see Appendix B.

❑ Holiday Care Service. Holds extensive details of accommodation, transport, guidebooks, provide insurance and many other services. Address: 2 Old Bank Chambers, Station Road, Horley, Surrey RH6 9HW
Phone: int+44-1293 774535

❑ RADAR (Royal Association for Disability and Rehabilitation). Publishes many books and pamphlets about everything that affects disabled people. Of particular interest may be the annual guide, *Holidays and Travel Abroad*. For a price list, send a large self-addressed envelope, with postage (international reply coupons, UK stamps or a check). Address: 12 City Forum, 250 City Road, London EC1V 8AF.
Phone: int+44-171-2503222
Fax: int+44-171-2500212
MiniCom int+44-171-2504119

❑ AA (Automobile Association). Publishes guides and pamphlets, reporting on all aspects of travel for motorists. For disabled travelers, *The AA Guide to Ferries* (available free from AA shops), amongst others, may be of use.

❑ Port of Dover (England). Publishes a useful leaflet as a guide to disabled passengers using port and ferry services, entitled *Happy to Help*.
Phone: int+44-1304-240400

11
Geography, History, and Geology

High in the Swiss Alps, meltwaters from the Grisons glacier form the beginnings of a great river which has helped to shape and define the destinies of four European countries and, at times, Western Europe.

The Rhine flows through four distinct geological regions. From source to Basel, it is the upper Rhine, from Basel to Bingen, the Rhine Rift valley. From Bingen to Koblenz is the Rhine gorge. The lower Rhine plain stretches from Koblenz to the Dutch-German border and the delta region, to the North Sea.

A dozen streams feed the upper reaches of the Rhine. The Hinterrhein (Upper Rhine) flows from the Zapport glacier on the Marscholhorn peak near the Saint Bernard Pass. This main source of the Rhine issues from an opening in the ice 5 meters (16 feet) high and 15 meters (49 feet) wide. The stream itself is 10 meters (33 feet) wide. The river rushes headlong towards the lower Swiss plain, adding to its waters from many tributaries on its journey. The Rhine brushes past the tiny principality of Liechtenstein, briefly forming the border between Austria and Switzerland, before flowing into Lake Constance ("Bodensee").

Lake Constance is especially vital to downstream shipping. The lake acts as a reservoir, holding the spring excess of melting snow and of summer rains, releasing those waters gradually, maintaining an even depth of water in the channel.

The navigation barriers of the Rhine have been overcome through the ages, but one remains; the Rhine Falls at Schaffhausen. This waterfall is the largest in Central Europe, being 23 meters (75 feet) high and 150 meters (488 feet) wide, with a maximum discharge of 600 cubic meters per second. It is most remarkable for its geological evolution.

At Basel (Basle, Bâle), the Rhine becomes a commercial waterway with access to the sea. Through the canal systems and Rhine tributaries, barges and ships can reach the Baltic, North, Black, and Mediterranean seas, as well as the Bay of Biscay, the English Channel, and other parts of the Atlantic Ocean coastline. With the inclusion of former Iron Curtain waterways, the Caspian and White seas can be accessed.

The Grand Canal d'Alsace, is the shipping waterway from Basel to Strasbourg. This marvelous feat of engineering with its great locks, almost made a desert of Alsace, as water seepage to the wetlands was cut off. The problem was quickly identified and resolved, though the water table has been permanently lowered.

The perennial problem of flooding in the lower Rhine was first tackled here by Johann Tulla, a civil engineer, in the mid-nineteenth century. Sections of the meandering Rhine were "straightened," allowing flood waters to drain away quickly. The scheme was abandoned before it was properly completed, however, thereby shifting the problem downstream.

Because the Rhine catchment area is in a number of climatic zones, water flow fluctuates by as much as half in its lower reaches. Upstream, the melting snow in spring, summer rainfall, regular inflow from tributaries and the balancing reservoir action of the Bodensee all combine to maintain a reasonably steady stream flow. There have been times of inordinately low water levels, as in 1972 when a warm winter produced no snow in the catchment areas.

More frequently, the Rhine tends to flood, and various flood levels can be seen marked on the walls of buildings along the river. The Rhine has risen over 9 meters (29 feet) at Cologne ("Köln") and 6 meters (19 feet) at Basel. In February 1995 the river flooded its lower reaches quite extensively. The little walled hamlet of Schenkenschanz (near Kleve /Cleves) was surrounded by flood waters and only the walls kept the water out.

Parts of the river bed slope steeply and produce faster currents, with all the problems that presents to shipping. At the Binger Loch (Bingen) the river bed slopes suddenly and with the narrowing gorge, presents the most dangerous section of the river to shipping. At least half the shipping accidents occur here and two tugs are on perma-nent standby at Assmanns- hausen for this reason.

Geological Formation

The Rhine is ranked eighth of all European rivers. It drains an area of over 224,000 square kilometers, discharges an average of 2,200 cubic meters of water into the North Sea every second and has a channel length of 1,360 kilometers (850 miles).

Through the ages, the river course has undergone tremendous changes, even reversing direction at times. The upper Rhine once flowed from its sources in the Alps into the river Danube. Later it changed course to enter the Rhône-Saône corridor. During the last ice age, the lower Rhine flowed northwards to connect with the river Ems, draining into an ice lake in the North Sea, along with the British rivers Humber and Thames.

Around 45 million years ago, the Rhine Rift Valley began its slow subsidence, with the bordering land masses tilting and rising simultaneously. The Rhine Rift Valley stretches from Basel in Switzerland to Bingen in Germany, a distance of 250 kilometers (156 miles), and is 35 kilometers (22 miles) wide on average. In time the upper Rhine broke through its northern barriers, capturing southern streams to create its modern drainage system.

As the glaciers of the last ice-age receded from the Netherlands coastal areas, the river found more outlets to the sea, the primary course swinging west. Major distributaries like the north-flowing IJssel remained, while floods, erosion, and later intervention by early settlers created a massive network of waterways stretching from the German border to the North Sea.

The mouth of the Rhine gradually moved southwards, as greater tidal falls in the south encouraged the river to gouge out channels, whereas in the north channels silted up.

The upper Rhine was formed mainly by Alpine glacial action, which created varying stream flow patterns and differing conditions of erosion and sedimentation. A section of the upper Rhine flows along one of Europe's most important fold valleys (Chur to Martigny) and Lake Constance itself lies in a fold valley. Ice action during the Pleistocene glaciation carved the Lake Constance out further.

At Schaffhausen, during the last glaciation, the old bed of the Rhine was filled with ground moraine and river gravels. After the glaciers retreated, the Rhine cut into these deposits. Downstream from the present site of the Rhine Falls, the river quickly cleared away loose deposits, while upstream it came across hard Jurassic limestone. The inequality of erosion caused first rapids, then the waterfall, at exactly the point where the river reached its former glacial valley. The waterfall wall was once the left wall of the Rhine valley. The Rhine Falls is relatively stable, having moved only about 30 meters (98 feet) upstream in the 15,000 years of its existence.

The Rhine Rift Valley was created by downward tectonic movement, while the slate mountains at its northern extremity were shifted upwards. From Basel to Lauterbourg, the Rhine drops 184 meters (600 feet) in as many kilometers. From there to Bingen, a similar distance (174 kilometers), the gradient drops only 28 meters (91 feet). The Rift Valley came into being in the Tertiary period, with a length of 250 kilometers (156 miles) and an average width of 35 kilometers (22 miles). This eventually provided a northern outlet for the Alpine Rhine, which had previously flowed into the river Danube.

During much of the Tertiary period, the Rift Valley formed a long arm of the sea, opening southwards, which later became a brackish inland lake, draining to the southwest. During the Pliocene period, earth movements caused a depression to the north, forcing the proto-Rhine to make a right-angled bend at Basel and flow northwards. The valley itself is terraced, bordered by a number of stepfaults, geological indicators of rift valleys; a distinct step of about 6 meters (19.5 feet) at the eastern edge of the river terraces marks the descent to the flood plains of the Rhine.

These upper Rhine flood plains are composed of gravel sheets deposited by swollen rivers towards the end of the last Ice Age. They vary in width from 1 kilometer (1,100 yards) at Basel, to nearly 5 kilometers (3.125 miles) near Strasbourg. The river is now contained between reinforced banks, so its former meandering course and the extent of its flooded areas are only evidenced by partly silted backwaters, cut-offs and minor channels as well as swampland. Much of this area, called the Rhein-Ried or Rheinwald, is unreclaimed as the soil is unsuitable for agriculture, though a few pastures have been established.

Between the Binger Pforte (Bingen Gate) and Koblenz the Rhine meanders between 300 meter (975 feet) high hillsides. This, the Rhine Gorge, is one of a number of examples of active stream bed erosion along the course of the Rhine. Movements of the earth's crust and the resultant intensification of stream bed erosion caused these meanders, a phenomenon of the plains, to be retained as a foreign element in a mountainous landscape. Other examples occur at Schaffhausen and near Basel. At Bingen the gradient increases by more than four times for a short distance, then halves around Oberwesel, gradually reducing to very little (0.03%) through the Lower Rhine flood plains.

This variation would in the natural course of events, and given time, even out through erosion and sedimentation. However, with the waterway being increasingly controlled and adapted to the needs of mankind, this smoothing out process may either be accelerated or may never happen. It is estimated that it would take the Rhine (above Bonn) 30,000 years to lower its catchment area by one meter.

The most recent Ice age, the Pleistocene, lasted 1,600,000 years and ended about 20,000 years ago. Repeated southerly advances of the ice cap in northern Europe, through alternating warm and cold periods, brought the glaciers to the present day lower Rhine and its tributary the Ruhr river. Particularly along the north bank of the Neder Rijn, ranges of steep, long hills were created by the pressure of the ice on the earth (peripheral uplift) which presented a barrier to the river causing it to flow alongside, much like a natural dike.

During the late Tertiary period, the Rhine delta lay in the region of present-day Cleves ("Kleve") in Germany, 125 kilometers (78 miles) from the modern coastline of the Netherlands. In the last Ice Age, the lower course of the river was deflected south-westwards by advancing ice sheets. Sands and gravels were raised ahead of the ice by its weight, and a bulldozing action caused these "moraines de poussée" to divert the river around them. These extremely high

and steep ridges are still evident at places such as Rhenen on the Neder Rijn in the Netherlands.

After the glaciers retreated, the Rhine turned north again. At this time, about 8000 to 7000 BC, much of today's North Sea was land, as a large proportion of the earth's waters were captured in the extensive ice sheets, glaciers and snow fields of the era. The mouths of many rivers, including the Rhine, Meuse, Elbe, Weser, Thames, and Humber, lay in the vicinity of the Dogger Bank, the North Sea fishing grounds of today, and formed a common river system.

As the sea rose, these rivers developed their own mouths as coastlines moved inland. The first stages of the Rhine delta region began about 6,000 years ago. With climatic regions moving from the south towards the shrinking polar regions, more variable influences were brought to bear on the Rhine.

The Human Element

Water is one of mankind's primary needs and rivers have played a major role in the development and growth of humanity. Early man was dependent on rivers for drinking water and food in the form of fish. Nomadic tribes used rivers for orientation, but often they represented barriers and danger because of their size and unpredictability.

Over millions of years, man learnt to live with rivers, to use them in practical ways. Irrigation was practiced in advanced early Oriental societies and dikes were constructed against flooding. Early developments in controlling and utilizing the elements of rivers have resulted in our ongoing exploitation of waterways and increasing reliance on them.

In terms of utility, trade, culture, and human achievement, the Rhine river is the most notable and important waterway in Europe. The Romans are credited with initiating the building of dikes and canals in the Rhine area, especially in the Netherlands. Early settlers in the swamps and mudlands of the Netherlands built mounds and earth walls to keep their settlements above the waters of the Rhine delta. From these simple activities, greater settlements grew, but sea tides and storms, as well as the river floods ever held sway.

In AD 10, the Roman general Drusus organized the building of dikes in the Netherlands. The drainage of wetlands and land reclamation carried on from these beginnings, but the great storms which prevailed between the eleventh and fifteenth centuries undid much of this work. Until the introduction of the windmill, the construction of dikes along river banks and barriers built against the sea were not enough to hold back the encroaching waters.

At Wijk bij Duurstede, where the Old Rhine swings northwards around the barrier imposed by glacial action, the river Lek flows west to join the major channel of the Rhine mouth, the river Waal. About AD 50, the Romans built canals at this former loop of the Rhine's major course. Later flooding drastically changed the channel and the river broke through to promote the Lek to a major outlet for the Rhine, to the detriment of its former course through Utrecht and Leiden.

During Roman times, the Rhine also entered the North Sea by way of the present-day IJssel river, which flowed into Lake Flevo (later the Zuider Zee, presently the IJsselmeer

and Waddenzee), then into the sea where the Frisian Islands are today. Another outlet was the Old Rhine with its mouth at Katwijk-aan-Zee. The principal mouth of the Rhine eventually became the Waal river mouth, which is the old course of the river Maas.

The opening and extension of the English channel, took place at the beginning of historical time; the final breaching of the Strait of Dover is placed at about 5000 BC, the end of the Lower Holocene. This opened up the North Sea, formerly contained by the southern land bridge, to the storms and currents of the greater Atlantic Ocean. Subsequently, the Rhine river mouths were gouged out by storms and floods, and the southward shift began.

Gradually the people of the Rhine delta gained ascendancy over the elements, through hard work and ingenuity, but time and again storms and floods destroyed large sections of the barriers, exacting great tolls in terms of human life, domestic stock, crops and buildings. In the Middle Ages, violent floods broke through the coastline of the Netherlands, the sea inundating Lake Flevo, which became the Zuider Zee, as well as flooding the northern Zeeland region.

The introduction of the windmill gave the Dutch a more effective way of draining land, even below sea level. With these machines working day and night, over the centuries more land was reclaimed for settlement and agriculture.

The mouth of the Oude Rijn at Katwijk aan Zee is protected by a triple lock built between 1804 and 1807. This prevents the sea flooding inland and allows the silted mouth to be cleared when the locks are opened at low tide to expel excess water.

The ongoing reclamation process has been interrupted in modern times by massive floods. In 1953 about 160,000 hectares (400,000 acres) of land were flooded, 47,000 houses destroyed and some 1,800 people lost their lives. The Delta project, however, has progressed to a stage where the Dutch are confident they can prevent such disasters recurring.

Without the intervention of man, more than two-fifths of the present-day Netherlands would be under water, the sea would have encroached as far up the Rhine as 's Hertogen- bosch and the entire Randstad area submerged. Despite enormous difficulties, nearly two million hectares (4.5 million acres) of land has been recovered by the Dutch.

The introduction of the chamber lock in the fifteenth century gave fresh impetus to canal construction in Central Europe. Major rivers like the Rhine, having the great volume of water required, as well as being developed shipping lanes, were linked by locked canal systems across watersheds. The Rhine became the main artery of inland navigation in western Europe. The Rhine–Rhône canal was completed in 1834 and the Rhine–Marne canal in 1853.

The Rhine in its natural state, however, could only take ships with a displacement of 400 tons, which was not particularly efficient. From the beginning of the twentieth century, new canal construction in Germany made provision for ships of 1,000 tons displacement and more efficient lock systems such as ship lifts were planned. In recent years, new and larger capacity canals have been built to replace older fore-runners, with fewer locks and less water wastage.

Since major restructuring of the Rhine between 1817 and 1914, shipping capacity has improved drastically. The Rhine now takes ships up to 3,000 tons to Mannheim and further upstream to Rheinfelden, of 2,000 tons. The common European ship that plies its trade on the major inland waterways of Europe has a displacement of 1,350 tons.

As a result of works begun in 1817, the main river has been confined to a straightened, diked channel. This regularization reached upstream as far as Mannheim by 1866. The river was increasingly regulated between Basel and Mainz in the decade after 1906 and the channel shortened by more than 80 kilometers (50 miles). This increased river bed erosion, due to faster water flow. By the 1920s, the river bed at Basel had deepened by over 2 meters and from Rheinweiler to Neuenburg by about 5.5 meters (18 feet). This increase in current made navigation on the Upper Rhine very difficult and with the extension of the railway system, navigation above Mannheim almost ceased in the late nineteenth century.

From 1907 to 1914, more regularization of the river was carried out between Mannheim and Strasbourg. Between the two world wars, further improvements were made, particularly at the Istein rapids below Basel.

The lateral canal on the French side of the Rhine between Basel and Breisach has caused the Rhine along this particular stretch to almost dry up. The hydroelectric power barrages between Breisach and Kehl have "looping" flows which allow the water to flow back into the Rhine to prevent this situation worsening.

After World War I (1914–18), Alsace was returned to France. The French interest in a lateral canal then increased, with the purpose of bypassing the Upper Rhine as well as using its potential for producing hydro-electricity. A clause in the Treaty of Versailles allowed France to divert waters from the Rhine except where shipping was affected. Despite protests from Germany and Switzerland, the French embarked upon this project. The Istein bar below Basel was tackled first, as it had deteriorated into rapids for most of the year. The Kembs barrage was constructed here, reaching completion in 1927. A bypass was cut, locks connecting both ends with the Rhine waterway. After completion in 1933, this canal was used by shipping to Basel, and that section of the Rhine river thereafter neglected for shipping.

In 1950 the French government began the next stage, and further stages were completed as well. Barrages and hydro-power stations were built at Ottmarsheim, Fessenheim and Vogelgrun. During Franco-German negotiations in 1956, they agreed to jointly improve navigation along the Rhine. Since then, more works have been completed along the left bank of the river, at Marckolsheim, Rhinau, Gerstheim, and south of Strasbourg.

With the reclamation of land and anti-flooding measures constructed over the years in the delta region, the Rhine no longer has a natural outlet to the sea. The main outfall is now through the Nieuwe Waterweg (New Waterway), specifically cut through the dunes at Europoort/Hoek van Holland to aid shipping and to prevent inland flooding from the sea.

In the late seventeenth century, as a result of the meander crossing the German-Dutch border, the Waal was taking an inordinate amount of the Rhine water, and the IJssel and Neder Rijn were rapidly silting up. To rectify this, in 1710 a 16 kilometer (10 miles) channel was cut from the Waal to the Neder Rijn at Pannerden (just inside the Netherlands) and the meander cut off from the main stream. This adjustment also helped prevent serious flooding.

Waste water factories were naturally sited alongside rivers, including paper-mills, dye factories, tanneries and chemical works. In the Rhine area various industries, including iron and steel foundries and petro-chemical producers, increased manufacturing output five-fold in the first two post-war decades alone, but not without negative effects.

Pollution of the Rhine waters from heavy industry situated alongside the river and its tributaries, created major problems. By 1980 the Rhine was in such a bad state, that the once salmon-rich river sustained little biological activity, especially in its lower reaches. Industrial spillage from as far upstream as Switzerland's chemical factories were fast destroying the cycle of riverine life. With 20 million tons of waste material dumped into the river every year, including 15 million tons of salts, the river was rapidly being killed. Another problem arose with the temperature of the water being raised by factory emissions, particularly through the cooling process employed in nuclear power stations.

Although these problems have not been fully eliminated, increasing efforts to overcome pollution have had a substantial effect in the past two decades. Not all pollution has been caused by riverside industries or cities, but indirect pollution has come from farmland pesticides and suchlike chemicals carried by runoff or ground-water. Sometimes these pollutants are carried in the atmosphere, some from a long distance away.

In 1880, the riparian states of the Rhine signed a treaty to protect the salmon in the river. After regional wars and worldwide conflicts, the salmon may well wonder if this treaty will ever be honored. But all is not lost, for salmon have been re-introduced to parts of the Rhine and are surviving.

An International Commission for the protection of the waters of the Rhine was set up in 1965 by the Netherlands, Germany, Switzerland, Belgium, and Luxembourg.

Some Rhine Facts and Figures

❑ The Rhine is navigable by sea-going ships to Mannheim and by Rhine ships to the Rhine falls at Schaffhausen. The port furthest upstream is Basel, Switzerland's only access to the sea.

❑ Duisburg, at the confluence of the Rhine and Ruhr rivers, is the largest inland port in the world. Duisburg is also the center of the largest iron and steel manufacturing area in Germany.

❑ The Rhine reaches its greatest width of almost one kilometer (1,100 yards) near Wesel, close to the German-Dutch border.

❑ At Arnhem the Neder Rijn is 90 meters (293 feet) wide, after the IJssel diverges northwards. Under normal conditions, the Neder Rijn–Lek waterway can take 2,000 ton barges.

❑ The waterway is regulated by the Central Commission for the Navigation of the Rhine, based at Strasbourg. It was created at the Treaty of Vienna (1815) after the Napoleonic Wars. Member countries include the riparian states (Switzerland, France, Germany and the Netherlands) as well as Belgium, Luxembourg, and the UK. Italy was dropped from membership after 1945 and replaced by the USA, which later relinquished its seat.

❑ After World War II, the Commission was responsible for clearing the river. About 1,500 air raids on Rhine installations had destroyed every bridge from Switzerland to the Netherlands. More than 200,000 tons of steel and concrete had to be moved. Between Bonn and Emmerich, nearly 1,000 large barges, 185 tugs and more than 200 other vessels were sunk and damaged.

12 Peoples and Nations

In prehistoric times, the migrations of hominids into present-day Europe began about a million years ago. The earliest surviving wooden tool, a spear estimated to be 400,000 years old, was found at Schöningen (between the Rhine and Berlin) in Germany. Fossil finds near the Rhine include Neanderthal remains from the Neander valley near Düsseldorf. Steinheim, near Paderborn (near the source of the Lippe river, a Rhine tributary), has human fossils of uncertain origin. The lower jaw of Homo heidelbergensis was found at Mauer, not far from the Rhine valley.

About 40,000 years ago modern man, homo sapiens arrived in Europe, 100,000 years after evolving in Africa. The period of co-existence of Neanderthals and modern man lasted about 12,000 years, when the Neanderthals disappeared.

Modern man adapted to living in colder climates, hunting on the grasslands and plains of Eurasia. During the last glaciation of 18 000 years ago, the course of the Rhine was the central artery of the western tundra.

The transition to agriculture in the Rhine region began about 8,000 years ago, 2,000 years after the last glaciation ended. Megalithic tombs date back to this period. Some have been found in the Netherlands and in Alsace. The band-ceramic cultures, named for their decorative pottery, were the first farmers of central Europe. The pottery kilns found other uses, especially for smelting metals. Early remains of woven cloth and potsherds have been found along the Rhine. By 3500 BC, farming was established throughout Europe, practiced by late Neolithic cultures.

Excavations of early farming villages along the Rhine have been made at Langweiler, Köln-Lindenthal and Michelsberg, and a megalithic tomb was found at Aillevans.

Bronze working became widespread throughout the farming cultures of Europe after 2000 BC and large communities developed as aristocratic chiefdoms. Bronze age settlements north of the Alps were often built on islands in lakes, as at Baldegg at Lake Constance (Bodensee). Late Bronze age "Urnfield" cultures (referring to burial practices) were rapidly replaced by the Celtic Halstatt aristocratic iron-using culture between 750 and 600 BC. The heartland of this Celtic settlement was east from the Rhine valley, the Rhine itself acting as barrier and border, which it continued to do well into the twentieth century.

About the sixth century BC, Frisian tribes arrived in the Rhine deltar egion. German tribes settled to the north, around the Baltic Sea.

The trans-Alpine trade route became established alongside the Rhine from its source to the North Sea. The Celts spread through western Europe into Spain and Britain, continuing to dominate the Danube and Rhine basins. The Romans, however, brought the Celtic lands into their domain by conquest. The Roman border extended northwards to the Rhine–Danube line and by 1 BC the only independent Celts were living in parts of Britain and in German territory north of the Danube.

During the time of Julius Caesar, Roman expansion through Gaul was rapid and vicious, stopping only at the Rhine. The Raurici (a Swiss tribe) were defeated near Basel in 52 BC and the Belgae at Aduatuca (Maastricht) in 54 BC. The Romans crossed the Rhine at Koblenz, invading the lands of the Germanic tribes, but did not make great inroads into Germania Magna, the territory north and east of the Rhine. In 44 BC, when Caesar died, the Rhine was the defined northern border of Roman territory.

After their defeat at the hands of Arminius (Herman) in the Teutoburger forest in Saxony, the Romans withdrew permanently to the Rhine, though the Germanic tribes were later severely punished by the Romans. By AD 117, at the death of the Roman Emperor Trajan, little territory across the Rhine had been gained. Further south, the Romans established the Limes, a series of fortresses and walls, defending a line from the right bank of the Rhine to the Danube, a distance of 550 kilometers (344 miles).

By then the Germanic tribes were settled at the Roman-held Rhenish borders, but the Rhine and the Limes were barriers too difficult for them to overcome. The Rhine continued to be a major trading and shipping route, trade flourishing on both banks. The needs of the Roman army had to be addressed and the Rhine valley became highly developed agriculturally. Fleets of supply ships serviced riverside garrisons. The Romans introduced grapes, and wine production became an important industry.

As the Roman Empire crumbled, northern invaders broke through the Limes and crossed the Rhine in increasing waves. The Burgundians migrated from the Baltic Sea in a southeasterly direction, at the same time (AD 150) as, and on a parallel course with, the Swedish Goths. However, at the Vistula, the Burgundians turned south-west, arriving at the Rhine at Worms. Here one of the great sagas played out its bloody course. The story of the hero Siegfried, his wife Kriemhild, her brother, Gunther, King of the Burgundians, his wife, the doughty Brunhilde and Gunther's faithful warlord Hagen, begins further down the Rhine at Xanten, Siegfried's birthplace. The tale unfolds in Worms and reaches its bloody conclusion at the court of Attila (Eftel) the Hun, at Vienna.

The Burgundians moved on to the area in present-day France, now naturally called Burgundy. The Huns came to the Rhine, conquering up to Cologne, and there is a legend of eleven thousand (English) virgins who met their end there at the hands of that barbarian tribe. The vacuum created on the Rhine at Worms was soon filled by Germanic conglomerate tribes, the Alemanni.

The Franks moved southwards into the low countries, displacing romanized Celtic tribes and conquered much of France. Virtually the whole of

Europe was in turmoil, with migrating tribes roaming and plundering. The Huns extended their control as far west as the Rhine, but after the death of Attila (AD 453) their confederation crumbled and they returned to the steppes.

From AD 486, the Frankish king Clovis ruled Gaul. By 600 the Frankish kingdom stretched from the Pyrenees to the Elbe, encompassing the entire Rhine region. This kingdom declined through the late seventh century but was revived by the Carolingian dynasty.

Charlemagne's Frankish empire had brought a measure of stability to the sub-continent by his death in AD 814. Charlemagne's kingdom was divided amongst his three grandsons at Verdun in 843 and parts of the Rhine became a border again. By AD 900, Vikings raided freely across Europe, as far up the Rhine as Mainz and the Moselle to Nancy. Magyars made forays into western Europe, reaching Mainz by AD 932 and the Bodensee (Lake Constance). One party passed through Speyer and Strasbourg to attack the Burgundians in AD 937. However, Otto the Great of Saxony inflicted a decisive defeat on the Magyars in 955 and adopted the title of Roman Emperor, founding the Holy Roman Empire in 962.

By AD 1000, Europe had settled down with the Holy Roman Empire as its stabilizing center. At the beginning of the thirteenth century, most of Europe was christianized and schools and universities flourished. At the same time, the feudal system in its various forms kept the continent in a state of flux, as minor rulers attempted to gain influence and territory.

By the end of the twelfth century, along the length of the Rhine there was intense rivalry amongst feudal lords, including churchmen. The Hohenstaufen emperors failed to assert their authority over the German princes and Germany disintegrated into a loose federation of states. The inter-regnum in Germany during 1254–73 caused further political chaos and its principal rulers took advantage of this to increase their power bases.

The fourteenth century in Germany continued in much the same way. The Bavarian Wittelsbachs gained ascendancy over the Austrian Habsburgs and then lost power to the Luxembourg dynasty. In the meantime the Rhineland cities had asserted their independence and the German princes were forced to unite to limit the influence of these cities.

The Swiss too were fighting for their independence and in 1388 the Swiss confederation of eight cantons threw off the Habsburg yoke after a century of rebellion.

However, the most significant event of the fourteenth century was the onset of the Black Death, a combination of bubonic and pneumonic plague, exacerbated by malnutrition and overcrowding. The people of the Rhine suffered greatly, as the plague spread along the major trade routes throughout Europe. For the following 250 years, plagues and pestilence took their toll. Anarchy, riots, pogroms and general hysteria followed every outbreak of disease and populations fell dramatically. By the sixteenth century, many cities had not regained their pre-plague population levels.

The fifteenth century saw the Burgundians extending their possessions in the Netherlands, but eventually the territory devolved upon the Habsburgs through marriage. The Habsburgs had become Holy Roman

Emperors in 1438, with the election of Albert II of Austria. The office remained with the Habsburg family until it was abolished in 1806.

In 1455, probably the most significant event of the century in Europe, was the creation of the first ever commercial printing press, in Mainz. The plague had given the surviving common people a measure of freedom from serfdom, by increasing the value and wages of their labor. The printing press would give them the opportunity to escape the prison of their ignorance.

Powerful dynastic families came to the fore in the fifteenth century. The Medici family of Florence are probably the best known, but in Augsburg the Fugger family held sway. The Fuggers owned many mines and ironworks, using networks of towns and cities to increase their wealth and Cologne became an important gateway to the west for their trade.

In the sixteenth century, much of Europe was divided up into bishoprics by the Roman church. The rivalries between archbishops led to conflict involving the people of each area, willing or not. The Rhinelanders, from Switzerland to the sea fell under four different archdioceses, with the concomitant problems. However, most of the Rhine remained within one country.

The partial dissolution of the Holy Roman Empire and the division of the Habsburg dominions from 1556, brought the Rhine lowlands and delta region under Spanish control. The Union of Utrecht in 1579 created a Dutch resistance to Spanish rule and the seven northern provinces of the Netherlands united to fight for independence.

By 1560 there was a marked religious division throughout Europe. The Rhinelanders from Switzerland to the Netherlands were embroiled in the Reformation, which had gained impetus since Luther nailed his theses to the door of Wittenberg cathedral in 1517. In 1531 the Schmalkaldic League of most of Europe's protestant princes allied themselves against the Holy Roman Emperor Charles V whose ongoing wars with the French would only come to an end after his abdication in 1556. The catholic Swiss cantons attacked protestant Zurich, and Zwingli was killed in the fighting. Basel had aligned itself with the protestant cause in 1528. In 1542 the Universal Inquisition was introduced by Pope Paul III in an attempt to repress the Reformation. The Spanish sent troops to the Netherlands in 1567 which revitalized the Dutch struggle for independence.

At the beginning of the seventeenth century, the formation of the Protestant Union and the Catholic League drew the boundaries of the ongoing religious conflict. With the rising of the protestant nobility of Bohemia against the Habsburg Emperor, the Thirty Years' War (1618–48) began, becoming Europe-wide as it drew in Denmark, Sweden, France and Spain. Germany, especially the Rhine valley became the main theater of war, with widespread devastation resulting in famine and depopulation. Switzerland and the Low Countries were finally lost to the German Empire and imperial power declined with the rise of the Prussians.

After the Peace of Westphalia in 1648, the United Provinces (of the Netherlands) administered a section of land along its southern borders, which it had seized from the Spanish Netherlands. This area, called the Generality, ultimately became part of the Netherlands. France had also gained territory during this period, particularly in the upper Rhineland. The cities of Landau and Hagenau and some surrounding territory were taken, as well as the Sundgau, on the French side of the Rhine near Basel.

Between 1648 and 1697, the French invaded the Rhine area and devastated many towns and villages, laying waste to the countryside as well as destroying as many castles and citadels as possible. The Alsatian plain was taken by the French, and they now occupied the left bank of the Rhine from Basel almost to Speyer.

In 1701 the War of Spanish Succession broke out. The Duke of Marlborough's forces marched up the Rhine from the North Sea coast via Mainz to victory at Blenheim in 1704. Prince Eugene of Austria had himself led his troops in the reverse direction to the Battle of Malplaquet.

By 1750 the European powers had expanded their colonial territories and were jostling for world trade domination. The Netherlands was particularly well established in the East Indies and

Remains of Duurstede castle, Wijk bij Duurstede, the Netherlands.

its maritime power was in the ascendant. The Rhine became an increasingly important trade route for Dutch goods. Commodities from Britain and France were also traded up the Rhine.

The Holy Roman Empire still existed in 1721, but its territories and its boundaries were changing. The Rhine flowed through various Austrian controlled territories as well as Germany, along the border of France, through some Brandenburg territory (Cleves), to reach the North Sea in the Netherlands.

Napoleon Bonaparte changed the map of central Europe between 1798 and 1812. Much of present-day Germany and Switzerland was lumped into the Confederation of the Rhine. From Basel to Bonn the western border was the Rhine. After the Congress of Vienna the German Confederation gained the Saar region, Luxembourg and the Palatinate, as well as other territories on the left bank of the Rhine. However, the Congress allowed Germany to be split piecemeal into many Kingdoms, Grand Duchies, and Duchies, opening the way for the most militant to gain control of the entire country.

Between 1865 and 1871, Prussia unified the whole of Germany and by conquest added Alsace-Lorraine to Germany as well.

During World War I (1914–18), the German line extended west of the border of Lorraine and Alsace to Switzerland. By 1918 the Allied forces had advanced almost to the German frontier in this sector. The Treaty of Versailles awarded Alsace-Lorraine to France, as well as dividing the greater part of Prussia. French troops occupied the Rhineland to ensure the Germans paid the war reparations demanded.

In 1936 Hitler remilitarized the Rhineland. The French troops had withdrawn some years earlier. German Nationalists reiterated the assertion that the Rhine was not a border of Germany but an integral part of it and campaigned for the return of Alsace-Lorraine. Although the French expected German aggression to begin through Alsace-Lorraine and had built massive fortifications there to pre-empt this, the Germans invaded through the Netherlands and Belgium. The French Maginot line thereby became defunct and Alsace-Lorraine was once again incorporated into Germany.

With the Allied invasions of Normandy the tide turned against the Germans in Europe and by December 1944 the Allied forces were camped on the banks of the Rhine from the North Sea to Basel. Throughout the ages the Rhine had proved to be an almost impossible barrier to invading armies from either bank, and this occasion proved no exception. The bridge at Remagen provided the only access to Germany from the west bank of the Rhine and the Allies managed to get enough troops across here to form a bridgehead before the bridge collapsed.

World War II had devastated the structure and economy of the Rhine states and considerable effort was required to restore them. Every bridge from the Netherlands to Switzerland had been felled, and the towns, industries, roads and railways on both banks had been bombed and shelled virtually to destruction.

Switzerland had remained as neutral as any country surrounded by warring nations could, though its trade and economy could not help but be affected by the events. The Netherlands had been overrun very quickly by the

Germans at the outset, but had suffered immense damage in the initial blitzkrieg and the later fighting. Alsace, the frontier territory which had been fought across since the beginning of history, was once more left with the task of rebuilding its economy and infrastructure.

With the 1963 Franco-German friendship treaty signed in Paris, and the strong movement towards European political and economic union vigorously pursued by these two central states, the Rhine has now become a bond rather than a barrier. The Schengen agreement which abolished border controls between the Netherlands, Germany, and France has enlarged on this sense of mutual trust and common purpose.

13
Introduction to the Routes

In this chapter, we'll take a look at the general information common to all sections of the route. Even if you follow the route in this book, you'll still need maps. A good touring map requires clarity, detail and strength (durability). I prefer a scale of 1:50,000 for area maps and about 1:20,000 for city maps.

There are exceptions, the 1:100,000 VVV/ANWB Provincial maps of the Netherlands and the IGN Serie Verte (i.e. green) maps of France being two of them. IGN, the French national survey office, also print blue (1:25,000) and orange (1:50,000) series. In Germany I have found no suitable maps of a scale larger than 1:50,000. Some maps have pictures drawn on them, obscuring parts of the map. Many of the best maps are only available in the areas they cover. Bookshops are a fair source, but I have found gas station shops to be better stocked with cycling maps.

There is a broad choice of cycling-specific maps available, including those compiled by and for the ANWB in Holland, teh ADFC in Germany, various district authorities, and numerous tourist bodies. The problem with many of these maps is that routes indicated are not properly researched. Some green routes, supposedly scenic

and motor-traffic free, are the opposite in terms of traffic. Suggested bike routes can take you far out of your way through the countryside, when a short trip along a busy road will get you where you want to go with less effort.

Travel information dates very quickly. New roads, railways, bike paths, bridges, and canals are being planned, designed, and built even as I write this. The better the map you choose, the more chance you have of recognizing any changes and finding your way easily.

Key to Route Descriptions and Maps in This Book

Routes are numbered from 1 to 19. Those without suffix or with the suffix "A" are routes along or near the Rhine. Those with the suffixes "B" or "C" are diversions away from the main Rhine route. Where no diversionary routes are specifically described, suggestions are made at the end of chapters.

A9	Freeway (motorway) numbers
B56	Road numbers
E	East/erly

E43	European freeway (motorway) numbers	R-L	turn right and immediately left
F	Ferry	RHS	on your right hand side
hard R	90 degrees right, as in road swings hard right (also L)	S	South/erly
		STOP	mandatory stop
immed.	immediately; as in "past (the) church (turn) immed. R"	T	T-junction; intersection of road running blind into another road which crosses at right angles and continues in both directions, as per the shape of the letter "T." The presumption is that you have arrived at this junction along the "stem" of the T and face a choice of turning right or left only.
Info	information sign, map, or office		
(KM 334)	kilometer marker board along navigable waterways, indicating distance from a fixed point. The Rhine is measured from Konstanz [KM 0]		
L	turn left		
L-R	turn left and immediately right	U-turn	a continuous turn (L or R) which results in a 180-degree switch in direction, as in the shape of a U
LHS	on your left hand side		
N	North/erly	W	West/erly
N207	National freeway (motorway) numbers	X	crossroads; intersection of two continuous roads, or four roads intersecting at one junction.
Continue	continue straight on along the same road or across intersection		
		X (roundabout)	intersection at traffic circle (roundabout)
opp	opposite, as in "R opp. Hôtel de Ville (Town Hall)"	X (lights)	intersection controlled by traffic lights
P13208	Paddestoel (mushrooom,). In the Netherlands you will find these low, four-sided signs shaped like a pyramid with the top half removed. Numbered on the top surface, with directions and distances indicated on the sides.	Y	road divides (forks) ahead; you are approaching along the stem of the Y and face a choice of turning right or left
		Y-L	take left-hand route (Y-R = take right-hand route)
		(120 m)	distance (in this example = 120 meters) from last instruction or observation; e.g. R; (55 m) L, means that
R	turn right		

55 meters after the previous instruction (i.e. R = turn right), turn left

(½) L   half-turn (i.e. 45 degrees) Left (or Right, as indicated)

Navigation Distance Boards

Along the course of navigable rivers and canals in Europe, you will find distance markers. Distances along the Rhine are marked starting from the bridge at Konstanz where the water leaves Lake Constance on its 1 000+ kilometer journey to the North Sea. Markers appear on one or both sides of the river, every 100 meters. Sometimes, at the half-kilometer points, the marker is a +. At the kilometer marks, the number of kilometers is shown in numerals. Other markers are shown either as numbers 1 through 4 and 6 to 9, or as vertical lines. These navigation guides are extremely useful to riverside traffic as well.

The KM numbers in text and directions represent kilometer markers you will see alongside the river. Markers point towards the center of the stream. Often you will pass behind the indicator board and, unless you can read the marker across the waterway, you will have to dismount and peer around the board to read it. Some distance markers are marked both sides, mostly those on the French side of the river. Not all markers will be visible along the routes; those printed in the directions are markers you will be able to see.

Ferries

There are few bridges across the Rhine, especially the upper Rhine and this is compensated for by ferries. Ferries vary in size and usage, but they all take cyclists. If you plan to use ferries, make sure the ferry works at that time of year and on that day. A general rule is that major route crossings have year-round ferry services, whilst others operate only in "season"— usually mid-March to mid-November, some from mid-April to mid-October. After floods, ferry services may be temporarily (or even permanently) suspended. The map indicators for ferries are WF (vehicles and passengers) and PF (passengers/cyclists only). Not all maps are up-to-date and you could

Old style survey marker alongside the Rhine in Germany at KM 286.5.

find a ferry has been replaced by a freeway bridge a few miles away. Most ferry crossing places have restaurants on at least one of the river banks, though some only open for the season.

Naming of the River Banks

Facing downstream, the conventional naming of the river banks is left and right bank. When traveling upstream this nomenclature is unsatisfactory, as the bank on the right is the left bank, and vice versa. I name the left bank the West (W) bank, the other the East (E) bank, from the German border to Basel. The route from the North Sea through the Netherlands, being generally in an east-west direction, the left bank is called the South (S) bank, the right bank, the North (N).

Road Signs and bike route Indicators

Along the entire route you will come across indicators for the many regional bike routes. It's often difficult to ignore these signs, as they seem to be pointing towards your intended destination. It's best to stick to your planned journey, unless you have a map to go with the tourist route. In parts of the Netherlands you'll find road junctions with all sorts of signs urging you to take one route or another — many to the same final destination. But, unless you don't mind going around in circles, stick to your set route.

Although there seems to be some agreement about sign-posting bike routes, for leisure or for everyday commuting, you will still come across great variations in bike route signage. Coloring of signs is only limited by sign

makers' imaginations. Red and white are popular combinations, as are green and white. Black and white, blue and white, yellow and black combinations are used on this route. Most will display a bicycle pictogram, but others will rely on their small size or position somewhere nearby a bike path to indicate their function.

Global Positioning Systems (GPS)

These are hand-held (or attached to bicycle handlebars) sets with pre-programmed maps. A GPS can be of great assistance for plotting your position on a map or tracing your route in either direction. GPS receivers use a number of satellites (some use up to twelve) for positioning, including those of the US military. Because there are times when the US Defense Department considers civilian use of their positioning satellites undesirable, the Selective Availability Program can degrade the accuracy of GPS receivers.

Maps programmed into GPS receivers will not always have bike paths included, nor necessarily be up-to-date with information mainly of concern to cyclists. When, sometime in the future, these wonderful instruments are programmed with cyclists specifically in mind, my collection of maps will be framed and hung on the wall as souvenirs.

Compasses

A word of warning about using a compass. The deflection of the compass needle from true North varies throughout the world, even in the space of a relatively short distance. Your bike will create magnetic interference too, if you take a reading over the handlebars, for instance. If you don't have a deviation table or map for the area in which you are traveling, don't rely exclusively on a compass.

Navigation Tips

Even with the use of maps and other aids, you may sometimes doubt whether you are where you think you should be, if you are out of sight of the Rhine. Often you will be no more than a few hundred meters from the water's edge, but unable to see the river through the woods or over the dike.

If you look for a long thin line of tall trees (mostly in Germany), all about the same height, that will usually indicate the position of the river and give you some idea of how far away it is. The sun will always be due south at noon standard local time (13h00 CET March–October), when you are north of the Tropic of Cancer. In winter, the sun will be southerly all day.

he direction of river flow is not always evident, so look for an object drifting past or throw a stick into the water. The navigation distance boards indicate a reducing distance as you travel upstream, both in integers and fractions.

Many roads in cities and even in villages have different names for the same road. You might enter a village along Rue General de Gaulle, suddenly find yourself on Rue Hôtel de Ville and leave town along Rue Principale, all in the space of a few hundred meters and along the same straight piece of road. Roads and alleys leading to the Rhine commonly have "Rhein," as part of the name — Rheinweg, Rheingasse, Rheinallee, Rheinbrückenweg — or other words that are related to the river, such as "Hafen" (harbor), "Werft" (dock), and "Kai" (wharf).

14. Approach Routes

The routes described in this chapter show how to reach the starting point of the Rhine route from the major ferry ports and airports. Covered are both the approach routes in Holland to reach the mouth of the Oude Rijn (Old Rhine) at Katwijk aan Zee and a route from Frankfurt airport in Germany to reach the route approximately halfway.

A. Amsterdam Schiphol Airport to Katwijk aan Zee

Distance: 40 km/25 miles

Terrain: Level

Maps: FALK Plan Zuid-Holland Noord; 1:50,000 (2 cm = 1 km) (shows some positions but no numbers of route signs)

ANWB Provinciekaart Zuid Holland; 1:100,000 (1 cm = 1 km) (does not show all numbered route signs)

Directions:

Leave the arrivals hall and exit the building. Immediately turn R and follow the sidewalk as it curves to the L alongside the building. At the corner of the building you will find a red-surfaced track, which is the bike path. If you face half-right, you will see a large raised advertising sign, which reads Canon. Cycle towards and under this sign, up to the exit gate in the perimeter fence (950m).

Take the signposted bike route (left) toward Hoofddorp; Pass the Aviodrome; Pass the Sony sky-ad.

Cycle south alongside the A4 freeway (on your right hand side).

At signpost No. 3989 left toward Rozenburg, along service road alongside N201.

At signpost No. 15046/11 continue toward Aalsmeer.

Through subway

Right at Y-junction up ramp

At signpost No. 3174 X (lights), turn right alongside canal, canal on your left

Continue through Rijsenhout

Pass Westeinder campsite, on your right

Continue through Burgerveen (stop for a "palingbroodje," a smoked eel roll); under freeway bridge; pass statue of dancing fisherfolk

At signpost No. 3909/4, continue through Weteringbrug

Across aqueduct

Continue along Huigsloten Dijk

Continue through Buitenkaag

At signpost No. 3586/1, turn right

After 20m U-turn, left back along bridge

Continue between freeway (A44) and railway line

At signpost No. 4019/16 continue

At signpost No. 3939/17 continue toward Leiden

At signpost No. 4016/11 continue toward Leiden (7 km)

At signpost No. 4014 continue, freeway on your right

Cross Oegstgeester canal, immediately right

Under freeway bridge

Follow Oegstgeester weg (road) to the end

T R along Sandtlaan (road)

Cross bridge over Oude Rijn

Cross another bridge, immediately right along Valkenburgseweg (road)

Continue into Rijnstraat (road)

Cross N206

X-R into Koningin Juliana Laan

Immediately before bridge, left along Rijnmond (street)

Continue to seafront, with sea lock on your right at end of road

Route ends at sea lock

B. Europoort Ferry Terminal to Hoek van Holalnd

Distance: 30 km/18.75 miles

Terrain: Flat; paved bike paths and roads

Map: ANWB Provinciekaart Zuid Holland; 1:100,000 (1 cm = 1 km) (does not show all numbered route signs)

Directions:

Exit the ferry terminal

Continue past the Eurocentrum building to the perimeter fence

Turn left along bike path alongside canal (Hartelkanaal); pass Shell fuel depot

Under bridge, continue past wind turbines

Cross intersection and continue

Continue over bridge

At signpost No. 8858 continue towards Rozenburg, follow bike route LF1b

Cross canal (Calandkanaal)

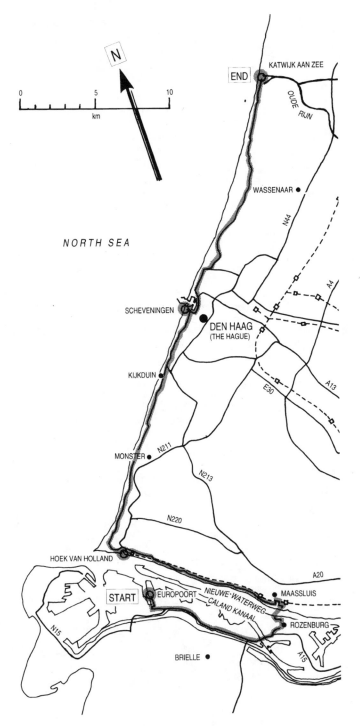

N

| 0 | | 5 | | 10 |
km

NORTH SEA

KATWIJK AAN ZEE

END

OUDE RIJN

WASSENAAR ●

N44

A4

SCHEVENINGEN

DEN HAAG
(THE HAGUE)

A13

KIJKDUIN ●

E30

MONSTER ●

N211

N213

N220

HOEK VAN HOLLAND

START

EUROPOORT

NIEUWE·WATERWEG

CALAND KANAAL

MAASSLUIS

A20

ROZENBURG

N15

A15

BRIELLE ●

Continue along bike path

Down ramp, R towards Rozenburg (2 km) and Maassluis (3 km)

Under bridge, continue alongside canal (Calandkanaal) going N

R towards Rozenburg (1 km) and Maassluis (3 km)

At crossing cross road and L towards Maassluis (4 km)

Through Rozenburg, off bike path, follow signs to Maassluis

R towards Maassluis (still in Rozenburg)

At T-junction, turn L along bike path leaving Rozenburg

R to ferry (costs DFl 1.00 and crossing takes about 7 minutes)

Off ferry (follow other cyclists if you're not certain)

Along cycle path, swings hard L

R over railway line, immed. stop and dismount

L (walk) across road and canal to far side, immed. L over railway line

Follow LF1b and Hoek van Holland route signs

R and then L along roadway directly towards canal (Nieuwe Waterweg)

R alongside canal towards Hoek v. Holland (ignore "Private" signs) (alternatively, cycle next to the railway line, parallel with canal)

Continue past the game park amongst the bunkers

Continue along the bike path deviation past the waterway flood barrier, then back alongside the canal

Continue past bunkers and alongside railway line

Cross railway line to R, at signpost No. 4146 immed. L along bike path

Continue straight through Hoek van Holland town

L at road intersection with traffic island to ferry terminal; Route ends here.

C. Hoek van Holland Sea Ferry Terminal to Scheveningen

Distance: 20 km/12.5 miles

Terrain: Undulating through the dunes, with some long, steepish hills, otherwise flat; compacted dirt roads, paved bike paths and roads

Maps: FALK Plan Zuid-Holland Noord; 1:50,000 (2 cm = 1 km) (does not show numbers of route signs)

Maps (cont'd): ANWB Provinciekaart Zuid Holland; 1:100,000 (1 cm = 1 km) (does not show all numbered signs)

Directions:

Exit the ferry terminal.

At signpost No. 1505/24 turn L (at traffic island) follow sign to "Strand" (beach) and Route LF1b

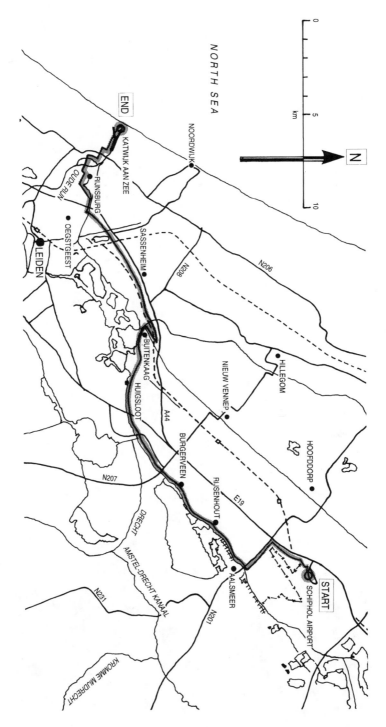

At signpost No. 15024 L towards "Strand"

At signpost No. 2331 L towards "Strand"

At P23697 R

At P24131 continue

At P24132 continue

At P24133 R

At P24134 continue towards Den Haag (16 km)

At signpost No.13058 continue

Stay on the LHS track (RHS track leads to glasshouses)

At crossing P23691 continue

At P23689 continue

At P23687 L

At P23686 R on top of hill, cycle N along coast

Arrive Kijkduin town square (public toilets, food and drink)

At P20972 L towards Scheveningen (3.6 km)

At P20655 continue towards Scheveningen (3.2 km)

At P23123 continue

At P23122 continue

Arrive Scheveningen

At P22678 L

Follow road as it swings R, continue to docks

Ends Scheveningen sea ferry terminal

Maassluis, the Netherlands. Ferry across the Nieuwe Maas, one of the main distributaries of the Rhine Delta and connecting the port of Rotterdam via the Nieuwe Waterweg to the North Sea at Hoek van Holland.

D. Scheveningen Sea Ferry Terminal to Katwijk aan Zee

Distance: 23 km/14.4 miles

Terrain: Undulating through the dunes, with some long, steepish slopes, otherwise flat; compacted dirt roads, paved bike paths and roads

Maps: FALK Plan Zuid-Holland Noord; 1:50,000 (2 cm = 1 km) (shows some positions but no numbers of route signs)

ANWB Provinciekaart Zuid Holland; 1:100,000 (1 cm = 1k m) (does not show all numbered route signs)

Directions:

Exit ferry terminal, cycle directly away from the sea

At crossing L through town

At crossing L towards sea

At Y-junction R

At T-junction (½)R parallel with coast going N

Pass pier, immed. R

At P20518 L along road

At P22726 L along bike path

Follow LF1b route signs

At P21733 L towards Katwijk aan Zee (5.5 km)

At P21734 R towards Katwijk aan Zee, also LF1b route

At crossing continue

At signpost No. 7343 continue

At signpost No. 7100/1 L towards Katwijk aan Zee, N along seafront

At signpost No. 3345 L to Rhine sea lock; route ends at Old Rhine sea lock.

E. Frankfurt Airport to the Rhine at Mainz

Frankfurt airport is Germany's major airport for international flight. There is a train station at the airport itself, with connections to many parts of the Rhine route.

There is an S-Bahn (urban train) connection to Frankfurt City train station. Train services from Frankfurt City Haupt- bahnhof (train station) will connect you to other destinations. You can use any of the express train ser-

vices, as well as the airport coach services. If you bring your bike along and it's still packed in its bag or box, you can take it as luggage, but not if it's unpacked.

If you prefer, you could cycle the 20 kilometers (depending on the route you choose) from Frankfurt airport to Mainz along a number of bike routes, or join the Rhine route elsewhere along the river.

15
The Netherlands

In the Netherlands, we are in the Rhine Delta. Tracing the river from its original (but now quite insignificant) mouth at Katwijk aan Zee through the provinces of South Holland, Utrecht, and Gelderland to the German border. The terrain in the western part of the route, through the province of Zuid

Holland is typified by waterways. Canals, rivers, drainage ditches, and peat-bog lakes (plassen) are part of the landscape. Most of this area was once nothing but a large swamp, and the land here has been drained and reclaimed over the centuries.

Route 1A: Katwijk aan Zee to Woerden

Distance: 54 km/34 miles

Terrain: Flat, alongside/nearby the Oude Rijn (Old Rhine); paved bike paths and roads

Maps: FALK Plan Zuid-Holland Noord; 1:50,000 (2 cm = 1 km) (shows some positions but no numbers of route signs)

ANWB Provinciekaart Zuid Holland; 1:100,000 (1 cm = 1 km)

Diversions: See Route 1B (dunes, lakes and tulips) and Route 1C (Gouda and Oudewater).

Description

The Katwijk sea lock, situated close to the sea mouth of the river, prevents the sea from flooding the Old Rhineland. This triple lock, built in 1804–47, is closed at high tide, being re-opened to allow the accumulated waters to wash sand from the mouth to keep it open. Here, where the mighty Rhine once spilt into the sea, the river nowadays carries only one five-hundredth of its waters.

Along the way you will find numerous interesting and entertaining gratuitous statues depicting the past as well as the present. Look out for them, as they can add so much pleasure to your journey.

From Katwijk the route takes you to Rijnsburg, where flower auctions are held on weekday mornings. Baruch

Spinoza the great philosopher lived here 1660–63.

Leiden translates to "place on the waterways" and is built around rings of canals. About 1670 Leiden was the second largest city in Europe. Its prosperity and importance grew when Flemish weavers settled here after the Black Death had ravaged Europe in the mid-14th century. The "Blue Stone" near the Stadhuis (Town Hall) was the place of execution as well as where faulty cloth, rejected by quality inspectors, was burnt.

De Burcht, a 12th century castle built on Roman and possibly Saxon (Frisian) ruins, offers great views from the battlements. Morspoort is one of the remaining town gates. The birthplace of the artist Rembrandt is along Weddelsteeg. Many other famous artists and Classicists were born in Leiden.

The University is the oldest and most important in the Netherlands and its botanical gardens are the oldest in Europe (open April–September, 09h00–17h00, otherwise 10h00–16h00, closed Sundays). The University was built in 1575 as the reward chosen by the citizens of the town after defying the Spanish despite suffering exceptional deprivation before being relieved by William the Silent. William cut the dikes and flooded the entire countryside between Leiden and Dordrecht to get his ships up to the town walls. Food was so scarce that the Burgemeester (Mayor) Pieter van der Werff offered to cut off his arm to provide food, rather than surrender to the Spanish. On 3 October there are fairs, ceremonies and processions to celebrate the relief of Leiden.

Associated with the University in the 17th and 18th centuries, are John Evelyn the diarist, Oliver Goldsmith, poet, playwright and novelist (Gulliver's Travels) and John Wilkes, British radical parliamentarian who supported American independence.

The Boerhaave Zalen in Lange St. Agnietenstraat was the world's first teaching hospital.

The Elzevier family, religious fugitives from Leuven in the Spanish Netherlands (now Belgium), worked in Leiden and contributed significantly to the development of printing.

The Pilgrim Fathers, religious dissenters from England, came to Leiden in 1609 looking for religious tolerance. They were unable to settle happily in this society and left for America via England in 1620. Their leader and pastor John Robinson, though he intended following the party, remained in Leiden until his death in 1625. The Pilgrim Press was run here by William Brewster, head of the Speedwell party of Pilgrim Fathers. The emigrants left via the Vliet waterway at the south end of the town. John Robinson's house is at Jan Pesijnshofje, Kloksteeg. There is a plaque on the 15th century Pieterskerk, commemorating the sailing of the Mayflower to America. The Pilgrim Fathers' Document center is open Monday–Friday, 09h30–16h30.

Museums include one of clay tobacco pipes, a collection from more than forty countries. The windmill museum, De Valk, is a tall corn mill with original machinery, workshop and living quarters. It's on the town ramparts, near Lammermarkt and opens Tuesday through Saturday, 10h00–17h00, Sundays and public holidays 13h00–17h00.

Alongside the canalized Old Rhine, in the center of Leiden, the former wharves at water level are now used as open air restaurants. Some are situated on floating platforms.

From Leiden, cycle alongside the Oude Rijn, through hamlets and villages to Alphen aan de Rijn. Across the river is Avifauna, a park where you can see 275 species of birds and animals. There are also replicas of well-known buildings. Boat trips are offered through Rhineland polder country, as well. The park is open daily, 09h00–21h00 (09h00–18h00 in winter).

At Bodegraven, cross the river in the center of town and continue alongside the Oude Rijn on the south bank. About 9 km south of Bodegraven is the town of Gouda, famous for its cheese market. Route 1C. will take you there from Woerden via an interesting route.

As you exit Nieuwerbrug you leave the province of South Holland and enter the smallest province of the Netherlands, Utrecht province. The swing bridge at Nieuwerbrug is a toll bridge where motorists are charged 50 cents per crossing. Bicycles cross free.

At Woerden, once a Roman outpost, you reach the end of this route. The center of Woerden is surrounded by a moat and there is a historical fortress and windmill. Nearby, to the north-east, is a campsite. At the railway station you will find an Info map as well as a bike shop.

Directions

Start facing south at the south side of the Rhine mouth lock

Cross the road

At signpost No. 3345/1, left towards Leiden (9 km)

Continue along Rijnmond (street)

City scene in Leiden, the Netherlands.

At roundabout, continue across along Kortenaarstraat

At the T-junction roundabout, turn right

Cross bridge

At traffic lights, turn left

At signpost No.1518/8 continue towards Leiden (5 km)

At signpost No. 1543 continue

Cross freeway (N206)

At Y-intersection, take the left fork

Continue along Rijnstraat

At signpost No. 1565/1 continue

Cross bridge (Zandsloot brug)

At traffic lights, cross to windmill

Continue along Valkenburgsestraat

Exit Katwijk, enter Valkenburg

Info map on your right

At signpost No. 3366/1 (on your left), turn left to pedestrian ferry ("Rijnsburg via Voetveer")

Cross on ferry

Continue along gravel track away from river

At T-junction, turn right along Rijnhof (road)

At signpost No. 12348/1 turn right towards Leiden (7 km)

Continue towards Leiden-Zuid (6 km)

At signpost No. 6441/1 turn right towards Leiden-Zuid

Under bridge (N206)

Under bridge (A44)

Under bridge

Enter Leiden

At signpost No. 12341/1 continue across roundabout

Continue direction "Duinpolder route" along Hogemorsweg

(Rhine on your right, pass park with picnic area, pass swing bridge)

Road swings left, railway on your right

1st left opposite apartment block, along Smaragdlaan

Right along Diamantlaan

At intersection, turn right along bike path under subway ("Dam Tunnel")

Immediately right, U-turn to roadway and left towards railway bridge

Under railway line

Cross bridge over Rhine (windmill on your left)

At signpost No. 8796/14 continue

Under subway

Immediately left towards "Centrum/ Leiderdorp" (Rhine on your LHS) (windmill ahead on your LHS)

Cross bridge over railway

Info map. [Note: Here you are in a good position to explore the center of Leiden. To remain on this described route, it is important that you exit Leiden under the A4 freeway along the North bank of the Old Rhine (i.e. with the river on your RHS)]

Continue along Noordeinde (street)

Continue along Breestraat

Left along Rapenburgstraat

Immediately right before bridge, alongside Rhine (on your left)

Continue along Aalmarkt

[In this area you will find: waterside restaurants; de Waag (weigh-house); Wednesday and Saturday all day markets; statue of flower sellers; Town Hall; small statue of a baker]

Left over Karnemelkbrug across river

Immed. R along Nieuwe Rijn (street)

Continue over hump bridge (corner Heerengracht/Nieuwe Rijn)

1st right over swing bridge (Rijnstraat)

Left along Utrechtse Veer

At T-junction, turn right along Zijlsingel

At T-junction, turn Left along Hoge Rijndijk

Left along Veerhuis (road)

Road swings right, continue alongside waterway (on your LHS)

Continue along Utrechtse Jaagpad, to end

At T-junction, turn left along Hoge Rijndijk

Over bridge, continue along Hoge Rijndijk

Left across bridge along bike path on left side of road

At T-junction, turn left

At signpost No. 9769/1 continue towards Alphen a. d. Rijn/Koudekerk a. d. Rijn

At signpost No. 4769/2 turn left towards Alphen a. d. Rijn/Koudekerk a. d. Rijn

Under A4 freeway bridge

At signpost No. 9769/3 continue towards Alphen a. d. Rijn, along Hoofdstraat

Right along alley (Chris Keijzerpad) opposite second church gate (church on your left)

Beware of blind corner and restricted passageway at end of alley

Left alongside Old Rhine, river on your right

Beware of mooring pegs in the grass verge

Under motor swing bridge, right under bridge steps

Continue alongside river

Left at sign "Doorgaand fietsverkeer"

Continue along lane (Rijnpad)

Right along Hoofdstraat

Cross swing bridge over Does waterway

At paddestoel sign P24125 right towards Koudekerk (4.5 km)/Alphen (11 km)

Left alongside river

At signpost No. 8287/3 continue towards Koudekerk (5 km)

Continue into countryside

Through Koudekerk aan de Rijn, Oude Rijn on your right

At signpost No. 4423/1 continue towards Alphen aan de Rijn (4 km)

At signpost No. 7684/1 continue towards Alphen

Bike path ends, continue along roadway

[On the far bank of the river is Avifauna bird and animal park]

Cross swing bridge over canal (Heimanswoud Wetering)

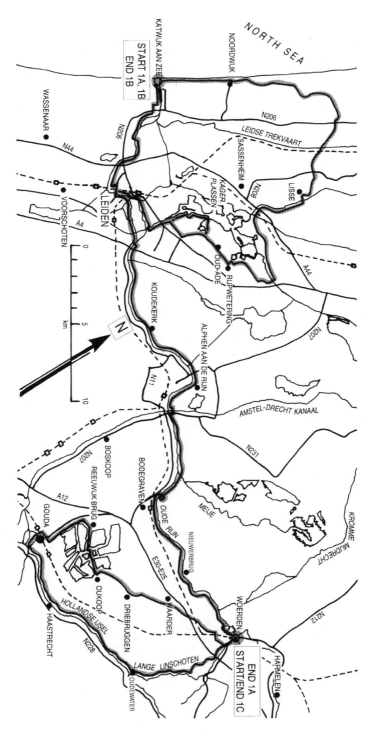

Continue along roadway, river on your right

Under bridge [cross river here to reach Avifauna]

Continue along Oudshoornseweg

Continue along Hoofdstraat

Under bridge

Continue through pedestrian area

Continue along van Boetselaarstraat

Left up bridge access road

Immediately right along bike path on left side of road

Cross bridge over Oostkanaal

At traffic light, continue

At signpost No. 4267/5 at T-junction, turn right towards river

Left alongside river

Continue past de Dikke Molen (1638 wind pump)

Continue through Zwammerdam

At signpost No. 1632 continue towards Bodegraven, river on your right

Under bridge

At signpost No. 9631/1 immediately left along Frank Habold Laan

At signpost No. 9631 T-junction, turn left

At signpost No. 2739/6 left and cross bridge over Rhine on left hand side bike path

Left alongside Old Rhine, along Damme Kort (street)

Info map on your left

Continue past windmill

At signpost No. 160/1 left along Brugstraat towards river

Right alongside river, along Rijnkade, river on your left

Continue past lock

At signpost No. 17832/1 continue towards Nieuwerbrug

Continue along Graaf Florisstraat

Cross swing bridge over Dubbele Wiericke

Continue along Bruggemeesterstraat

Continue past Toll Bridge, on your left

Left along Hoge Rijndijk towards Woerden (6 km), cross to left side bike path

At signpost No. 1396/2 direction "Doorgaand Verkeer;" cross road to bike path

At signpost No. 1396/4 left across road, immediately right towards "Centrum" (town center)

Continue along Gildeweg

At signpost No. 8740/6 cross road, immediately left towards "Centrum"

Continue across swing bridge

Continue past statue group working at a table

Continue to Railway Station entrance; route ends here.

Diversion Route 1B: Loop Route from Katwijk aan Zee

This is a circular route past coastal dunes, flower fields, peat-bog lakes, windmills and canals, beginning and ending in Katwijk aan Zee.

Distance: 58 km/36 miles

Terrain: Mostly flat, some hills through the coastal dunes; short distance on hard sand, otherwise paved bike paths and roads

Maps: FALK Plan Zuid-Holland Noord; 1:50,000 (2 cm = 1 km) (shows some positions but no numbers of route signs)

ANWB Provinciekaart Zuid Holland; 1:100,000 (1 cm = 1 km) (does not show all numbered route signs)

VVV Bulb Fields map

Description:

Starting at the north side of the Oude Rijn mouth, travel north along the coast through the sand dunes, passing through Noordwijk aan Zee. Along the way pass to the west of the European Space Center (ESTEC), but not on its access road; you can get a permit to visit from the VVV. Past Noordwijk the route takes you through the coastal forest and briefly into the Amsterdam Dunes.

Turning East, cross the renowned flower fields; if you're here at the right time of year, they'll be in full bloom (April–May most years). Pass Keukenhof Castle and the world-famous Keukenhof Gardens, the show-

case of Dutch floriculture. The gardens are open during the flower growing season, mid-March to the end of May (varies, so enquire at VVV offices), daily, 08h00–19h30. These 70 acre gardens were designed to show the produce of the many growers of the region, with both indoor and outdoor exhibits. There are ten miles of footpaths around the gardens, so you can walk to your heart's content.

Travel to the town of Lisse, the center of the multi-million dollar bulb growing industry. There is a newly established Museum of the Bulb District here. Cross the canal to enter the Province of North Holland. Following the canal, which is also the Provincial boundary, ride on the dike, passing through the village of Buitenkaag and the hamlet of Huigsloot.

After turning south and re-entering the Province of South Holland, swing west to reach the Kager Plassen. These peat-bog lakes were created when the peat was removed. Cycling south and west, you pass windmills and the little villages of Rijpwetering and Oud-Ade. Past Oud-Ade there are two route options. You can turn West towards the lake and cycle through farms to the quaint ferry over the Zijp waterway then on a roadway alongside the water to Leiden. Or you can continue past the Venne Meer and rejoin this route before cycling into Leiden and North to Oegstgeest. You then turn West along the canal to Rijnsburg and back to Katwijk.

Directions:

Start at the coast-side Oude Rijn sea lock. Travel northwards with the sea on your LHS

Continue along bike path which begins before the car park ("Rijwielpad Noordduinen")

Enter Noordwijk

Continue along Noordwijk promenade

R-L at end of promenade

Cycle around the lighthouse, sea on your LHS

Y-L along coast road

Continue along dunes bike path

At P21611 R

At Signpost No. 2590 T L

At P21736 X continue

At P21597 L

AT P21596 T R

At P21744 L

At P22573 continue towards Lisse (7 km)

At P21772 continue to roadway

At signpost No. 4119 cross road, L to face freeway underpass

At signpost No. 4122 continue under bridge (N206)

L towards Keukenhof along bike path

At signpost No. 4125 R towards Keukenhof (3 km)

At P10134/1 continue along Delfweg

Continue across railway line

[L to Keukenhof gardens]

X (lights) continue across N206 into Lisse

Continue to end of road

T-R along van Spijkstraat

L along Kanaalstraat

Cross swing bridge

Immed. R, canal on your RHS

Continue towards Kaag(dorp)/Buitenkaag

Continue through Buitenkaag along Huigsloter Dijk

R across first swing bridge on your RHS

Y-R (continue along main roadway)

At signpost 18777/3 R towards Oud-Ade (5 km) along Molenweg

Continue to windmill

At signpost No. 18778/1 L towards Oud-Ade

At signpost No. 18779/1 T R towards Oud-Ade (2 km)

R across swing bridge into Oud-Ade

Continue through Oud-Ade along Oud-Adeselaan

Continue past windmill and continue past road to Zevenhuizen on RHS

* Alternative Route: Immediately before the Venne Meer, turn Right to the Bungalow Park (signed) and sailing club. Follow the signs through farms, cross on the quaint ferry, continue alongside the Kager Plassen to rejoin the route near Leiden at Signpost No. 1757/1; this route is 1 km longer

Continue across Achtergat Voorsloot (waterway) along Leidse Weg

At signpost No. 10522 R towards Leiden

At signpost No. 1757/1 T turn L towards Leiden (3 km)

(Alternative route joins here)

At signpost No. 2738/4 continue towards Leiden, canal on your RHS

At signpost No. 1456/2 R across swing bridge (Spanjaardsbrug)

Continue through the Spanish Gate and over bridge (Spanjaardsbrug)

Continue along Lage Rijndijk

T-R along Herensingel

Road swings L, continue along Herensingel (waterway on your LHS)

Continue along Maresingel, waterway on your LHS

T-L along Morssingel

Road swings R, waterway on your LHS, continue along Morsweg

R over railway line, along Lage Morsweg

X-L along Damlaan

X continue along Diamantlaan

T-R along Smaragdlaan

X-L along Agaatlaan

Continue across Stevensbrug (bridge)

Immed. R along Rijndijk, Oude Rijn on your RHS

Immed. before freeway bridge R, then L under bridge

Immed. L, bike path swings R

Continue along Valkenburgseweg, Oude Rijn on your RHS

Under freeway (A44)

Continue along Valkenburgseweg, Oude Rijn on your RHS

T L along Rijnstraat

Over freeway (N206)

X (lights) R

L along Rijnmond

Route ends at Rhine mouth sea lock

Bicycle-friendly sculpture in Woerden, the Netherlands.

Diversion Route 1C: Loop Route from Woerden

This is a circular route from Woerden to the Emperor's honest witch scales, through Gouda, the world's most famous cheese town, and across peat-bog lakes and polders

Distance: 44 km/28 miles

Terrain: Flat; paved bike paths and roads

Map: ANWB Provinciekaart Zuid Holland; 1:100,000 (1 cm = 1 km)

Description:

Circular route from Woerden, along scenic routes to the witch scales at Oudewater and to Gouda with the largest cheese market in the Netherlands. Return to Woerden across the Reeuwijkse Plassen, through Driebruggen. A gentle ride through villages and polder- land, alongside streams and rivers. Cycle along roads surrounded by peat-bog lakes and through quiet lanes.

Directions:

Start facing the Woerden Railway station entrance, turn R and cycle past the face of the building on the bike path

Continue towards Linschoten (bicycle sign)

Through subway (Middelland tunnel)

Continue along Jaap Wijzerweg

Through subway (Wolwehorst tunnel)

Continue alongside N204

At signpost No. 13463 R along Polaner Zandweg

L across sloot (narrow drainage canal)

Signpost No. 13463/3 L

Continue under freeway (E30/E25)

(2nd) R after freeway, along Haardijk

Continue along Haardijk

Enter Oudewater

L over waterway, Immed. R

L along Nieuweringstraat (street), to town square

(De Waag, the witch scales, are on your LHS; 15 meters ahead is the VVV office on the RHS)

R to Marktstraat (street)

R along Noordekerkstraat (street)

L towards front of church

T-R along Noordijsselkade, quay and waterway on your LHS

Y-R along bike path, at end of quay

Under road bridge

Continue along lower roadway, waterway on your LHS

T-L along Hekendorperweg (street)

Continue along Hekendorpsebuurt

Continue through Wiltenburg

Continue through Hekendorp

At signpost No. 1339/1 continue towards Haastrecht (3 km) along upper road

Continue along Steinsedijk

At signpost No. 12976/1 L along bike path towards Haastrecht (3 km) and Gouda (7 km)

Through Haastrecht

At signpost No. 5776 continue

Enter Gouda

Pass windmill, on your LHS

Continue along Goejanverwelledijk

Continue along this route (as for Alphen aan de Rijn) until you come to a windmill on your RHS

R (after passing windmill) to Gouda Town Square and Cheese Market

Facing the Waag (weighing house), make your way to the LHS of the building and head for the subway under the railway line (signposts indicate direction to the ANWB office and Schouwburg train station)

Through subway under railway line

R along Count Florisweg (street)

Continue past hospital

Cross bridge over canal

X-L towards Reeuwijk (3 km) and Reeuwijkse Plassen (1 km) along Venteweg

Continue along bike path over wooden bridge

Through subway under motor road

T-L

R along 's Gravenbroekseweg (road)

At signpost No. 4003/1 continue towards Driebruggen along 's Gravenbroekseweg

Continue through Sluipwijk (Info on RHS)

P (21722) L towards Driebruggen

P (21723) R towards Driebruggen (4 km) along Nieuwebroeksedijk

Cross bridge

P (21725) continue towards Driebruggen

P 21214 L towards Driebruggen along Oukoopsedijk

P 21179 R towards Driebruggen along Wierickepad

Through Driebruggen (Info map)

At signpost No. 4551/1 R towards Woerden along Westeinde

At signpost No. 5650/1 T R towards Woerden

T-R (parallel with freeway)

Under freeway

Across railway line

Enter Woerden

Continue along Waardsedijk

At signpost No. 1402/13 X L, cross intersection, immed. R

At signpost No. 1402/11 R, immed. Signpost No. 1402/9 R

Under railway bridge ("viaduct Het Vintje")

Continue under another railway bridge

X (roundabout/circle) continue

Cross to bike path on LHS of road and continue in same direction

Cross bridge over canal

Halfway down the bridge off-ramp, immed. L along bike path

At end of ramp, cross road and L

L following sign "Fietsers/Station"

Through subway under railway (Spoor tunnel); ends at Woerden Railway Station.

Route 2A: Woerden to Driebergen-Rijsenburg

Distance: 44 km/28 miles

Terrain: Flat, alongside Leidse Rijn and Kromme Rijn; paved bike paths and roads, short sand track

Maps :   ANWB Provinciekaart Utrecht Province; 1:100,000 (1 cm = 1 km)

Falk CityPlan Utrecht; 1:12,500 (1 cm = 125 m)

Diversion: See Route 2B

Description

From Woerden, cross the East moat and the Old Rhine river, along the cycle path on the south bank of the Rhine. Continue along a cycles-only roadway past the hamlet of Breeveld. A country lane brings you to Harmelen, where you cross to the north bank of the river. This section of the Rhine is called the Leidse Rijn. Passing through the hamlet of Harmelerwaard and De Meern, you come to the city of Utrecht.

Utrecht, the fourth largest city in the Netherlands, is the capital of the smallest province and boasts the largest and second oldest University in the country. The city's history dates back to Roman times (AD 47) when the settlement was known as "Trajectum ad Rhenum" (ford on the Rhine). After the Great Flood of AD 839, when the principal course of the Rhine moved further south, the town became known as Oude Trecht (old ford), from which the present name is derived.

In the tenth century the Vikings raided up the Dutch rivers and sacked Utrecht. The German Emperors built a palace in the city which was used as their residence from AD 1080 to AD 1250. The only Dutch Pope, Adrian VI, had a house built here (Paushuisje). The Earl of Athlone (Godert de Ginkel, 1630–1703), a general in Ireland with the forces of King William III, was born here. The University was popular with Scottish students in the seventeenth and eighteenth centuries; James Boswell, "Doctor" Samuel Johnson's biographer, studied civil law here in 1763. Louis Bonaparte reigned as King of Holland (1806–1810) and used Utrecht as his base.

The Cathedral tower (Domtoren) is the highest in the Netherlands (112 m/364 ft) affording a spectacular view, if you brave the 465 steps. The weathervane depicts Saint Martin cutting off part of his coat to clothe a beggar. Martin was a Roman officer converted to Christianity. The first Bishop of Utrecht and founder of the Cathedral of Saint Martin, an Englishman who became Saint Willibrord, introduced Christianity to Denmark. This fact is commemorated by a copy of a Danish rune stone from Jutland presented to Utrecht by the Danes, kept at the Cathedral. On Saturdays, 11h00–12h00, you can hear carillon concerts at the Cathedral tower, played on one of the finest instruments in the Netherlands.

The Union of Utrecht (1579) was the treaty which eventually unified the seven Dutch provinces against Spain and led to the formation of the present-day Kingdom of the Netherlands.

The National Museum of Music boxes, street organs and other musical instruments can be found at Buurkerkhof 10, opening Tuesday-Saturday, 10h00–17h00 and Sundays and Public Holidays, 13h00–17h00. Tours are guided, multilingual and last about an hour, beginning on the hour. It's well worth a visit. During June you can also enjoy theatrical and musical performances in the streets and along the canals.

The Nederlands Spoorweg-museum (Railway Museum) has many British-built locomotives, some purpose built for the D-Day invasions of World War II. It's in the former Maliebaan station, open Tuesday–Saturday, 10h00–17h00, Sundays 13h00–17h00.

There are a number of other highly-rated museums in Utrecht, with exceptional architectural features and artistic exhibits. For pure nostalgia, especially for older countryfolk who will still remember such stores, don't miss the Grocery Museum (Museum voor het Kruideniersbedrijf) at Hoogt 6, open Tuesday–Saturday, 12h30–16h30.

Hoog Catharijne is the largest covered shopping center in Europe, with safekeeping facilities for bicycles. There is a general market on the Vredenburg on Wednesdays and Saturdays.

Along the wharves, below street level and next to the central canals, you'll find many restaurants and cafes. Prices vary, but you can check the menus and prices, which are always posted outside the entrances.

From Utrecht leave alongside the now renamed Kromme Rijn (Crooked Rhine), past the football stadium and through the Rhijnauwen estate country park. Pass the moated former Rhijnauwen fort and cycle through the village of Bunnik, to Odijk and Driebergen-Rijsenburg.

There are camp sites nearby on the East and Northeast sides of Driebergen-Rijsenburg.

Directions:

Start with your back to the railway station, at the western side. Cycle directly away from the station, along the bike path on the RHS of the road. Cross over the intersection with the traffic lights. **Very** Important Instruction: Immediately before the bridge ahead of you, next to the bridge railings, turn R along a narrow black tar path, with the Oude Rijn immediately on your LHS.

X continue (along Haarzuilers route)

X (lights) continue

At signpost No. 13460/1 continue towards Harmelen (5 km) and Utrecht (17 km)

At signpost No. 13464/1 continue towards Harmelen (2 km)/ Utrecht (14 km) along Breeveld (street)

Cross rail line

(From the lock, the waterway becomes the Leidsche Rijn.)

Enter Harmelen

T-L towards De Meern and Utrecht

At signpost No. 3436/1 T-L towards De Meern

Immed. R before bridge, along Kloosterweg (street)

X-L along (also) Kloosterweg

T-R

At signpost No. 13076/1 L to De Meern and Utrecht over swing bridge

Immed. R on bike path along Harmelerweg

Bike path crosses road

Exit Harmelen, with Rhine on your RHS

Continue along Harmelerwaard (road)

X continue along Zandweg

Through De Meern along Zandweg

At end of Zandweg, follow road R over waterway

Immed. L

Continue along bike path, waterway on your LHS

X continue along bike path on LHS of road

Continue under freeway

At signpost No. 1022/20 X R across road onto bike path to Utrecht (1 km), Route LF4A

Continue along Ds. Abernathy laan

Continue along Ds. Martin Luther King laan

Cross Amsterdam-Rijn canal on bowed iron bridge

U-turn L off down-ramp of bridge

T-R

Road curves R into Kennedylaan

Continue along Leidseweg

Cross bridge (Muntbrug) over Merwede kanaal

Continue along Leidseweg, canal (Leidsche Rijn) on your LHS

Move across road to bike path on LHS and continue

L across bridge (with statue group) into Damstraat

R along Kanaalstraat

X continue towards railway lines, then L along bike path

Continue under railway line subway (Daalse tunnel)

X continue along Nieuwe Kade

X-R along Sint Jakobs straat

Into pedestrian area and square and continue

L along Drieharingstraat (lane)

R along Oude Gracht

[This is close to many of the Utrecht attractions, with many interesting facets of Utrecht life being displayed down the Oude Gracht itself.]

Continue along Oude Gracht to the end — make sure you are in the right-hand traffic flow, with the waterway on your LHS; Oude Gracht becomes Tol Steeg Zuid

X (circle/roundabout) R along Ledig

L along Gansstraat

L along Albatrosstraat

Over bridge (Albatrosbrug), immed. R along Venuslaan

X-R along Kranerbergerweg

Cross bridge (Waterloobrug)

L along Bosch van Drakensteinlaan

T-L over bridge (Prinsenbrug)

R along Breitnerlaan

T-R along Israelslaan, swing L with the road

T-R along Tamboersdijk (road)

Cross Kromme Rijn

At signpost No. 8082/2 T-L along Koningsweg

Under bridge

Immed. L along Galgenaarwaardsepad (bike path)

Cross Kromme Rijn

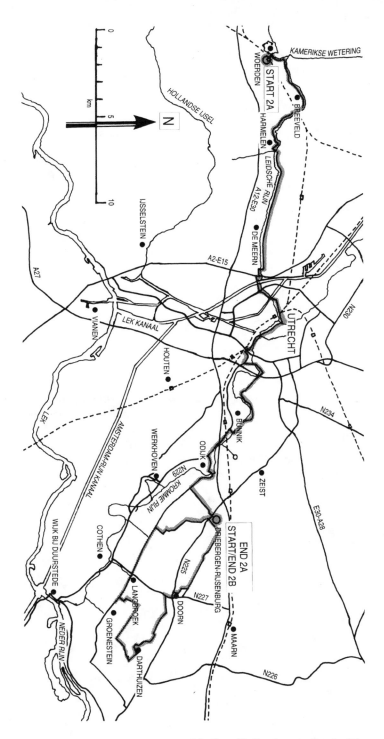

Continue into Stadium area

Bear R along bike path around perimeter of Stadium car park

Exit Stadium area, L-R along Weg tot de Wetenschap (not R to Bunnik)

Cross waterway

X (lights) R towards Wijk/Bunnik along Weg naar Rhijnauwen

Under freeway (A27) bridge

At signpost No. 17957/1 L-R along Vossegatsedijk

X R along hard sand road (Route LF4B)

X continue (remain on sand surface)

T-R towards Bunnik (1 km) (Route LF4B) along Rijnsoever

At signpost No. 1226 R towards Bunnik along Tolhuislaan

Cross Kromme Rijn

Continue along Dorpstraat

L along Smalweg

T-L along Stationsweg

At signpost No. 8100/5 continue towards Odijk/Driebergen along Stationsweg

Cross rail line

X (freeway junction) continue

Under freeway, river on your LHS

At signpost No. 9321/6 L into Odijk

At signpost No. 14611/2 L towards Driebergen (4 km)

[Look out for the Lakenvelder cattle breed, which have a band of white around their otherwise black bodies; also for the Roman encampment built to celebrate the coming of the Romans over 1950 years ago.]

Cross Kromme Rijn

At signpost No. 923/1 X-R towards Driebergen

At signpost No. 2220/1 L towards Driebergen

Continue past church

R along Hoofdstraat

Route ends at Driebergen-Rijsenburg VVV office/Stadhuis (Town Hall) (Hoofdstraat 87-89).

Diversion Route 2B: Loop Route from Driebergen-Rijsenburg

This is a circular route past castles and through woods.

Distance: 32 km/20 miles

Terrain: Small hills and gentle slopes; compacted dirt roads, paved bike paths and roads

Maps: ANWB Provinciekaart Utrecht Province; 1:100,000 (1 cm = 1 km)

VVV map Utrecht Oost, Heuvelrug en Eemland; 1:50,000 (2 cm = 1 km)

Description:

This area was once covered with forests and heaths, but has suffered badly from deforestation over the past two centuries.

The Langbroeker wetering (the waterway between the foot of the hills and the Kromme Rijn) had an inordinate number of castles built nearby during the early middle ages. The established farms date from before the seventeenth century and most of the chateaux were constructed during the nineteenth century. These chateaux are noted for their varied architecture and their park-like gardens.

The attraction of this area for the nobility stemmed mainly from the good hunting, whilst landed gentry appreciated the dry soil which could be cultivated with greater success than the heavy clays of the delta.

Begin at Driebergen-Rijsenburg and head directly for the town of Doorn and the retirement chateau of Kaiser Wilhelm II of Germany. The gatehouse itself is an impressive con-

struction with a golden weather vane. The gardens can be visited on foot without restriction. You can buy tickets for visits to the residence at the gate house (closed Mondays, Christmas and New Year; open afternoons only on Sundays and in wintertime 13h00 to 17h00, otherwise opens in summer 10h00 to 17h00). There are bike racks, but no lockup facilities.

Continue on through the hamlet of Darthuizen to Broekhuizen estate, then through the rich farmlands and woods past the castles and chateaux at Sandenburg, Walenburg, Lunenburg, Hindersteijn, Leeuwenburgh and Sterkenburg, then back to Driebergen-Rijsenburg.

Directions:

Start at VVV office in Driebergen-Rijsenburg. Exit the parking area

L along bike path along Hoofdstraat

L along Bosstraat

T-R along Arnhemse Boveweg

Exit Driebergen along Arnhemse Boveweg

Cross over to bike path on LHS of road continue

Enter Doorn, cross to bike path on RHS of road

X-R along Drift (road)

Continue along Berkenweg

P20086 T-L

Pass Stadhuis and immed. R along Raadhuisplein

(VVV office and Info board are 10 m past this turn, on Berkenweg)

Follow Raadhuisplein when it swings L

Along Kapelweg (towards church)

T-R along Langbroekerweg

(Doorn Chateau on your RHS)

L along De Beaufortweg

Exit Doorn

Continue along Bourtweg, follow Heuvelrugroete (route)

X-L along Heuvelrugweg (road)

T-R towards Leersum along Darthuizerweg (Heuvelrugroete)

*T-L along Broekhuizerweg, cross waterway and on your RHS is Broekhuizen chateau; no cycling, but walking permitted on designated pathways

Return to *T and continue along Langerbroekweg

T-R along Gooijerdijk

X-L towards Sandenburg chateau

**T-R to view front of chateau

Return to **T and continue

***T-L to view Groenesteyn

Return to ***T and continue

(Walenburg chateau on LHS)

Enter (Neder) Langbroek (village)

Cross waterway

Continue along Langbroekerdijk

X continue over N227

Exit Langbroek

(Lunenburg chateau on LHS; not open to public)

Continue along Langbroekerdijk

(Hindersteijn chateau on LHS; cycling permitted on designated paths)

Continue past church on LHS

(Leeuwenburgh chateau entrance on RHS; cycling permitted)

Continue along Langbroekerdijk

(Sterkenburg chateau on LHS)

R, cross bridge and continue away from waterway

L along Dwarsweg

R-L along Gooijerdijk

Through Sterkenburg hamlet

Road swings R

(1st) L and continue along Engweg

T-L along Hoofdstraat

Route ends at VVV office.

Route 3A: Driebergen-Rijsenburg to Rhenen

Distance: 44 km/28 miles

Terrain: Flat, alongside Kromme Rijn, Lek, and Neder Rijn rivers; paved bike paths and roads, compacted dirt roads

Map: ANWB Provinciekaart Utrecht; 1:100,000 (1 cm = 1 km)

Diversion: See Route 3B (forests and hills)

Description:

From Driebergen-Rijsenburg cycle to the Kromme (Crooked) Rijn and follow its meanders through the countryside. Cycle through Werkhoven, past Rhine chateaux, through Cothen with its windmill and Rhijnestein castle, to Wijk bij Duurstede.

Wijk bij Duurstede was founded as Roman Batavodurum. Local tribes were named Batavii by the Romans. Later the settlement was named Dorestad. The old ruins near the Neder Rijn river are called Duurstede. The castle dates from the twelfth century and was the Duke of Burgundy's residence (1459).

Here the Neder Rijn becomes the Lek river, flowing west and south towards Rotterdam. Lek means leak, an appropriate name, for the Rhine leaked away from its old course through Roman-built canals in the great flood of AD 839. The Neder Rijn river carries about one third of the Rhine waters, the other two thirds flowing down the Waal river towards the sea. The Neder Rijn is further diminished by the IJssel river which branches away at Arnhem.

It was here that the Christian Frankish king Pepin of Herstal defeated Radbod of Frisia in AD 689. The Franks had been settled here for some few hundred years before then. This was also the site of the capital of the short-lived Norse kingdom of Frisia in AD 850.

Astride the dike wall facing the confluence of the Lek, Neder Rijn and Kromme Rijn, is the only remaining windmill (Rijn en Lek, 1659) in the Netherlands which is built on a gate in the city wall.

From Wijk bij Duurstede, cycle under the Rijn and Lek windmill and across the Kromme Rijn lock. Continue along the dike-top road towards Amerongen, past the locks on the Neder Rijn. Arrive at Amerongen chateau, residence of Kaiser Wilhelm II, who lived here 1918–1920 before moving to his final residence at Doorn (see Route 2b). This medieval chateau was rebuilt in 1676, having been damaged during the French wars. It's open April to October, Tuesday–Friday 10h00–17h00 and Saturdays, Sundays, and public holidays 13h00–17h00.

Cross over the Neder Rijn on the ferry and continue East along the dike road. About 1 km past the next ferry crossing (to Elst), is a viewpoint. Carry on along the dike road past the hamlet of Bontemorgen, along the scenic road to the Rhenen bridge and over the river into Rhenen town.

Rhenen is associated with Saint Cunera, one of the eleven thousand (English) virgins who accompanied Saint Ursula on a pilgrimage to Rome in the fourth century. Whilst returning home, the party was slaughtered by the pagan Huns at Cologne, and Cunera was apparently the only survivor. A Frankish chief took pity on Cunera and brought her here to his estate. To assist her in her good works amongst the poor and suffering, the chief gave Cunera the keys to his store rooms. But the chief's wife wasn't pleased that her husband's wealth was being eroded, so she strangled Cunera, burying her body in the stables. When the horses refused to enter the stables, the dastardly deed was discovered.

A palace was built here in 1629 for the exiled Winter King, Frederick V of Bohemia.

Rhenen was a favorite subject for many famous Dutch artists and pictures of the surrounds were painted time and again by Rembrandt, van Goyen, Saenredam, Seghers, and others.

There is a viewpoint to the West of the town, just North of the N225. A few kilometers East along the North bank of the river is Ouwehand recreation park, which has an aquarium.

Directions:

Start at the VVV offices at Driebergen-Rijsenburg. Exit the parking lot and R along Hoofdstraat

L (towards church) along Kerkplein (follow road on LHS of church)

Continue along Rijsenburgerlaan

T-L along Langbroekerdijk (road)

R over bridge (farm on your RHS)

Immed. R through gateposts marked Bever Weert

Follow road as it swings L (hardened dirt road)

T (opposite Beverweert house) L along Jagdrustlaan

T-R along Steenovenweg

Cross Kromme Rijn

Immed. L

X continue across freeway (N229) along Steenovenweg

T-L

At signpost No. 1160/1 R towards Culemborg and Schalkwijk along Watertorenweg

At signpost No. 7391/2 L along Caspargauw (road)

(2nd) L along Ossenwaard

Enter Cothen village along Ossenwaard

X (roundabout/circle) continue along Willem Alexanderweg

T-R along Dorpsstraat (L to windmill and Rhijnestein chateau)

Continue along Groenewoudsestraat

Exit Cothen

At signpost No. 9336/5 X continue across N229 road

(De Pronckheer restaurant on RHS)

L-R along Groenewoudseweg

Cross Kromme Rijn

Immed. R along bike path

T-L

T-R along Melkwegsetiendweg (road)

T-R along bike path

Enter Wijk-bij-Duurstede

Cross Kromme Rijn

Immed. L alongside Kromme Rijn (river on your LHS) along bike path

Keep turning towards river when path allows

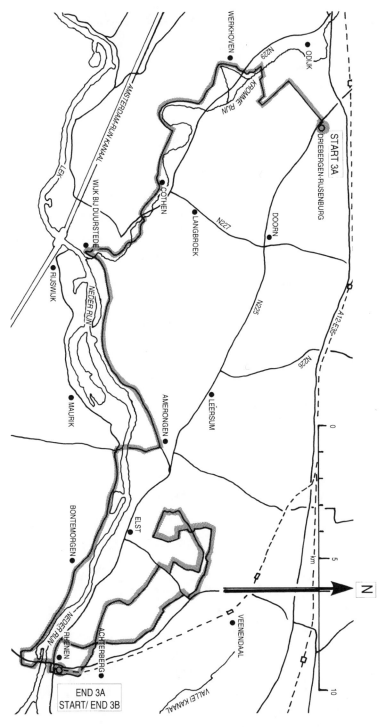

X-L-R across road (Nieuweweg)

Continue along Prins Hendrikweg

T-L along Hoogstraat

T-R (across the road you'll see the old town moat)

X (½) L, cross old town moat

At signpost No. 1014/1 L across bridge

(1st R to town square and VVV office)

Continue along brick paved road up to dike wall

At signpost No. 3778/1 L towards Amerongen along Dijkstraat (R to Duurstede castle ruins nearby)

Under old mill (Rijn en Lek, 1659)

(On your LHS you can see the Kromme Rijn lock)

Continue over lock and along dike-top, Neder Rijn on your RHS

Continue towards Amerongen

At signpost No. 1506 X R towards ferry along Rijnsteeg (road) (but continue to Amerongen chateau nearby)

Cross Neder Rijn on ferry (about 90 cents)

At signpost (no number) T-L

At signpost No. 412 L along dike, Neder Rijn on your LHS

At signpost No. 1811 continue along Rijnbandijk

At signpost No. 1811/2 continue

At signpost No. 14649/1 L along Marsdijk

At signpost No. 1529/1 R (sign reads "Doorgaand Verkeer")

T-L along bike path (Hogeweg)

Over to LHS of road on bike path when instructed ("Fietsers oversteken")

Continue towards bridge

At signpost No. 5504/18 R across road-way to far side

Immed. L

(On RHS is Info map)

L into Stationsplein

Immed. R and under road bridge

Ends at Rhenen railway station.

Diversion Route 3B: Loop Route from Rhenen

This is a circular route around the eastern limit of the high ridge formed during the last Ice Age, along trails through the forests.

Distance: 30 km/19 miles

Terrain: A mixture of hills with slopes varying in grade (gradient) from very steep to easy, with some flatland riding, on a number of different surfaces, from tar to loose sand.

Maps: VVV Utrecht Oost, Heuvelrug en Eemland; 1:50,000 (2 cm = 1 km)

ANWB/VVV Recreatiekaart Gelderland; 1:40,000 (2,5 cm = 1 km) ANWB Provinciekaart Utrecht; 1:100,000 (1 cm = 1 km)

Description:

During an earlier Ice Age, 150,000 years ago, the ice cap extended as far south as the present-day Rhine. The weight of the ice pushing down on the earth, as well as the bulldozing effect of the advancing ice, created steep, high ridges of soil ahead of the ice. From Utrecht to Rhenen, this ridge is know as the Utrechtse Heuvelrug.

Around Rhenen the forests are criss-crossed by tracks, paths, bridleways, and bike paths. There are endless opportunities to cycle along tree-lined avenues away from motor traffic.

There are also marked trails (maps at Rhenen VVV office) which lead to ancient burial mounds (grafheuvels),

with cryptic messages for the searcher. Many treasures uncovered in the forests and nearby settlements (such as Achterberg) can be seen in the Rhenen museum (Kerkstraat 1, open Tues–Fri 12h00–17h00, weekends 13h00–17h00, closed Mondays, Christmas Day, New Year and Ascension).

Deer were re-introduced to a park on the lower slopes of the Heuvelrug at Remmerden and you may catch a glimpse of them as you cycle this route.

Tobacco was once grown at Elst, and on this plantation William III had a 100 hectare (247 acres) forest of oaks planted on the south slopes of the ridge, down to the Neder Rijn. These plantations are maintained to allow the fauna and flora of the heights and the river to interact freely as in the past. There is also a program to replant trees along the entire ridge and to restore the area to something like its former self before major deforestation began two centuries ago.

There are many trails for walkers or horse riders throughout the area, so you can modify the route to your own taste.

The VVV office in Rhenen is behind the Cuneratoren (you can't miss the tower, it's visible for miles around), through an archway on the river side of Herenweg, the main road through the town, parallel with the Neder Rijn.

Directions

Start at the railway station. Exit the station car park and turn L along Zwarteweg

X (lights) continue along Castanjeweg

Continue along Boslandweg

At signpost No. 8966 L along Bergseweg

T-L

Cross railway line, cross freeway (N233)

Y-R

X continue along Autoweg

X continue along main road

R along Defensieweg (be careful not to miss this turn)

T-R along bike path alongside road (N416)

At restaurant 't Koetshuis, L across road (N416), through gate (bike sign), into Prattenburg forest (sign on tree) and continue away from N416

X-R along avenue of hardened gravel

X continue (bear slightly L) (some loose gravel on road)

X continue towards asphalt road ahead

T-L

Road swings L

X continue through parking area, along bike path ("Fietspad")

P22828 continue towards Amerongen

P22827 L towards Elst

* Caution sharp L turn (striped red/ white warning boards)

P22820 continue towards Rhenen

[On your LHS you will see a cast bronze wedge on a short post; this is a marker for the Grave Mound Route, in this case, the Third step]

Bike path jogs to R and L, then hard R and hard L

Immed. L and continue directly up the hill (soft sand to start, then harder surface)

On LHS is another marker for the Grave Mound Route, the Fourth step)

Continue towards top of hill

Y-L (uphill for 10 meters)

X-L (now heading West)

X continue

* Caution X R down hill (steepens as you descend, loose gravel)

P22828 X continue towards Overberg

P22829 X R along asphalt road

[Road crosses Het Egel Meer (Hedgehog Lake) named by the Romans Aegil Marum, see information board]

P22853 X through Parking area, continue towards Prattenburg

At signpost No. 2634/18 T R along bike path

At signpost No. 2634/19 R along Veenendaalsestraatweg (road)

L along Oudeveensegrindweg

T-R along Nieuwe Veenendaalseweg

* Caution Y-R down very steep hill (Paardenweg) along bike path

T-L along Herenweg

Immed. before bridge, R

X-L

T-L along Zwarteweg

L into railway station car park; route ends here.

Route 4A: Rhenen to Arnhem via Wageningen, Doorwerth, and Oosterbeek

Distance: 30 km/19 miles

Terrain: Flat with some minor hills; paved bike paths and roads, compacted dirt roads

Maps: ANWB Provinciekaart Gelderland (part 1 of 3); 1:100,000 (1 cm = 1 km)

ANWB/VVV Recreatiekaart No. 23, Gelderland – Veluwe Zuid 1:40,000 (2,5 cm = 1 km)

Diversion: See Route 4B (De Hoge Veluwe National Park)

Description:

From Rhenen cycle east along the north bank of the river, through the Grebbeberg park and along the Grift. The Grebbeberg is the easternmost point of the Utrecht ridge (Info board).

Travel south to leave Utrecht Province and enter Gelderland. Follow the Neder Rijn along its north bank on the dike road to Wageningen.

Wageningen is thought to be Roman Ad Vada, but there is no conclusive proof. In 1263 it was granted its charter. The largest center of agricultural science in Europe is situated here.

On 5 May 1945 at the Hotel de Wereld, General Blaskowitz representing the occupying German Forces surrendered to General Foulkes, Commanding Officer of the First Canadian Corps.

Before crossing the Neder Rijn, take a short trip east along the north bank of the river to the viewpoint called the Wageningse Berg (Wageningen mountain). Cross the river and turn east along the dike road. Pass through the villages of Randwijk and Heteren. Continue along the scenic route to Driel and take the ferry to the north bank of the river between Doorwerth and Oosterbeek.

During the World War II Arnhem airborne offensive in 1944 (Operation Market Garden), the British parachute and glider landing area was north west of here, near Heelsum. The Airborne Museum at Oosterbeek opens Mondays to Saturdays 11h00–17h00, Sundays and public holidays 12h00–17h00.

Arnhem is the Provincial capital of Gelderland. In Roman times it was called Arenacum. In 1433 Arnhem became a member of the Hanseatic League, a powerful trading cartel of European cities. Sir Philip Sidney, a famous English gentleman soldier, died here after being wounded at the siege of Warnsveld during the Spanish wars.

The IJssel, a distributary of the Rhine, branches away to the northeast, ultimately discharging into the former Zuider Zee, now a fresh water lake called the IJsselmeer. The IJssel river carries about one tenth of the Rhine waters.

Stretching north from Arnhem is a massive open space of woods, moors, heaths and barren wastelands. This is for the most part the Hoge Veluwe National Park (see Route 4B). Within the park lies the impressive Kröller-Müller Museum, with an extensive Van Gogh collection, modern sculptures, and Oriental pieces.

The Openlucht (open air) museum north of Arnhem illustrates the daily life of ordinary people from past times, with an emphasis on the nineteenth century. It includes a hundred original buildings from all over the Netherlands. There are special exhibits of regional costumes and craft demonstrations. The museum is open daily from April to October, 09h00–17h00. In the Alteveer suburb is the excellent youth hostel. Camp grounds are to the north west of Arnhem, including the overall best campsite I used anywhere along the Rhine, Camping Warnsborn, at the end of Bakenbergseweg. The ANWB and VVV offices are near the central railway station.

In the Arnhem railway station building is a bike repair and spares shop, at the bike lockup. Open 05h15 to 01h15 (yes, 5:15 a.m. to 1 a.m. the next morning). Holidays and Sundays, later openings, to fit in with train schedules. Repairs done during normal working hours, Mon–Fri. Used bikes also sold here.

Directions:

Start at Rhenen railway station. Exit station car park, R along Zwarteweg, continue along the road leading to the river alongside the bridge, bridge on your RHS

At signpost No. 5504/8 Continue towards river

T-L along Cuneralaan

Continue, waterway on your RHS T-R along Nude (road) (Info about Grebbeberg on your RHS)

At signpost No. 1266/5 R along Grebbedijk

At signpost No. 7012/1 continue towards Wageningen and Arnhem exit Utrecht Province, enter Gelderland

enter Wageningen (remain on road parallel with Neder Rijn)

At signpost No. 12909/1 T-R towards Renkum (4 km) and Arnhem (17 km), along Veerweg

At signpost No. 7357/7 R towards Renkum and Arnhem (16 km)

At signpost No. 13798/1 R to ferry cross Neder Rijn on ferry (Lexkesveer, 90 cents)

Continue along Veerweg T-L

At signpost No. 2728 L towards Heteren and Driel along Randwijkse Rijndijk (road)

Continue along dike road, Neder Rijn on your LHS pass Randwijk

At signpost No. 630/1 continue along Kastanjelaan, pass Heteren

Continue along Drielserijndijk under freeway bridge (A50) (immed. RHS is Airborne Monument) [to visit Doorwerth Castle and hunting museum, cross this bridge over Neder Rijn, 1st R and keep R to the Castle

To rejoin the described route, exit Castle, R along river road to foot ferry (voetveer)

At signpost No. 2719/4 continue towards Arnhem (5 km) pass Driel

At signpost No. 2718 L towards Oosterbeek ferry (voetveer) (April to mid-Oct.; Mon.–Fri. 07h00–18h00, Sat 09h00–18h00, Sun. 10h00–18h00. Not weekends mid-Oct. to end Nov. and March. Closed Dec. to end Feb.)

* Caution: take care as you near the jetty, as the last section of road is steep and awkward to negotiate; it's better to walk.

Cross Neder Rijn on ferry

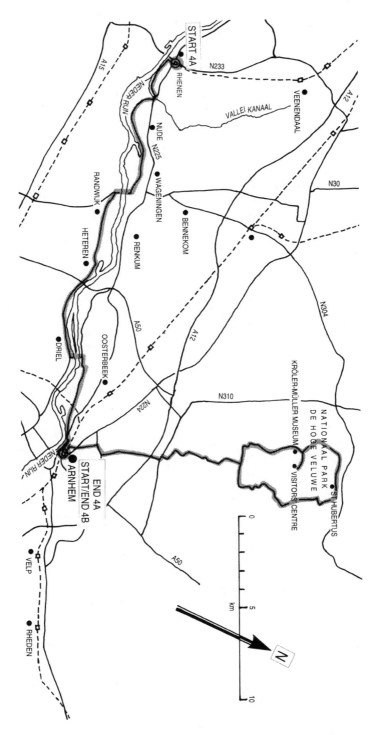

Exit parking area

At signpost No. 1591/1 T-R towards Arnhem (6 km) and Oosterbeek (1 km) (alternative route via Doorwerth Castle joins here)

At signpost No. 8643/1 R towards Arnhem (6 km) along Benedensdorpsweg enter Oosterbeek continue along Rozensteeg

At (signpost No. 8642) lamppost 31, Y-R along Benedensdorpsweg exit Oosterbeek under railway bridge

Continue along Klingeldeekseweg

Enter Arnhem

At signpost No. 9343/2 T-R along Utrechtseweg

Continue across Oranjestraat, cross to left-hand lane of cycle path

Y L, up hill

Continue past Museum of Modern Art

L to Arnhem railway station; route ends here.

Diversion Route 4B: De Hoge Veluwe National Park

Distance: 58 km/36 miles Note: from Arnhem railway station to Park entrance is 7.3 km (4.6 miles). Inside the park you can choose any route. Marked with "paddestoel" signs at all intersections. Get maps at the Visitors' Information Center.

Terrain: Easy hills to and from the park, flat in the park; paved bike paths and roads

Maps: ANWB Provinciekaart Gelderland (part 1 of 3); 1:100,000 (1 cm = 1 km)

ANWB/VVV Recreatiekaart No. 23 Gelderland – Veluwe Zuid; 1:40,000 (2.5 cm = 1 km)

Description:

The Hoge Veluwe National Park is the largest Nature Reserve in the Netherlands, covering an area of over 5,500 hectares (13,300 acres). The Park consists of a mix of woodland, heath, sand dunes and fens. It boasts herds of red deer, wild boar and other animals. Open every day 09h00–17h00, longer in summertime.

The Kröller-Müller museum displays a massive collection of nineteenth and twentieth century art. The 276 van Gogh works make this the world's greatest collection of his works. There are outdoor sculptures as well as indoor pieces, including some Henry Moores. The Oriental rooms display Tang horses. Open April through October, Tuesdays to Saturdays 10h00–17h00, Sundays and public holidays 11h00–17h00 and November-March 13h00–17h00. Closed Mondays and 1 January.

At the Visitors' Center is the Museonder, an underground exhibit that is unique in that it displays the living underside of the park, besides other underground treasures.

The General Christiaan de Wet monument was sculpted by Jos. M Mendez da Costa in 1915–16.

Christiaan de Wet was a Boer general who dedicated his life to his country and was sacrificed on the altar of expediency by his fellow-countrymen, to their great and everlasting shame.

There is also a Statue of President Steyn, President of the Orange Free State at the outbreak of the (second) Anglo-Boer War in 1899. His was the only country ever to declare war in support of a promise to do so against British aggression, with nothing to gain and everything to lose, as a matter only of honor.

The St. Hubertus hunting lodge was built between 1914 and 1920. Saint Hubertus, Patron Saint of hunters, was born in Flanders during the seventh century. After an incident involving a stag with a blazing cross between its antlers, Hubertus devoted his life to the church and became the Bishop of Luik (Liege). This lodge represents Hubertus' life and conversion to Christianity. The view from the tower is stupendous.

Directions:

Start at Arnhem railway station. Exit at traffic lights and R along Utrechtsestraat

R along Brugstraat continue over railway bridge

Immed. L along Noordelijke Parallelweg R along Brouerijweg

Continue along Bakenbergseweg

P22721 R along Schelmseweg

St. Hubertus hunting lodge with lookout tower in the Hoge Veluwe national park, the Netherlands. Note the white bicycles that are available free of charge to visitors throughout the park.

Signpost No. 6032 L along Kemperbergerweg under freeway (A12-A50)

Signpost No. 6033 T (lights) L along Koningsweg towards Hoge Veluwe (very busy road; you can cycle on dirt track on LHS of roadway)

Signpost No. 4849/1 R towards De Hoge Veluwe Park entrance (buy ticket at office, about HFL 8,50, includes entrance to Kröller-Müller museum, Museonder and use of white bicycles. Open 08h00 to 22h00. Bike racks at all major areas and foot pumps for tires with Presta valves. No security for bikes; if you're using your own, take a lock and remove loose bags and equipment if you leave your bike unattended)

Enter Park

P21479 (LHS of entrance) L along road

P21701 R along bike path

P23682 T-L towards Kröller-Müller Museum

P22109 T-R towards museum

P21303 R to museum exit museum

P21303 R

P21360 R towards Bezoekerscentrum (Visitors' Center)

P21068 L to visitors' center, underground museum, shops, restaurant, maps; buy tickets for St. Hubertus hunting lodge here

P21068 R towards museum, monument and hunting lodge

P21360 continue to de Wet monument and hunting lodge (1st) R

P21426 R towards de Wet monument X continue towards de Wet monumen

Continue past General Christiaan de Wet monument, on your RHS

P20968 L towards hunting lodge

P20117 Info board, St Hubertus lodge on your RHS

R past front of lodge, swing R along bike path and continue

P21235 T-R

P21302 L towards Schaarsbergen

P21353 T-R towards Schaarsbergen

L to Deelense Was

Info (libellen = dragonflies) return to bike path and L

P23682 L towards Schaarsbergen and park exit (where you entered)

P21701 L towards gate P21479 R to exit

T-L along Koningsweg

Signpost No. 6033 R at traffic lights along Kemperbergerweg

Signpost No. 6032 R along Schelmseweg

P22721 L along Bakenbergseweg

Continue along Brouerijweg

T-L along Noordelijke Parallelweg

R over railway bridge along Brugstraat

T-L along Utrechtsestraat

L towards Arnhem railway station; route ends.

16
Germany

The following routes are in whole or partly in Germany. The first of these starts in the Netherlands at Arnhem and ends in the German city of Emmerich, with a detour to the city of Cleves (Kleve).

Route 5A: Arnhem to Emmerich via, Pannerden and Spijk

Distance: 42 km/26 miles

Terrain: Flat; paved bike paths and roads

Maps: ANWB Provinciekaart Gelderland (parts 1 + 3 of 3); 1:100,000 (1 cm = 1 km) roads not shown alongside Pannerdenskanaal

ANWB/VVV Recreatiekaart No. 23, Gelderland; 1:40,000 (2.5 cm = 1 km) partway only

Landesvermessungsamt NRW/Kreis Kleve Radwanderkarte; 1:50,000 (2 cm = 1 km) partway only

Diversion: See Route 5B to Cleves

Description:

Leave Arnhem, following the Neder Rijn east and then south along the IJssel to where the waterways divide. The Rhine becomes two separate rivers as it crosses from Germany into the Netherlands [KM 868]; the Waal and Neder Rijn. Formerly this junction was further inside Germany, as evidenced by remnants of past waterways, particularly ox-bow lakes. About two thirds of the waters flow in the Waal river, the remainder branching into the Neder Rijn through the Pannerdens canal. The Pannerdens canal waters are divided between the Neder Rijn and the IJssel, the former receiving two-thirds (or two-ninths of the Rhine waters) and the latter one-third (one-ninth).

The Pannerdens canal was cut as the Waal river was silting up the Rhine take-off and starving the Neder Rijn-IJssel distributaries of water. The little town of Pannerden gives its name to this waterway. At the point created by the dividing rivers, is the former Schenkenschans fortress.

Cycle alongside the Bijlands kanaal, cut to bypass the loop in the old Waal river, now a recreation area called De Bijland. Continue along the north bank of the Rhine through Tolkamer [KM 863] and Spijk [KM 859] and soon afterwards, cross into Germany [KM 858] from the Netherlands. There are no border formalities.

Having entered the German state (Land) of Nordrhein-Westfalen, continue through the village of Hüthum to Emmerich.

Emmerich [KM 852], the last German town on the Rhine, was the worst bomb-damaged German town in World War II. Much of the damage has been repaired, but some buildings were only partially restored. Here the Rhine is one kilometer wide (1,100 yards) and spanned by the longest suspension bridge in Germany (1,200 m/ 1,343 yards). The chief customs point for German shipping is here, with more than 200,000 ships passing annually.

Formerly the Roman town of Embrica and later a free town and member of the Hanseatic league, Emmerich boasts the oldest (town) coat of arms in Germany. As in Utrecht in the Netherlands and further up the Rhine at Wesel, St. Willibrord established a church in Emmerich. In the treasury of the eleventh century church of St. Martin is the tenth century chest-reliquary of St. Willibrord. This is the oldest surviving example of lower Rhineland goldsmith art. The church was rebuilt in simplified form after being destroyed in World War II.

The 91 meter (300 feet) tower of the restored fifteenth century gothic church of St. Aldigond (Aldegundis-kirche) offers a marvelous view. The church itself has an interesting interior.

The Rhine museum at Martini-Kirchgang 2, celebrates the history and development of shipping on the Rhine. Don't miss this.

Directions:

Start at the railway station at Arnhem. Exit at the traffic lights and turn L along Utrechtsestraat

X-R towards Nelson Mandela Brug (bridge)

X (lights) L under Mandela bridge

Across intersection, R along Roermondsplein

T-L along Boterdijk alongside Rhine, river on your RHS

Under John Frost bridge

At signpost No. 10570 T-R along Westervoortsedijk

At signpost No. 1117/9 L towards Westervoort (2 km)

At signpost No. 11174/12 R (over bridge) towards Westervoort

Cross bridge

Before end of off-ramp, U-turn R back alongside bridge

T-L along IJsseldijk

R along Veerdam (also Route LF3a)

Continue along Pleijdijk, alongside IJssel river, on dike-top road (Route LF3a), river on your RHS

Continue past Neder Rijn–IJssel divide

L away from dike, road swings L

T-R along dike road (also LF3a)

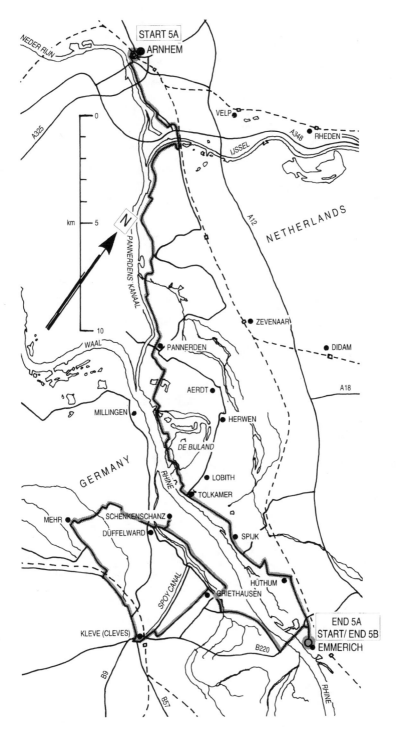

At signpost No. 60120/1 (Looveer) Continue along Loodijk towards Loo

At signpost No. 2389/1 Continue (also LF3a)

Y-R through barrier (also LF3a)

R along dike-top road (also LF3a)

T-R along Rijndijk (Info)

At signpost No. 64401 X Continue along Rijndijk to ferry

R along Opperdenseweg towards Millingen voetveer (ferry) (also LF3a)

T (at Rhine) L towards "Voetveer and De Bijland" (also LF3a)

R towards Voetveer Millingen, along bike path

* Caution: cross lock (narrow passage; take care)

Continue along concrete bike path

[KM 866] Continue past foot ferry

Bike Path swings L away from Rhine

At signpost (no number) R towards Lobith and Tolkamer

Past watersports center, on your LHS (De Bijland)

T (parking lot) L

At signpost No. 17060/1 (at Rhine) T-L towards Tolkamer and Lobith

Cross bridge

R to road on dike

L along roadway

[KM 863] Through Tolkamer village

Continue along Swarteweg

At signpost No. 8363/1 R along dike-top bike path, towards Tolkamer and Spijk

X Continue along Polweg

L along dike-top, alongside Rhine

T-R towards Spijk and Elten

Continue along Spijksedijk (pass turning to Spijk)

[KM 859] (The road from the Rhine at [KM 858] marks the Germany–Netherlands border)

Continue along dike-top bike path towards Emmerich

Road turns hard left and off dike top

Continue along Rundestrasse

T-R along Hofstrasse

L along Kleischestrasse towards Hüthum

X-R towards Hüthum on LHS bike path along Eltenerstrasse

Continue through Hüthum

Enter Emmerich (Rhine bridge on your RHS)

X continue towards Emmerich center

Continue to town square with statue of a ferryman

R to Rheinmuseum and Info center (Martinikirchgang) (Touristik-Information, Sun–Weds 10h00–12h30 and 14h00–16h30, Thurs 10h00–12h30 and 14h00–18h00, Fri 10h00–12h30). Route ends here.

Diversion Route 5B: Loop Route from Emmerich to Cleves

This is a circular route to Cleves (Kleve), via Griethausen, returning past Donsbrüggen and through Die Düffel, via Mehr and Düffelwaard. Cross the Griethauser Altrhein by foot ferry, cycle to Schenkenschanz and return to Emmerich.

Distance: 42 km/26 miles

Terrain: Mostly flat, with some long easy graded hills. In Kleve are a few short steep hills; paved bike paths and roads, compacted dirt roads

Map/s: Landesvermessungsamt NRW/Kreis Kleve Radwanderkarte; 1:50,000 (2 cm = 1 km)

ADFC Radtourenkarte Münsterland Niederrhein; 1:150,000 (1cm = 1.5 km)

Description:

The Rhine bridge at Emmerich, the longest suspension bridge in Germany (1,200m/1,343 yards), spans the widest point of the river. At this point the Rhine is one kilometer wide (1,100 yards).

Griethausen lies next to the Old Rhine. The old iron bridge here was the first iron railway bridge in Germany. The railway route between Griethausen and Kleve now provides a motor free bike path.

Kleve (Cleves) was originally situated on the Alter (old) Rhein which has since moved 6 km (4 miles) away. Connection with the Rhine is maintained via the Spoy canal, constructed in the eleventh century, and a section of the Alter Rhein, through the Brienen lock.

At the Brienen lock inn is a plaque bearing a Latin inscription, moved from the house (monument) of a seventeen year old heroine, Johanna Sebus, who swam a number of people to safety during the 1809 floods. She continued bravely with her task until she was drowned. There is a monument to her on the inner dike near the lock. Inscriptions in French and German tell the sad story and a Goethe poem completes the wording.

Once the capital of the Duchy of Kleve (Cleves), the town is built around the fifteenth century Gothic Schwanenburg (also Schwanburg) castle, now in ruins. The Schwanenturm (swan tower) dates from the early fifteenth century extension of the castle. It was built in Gothic style with parapet, corner towers and a spire. On the south side is the Spiegelturm (mirror tower), built in 1429. Fragments of the Romanesque wing were dismantled in 1771 and incorporated into the newer section of the castle. Nothing remains of the eleventh century Schwanenburg (swan castle) of the Counts of Kleve. The English king Henry VIII married Anne of Cleves as his fourth wife in 1540, but "put her aside" after six months.

To the south is the Reichswald (Imperial forest), which is largely a war cemetery. The Tiergarten (zoo) created by Johann Moritz of Nassau in the mid-seventeenth century is in the hilly area to the north west. A terraced garden (1660) based on Italian models, with a statue of Pallas Athene in the center, lies in the amphitheater of a natural gorge below the Tiergarten.

The legend of the Knight of the Swan has found a home here, having probably been transferred from the Dutch town of Nijmegen. This story of Lohengrin who came here to champion and subsequently marry the fair Elsa (Beatrix in some accounts) created a unique connection between French and German mythology. Wagner wrote his Lohengrin opera in 1850.

The youth hostel is towards the south west of the town, on top of a very long and steep hill. There are no campsites nearby.

The center of this lovely and lively town has been pedestrianized and provides good shopping. It is also surprisingly hilly. The town museum at Karavinerstraße 33, is in the former house of the nineteenth century landscape painter B.C. Koekkoek and exhibits Lower Rhine art since the Middle Ages.

The church of St. Mariae Himmelfahrt (Assumption), is the first example of a Kleve stepped hall church. It was almost totally destroyed during World War II. Like many of the Rhineside towns, Kleve suffered great destruction from bombing during World War II.

Die Düffel is a farmed nature preservation area. These wetlands have been drained over the ages and the dense networks of ditches and sloots are still maintained. The old corn mill at Donsbrüggen is a working mill, open May–November. On Saturdays during this period you can buy bread freshly baked from corn ground at this mill, between 12h00 and 17h00.

The foot ferry across the Old Rhine at Düffelward can take only a few passengers per trip. It costs DM1.60 in each direction.

Get your bread fresh from this working windmill at Donsbrüggen, near Kleve (Cleves), Germany.

Schenkenschanz is a tiny walled hamlet in the Salmorth Nature Reserve. Its walls are certainly good protection against the floodwaters of the Rhine, evidenced as recently as during the February 1995 floods. If you ask at the house near the wall gate, you can buy a large color postcard aerial picture of Schenkenschanz completely surrounded by water during those floods.

Directions:

Start at Emmerich Info office. Cycle away from the Rhine, turn L and continue through the pedestrianized area

X (lights) L along Eltenerstrasse towards Rhine bridge

L towards bridge and Kleve

T-L across bridge

R off bridge towards Griethausen, along Oraniendijk

Pass pump house, on your LHS

Immed. R along dike-top bike path

X continue past Griethausen, along dike-top track

L along the compacted dirt road directly opposite the old iron bridge (monument)

R along Steinstrasse (asphalt road)

T-L alongside Spoykanal (on your RHS) towards Kleve

R (immed. before overhead bridge) along bike path alongside canal

Continue under bridge

Continue over Railway line

X continue

(On the far RHS of this intersection is a shoemaker statue which exhibits the supposed peculiarity of certain shoemakers — wait and watch)

T-R over bridge along An der Münze

Continue into pedestrianized area; dismount and continue

L (1st square) along Grosse Strasse

R (2nd square, with overflowing fountain) along Karavinerstrasse (look back and up to see Schwaneturm)

R down lane opposite bookshop and bakery, to Rathaus (Info)

L to car park exit

L along Minorietenstrasse

Continue along Tiergartenstrasse, along bike path

Cross to LHS bike path and continue (at intersection with Wasserburg Allee)

Pass entrance to Tiergarten (zoo), on your RHS

Pass entrance to Schloss Genadendal, on your RHS

Enter Donsbrüggen

R immed. past church, towards Niel and Mehr

Pass old corn mill, on your RHS (or stop for bread)

X continue towards Mehr

Enter Mehr

X-R along Boursweg towards Keeken

R towards Keeken and Düffelward

L along Keekener Strasse

Continue towards Düffelward

Enter Düffelward village

X continue across K3 freeway

Continue along road skirting LHS (river side) of Düffelward, below dike wall (when possible, take the dike-top road)

L to Schenkenschanz foot ferry

Across Griethauser Altrhein on ferry

Continue to Schenkenschanz

Back towards ferry

L along dike-top road, Altrhein on your RHS (further on, the Spoykanal lock is on your RHS across the Altrhein)

Y-R, before iron bridge

Continue under bridge

T-R towards Griethausen

Through dike (gate)

Immed. L up ramp onto dike-top bike path

Continue towards Emmerich

T-L towards Emmerich

X-L towards Rhine bridge

Cross Rhine bridge

R (lights), along bridge off-ramp

X (lights) R along Eltenerstrasse

Continue to town square with statue of a ferryman

R to Rheinmuseum and Info center; route ends here.

Route 6A: Emmerich to Wesel via Rees and Mars

Distance: 55 km/34 miles

Terrain: Flat; paved roads and bike paths, compacted dirt roads

Maps: Falk Wanderkarte Niederrhein 1 (No. 1615); 1:50,000 (2 cm = 1 km)

Kreis Kleve Radwanderkarte; 1:50,000 (2 cm = 1 km) partway only

ADFC Radtourenkarte Münsterland Niederrhein (No. 10); 1:150,000 (1 cm = 1.5 km)

Diversion: See Route 6B (Xanten, Roman settlement)

Description:

From Emmerich cycle south alongside the east bank of the Rhine to Dornick, around the Old Rhine meanders through Steegh, Praest and Bienen, then back to the Rhine at Rees [KM 838]. Rees has surviving early fortifications, such as the thirteenth century Mühlenturm, the Toelder gate and the riverside bastion.

From Rees you can make the short trip to Kalkar, a return trip of some 16 kilometers (10 miles). Kalkar is situated on what was once an island in the Rhine. It is still surrounded by waterways, but the course of the river has moved north-east. In the Middle Ages, Kalkar was an important trading town and a member of the Hanseatic League. During the period 1490–1540, it was the centre of Rhenish woodcarving. The fifteenth century St. Nikolai church has seven carved altars

by the Kalkar school. The church museum opens daily 10h00–12h00 and 14h00–17h00.

The main attractions in Kalkar relate to its architectural heritage. St. Nikolai church is a three-aisled Lower Rhenish version of a Gothic hall-church. The mid-fifteenth century Rathaus (Town Hall) boasts a hipped roof, battlements with corner towers and an octagonal staircase tower. The Beginenhof has a medieval wall and ceiling paintings. You can also see the twelfth century Romanesque twin towered basilica of St. Clemens and fifteenth century brick houses on the Marktplatz (the market square).

The town museum (Hanselaarstrasse 5) exhibits local history, ancient manuscripts and an edition of the Sachsenspiegel (Saxon mirror), an early thirteenth century law book.

From Rees move away from the Rhine around Old Rhine meanders, through wetlands and meadows to Haffen and the outskirts of Mehr. Continue through the countryside towards the Rhine, along a dike-top bike path and follow the Rhine to Bislich, Marwick and even Mars. Cycle past the Auesee (island lake) to Wesel.

Wesel [KM 815] is situated at the confluence of the Lippe and Rhine rivers. Originally established as a fort by the Romans, it was made into a citadel by the Spaniards a thousand years later and re-fortified by the Prussians. The 1718 Zitadellentor and 1772 Berliner Tor remain after the town was almost totally destroyed in World War II. In the citadel is the Schill museum, displaying the history of the Schill Freicorps.

In Willibrordplatz is the church of St. Willibrord, founded in the eighth century, extended and altered in the tenth, twelfth, thirteenth and fifteenth centuries and finally completed in the nineteenth century. During World War II large parts were destroyed. It remains much as it was in the fifteenth century, with ornate net and stellar vaulting, the double portal of its tower and tracery windows.

The museum at Ritterstraße 14 contains 16th and 17th century gold and silversmiths' work and nineteenth and twentieth century art of the Rhine.

Upstream are the Wesel–Daffeln and Wesel–Seifen canals which link the lower Rhine to the what used to be East Germany and Poland.

A local legend involves a soldier and a local girl whose parents objected to their relationship. The couple put their heads to the muzzle of a cannon on the ramparts and set it off. It is said that they appear on the ramparts together immediately before the sound of a cannon shot is heard.

Directions:

Start at Emmerich Info center

Cycle directly away from the Rhine and turn R

(1st) R towards the Rhine

T-L along Rhine promenade, Rhine on your RHS

L (before War Memorial)

L along Hafenstrasse

T-R over rail lines, along bike path

R along Deichstrasse

X continue along bike path

Bike path ends

Rhine traffic between Emmerich and Wesel, Germany.

Cross rail line

L along Deichstrasse, Rhine on RHS

Continue along hard gravel track on dike-top

Continue along tar road on dike-top

T-L through Dorneck village (R to viewpoint)

X-R past military area (on your RHS)

L along Pionierstrasse

X-R along Reeserstrasse on bike path

Through Praest village

Continue along Emmericher Strasse

Enter Bienen village

R along Kemnadenstrasse

R along Schulstrasse

X continue (also cycle Route 17)

T-R (also Route 17)

Exit Bienen

L along Zur Rosau (road) on dike-top

Off dike and L

Continue along Zur Rosau

X-R along Esserdenerstrasse

R and up dike

Continue along Spijkweg

T-L along Waardstrasse

[Optional diversion to Kalkar:

Cross Rhine along RHS bike path on freeway (B67) bridge

R along L8 (road) to Mühlenfeld

L along L41 to Kalkar

(Alternatively, follow cycle route "via Romana" from Mühlenfeld)]

Cross road to LHS bike path

Continue under Rhine freeway (B67) bridge

Enter Rees

X-R

L alongside Rhine, on your RHS

Continue along Rhine promenade

[KM 837]

(Continue around town on Rhine side)

R along bike path and down dike

R along Am Damm

R along bike path (also cycle Route 6)

Road swings R

Off bike path, onto roadway

L immed. before dike-top, continue alongside dike on bike path

Cross quarry conveyor

Bike path ends, continue along roadway

Continue along Doelenweg

Continue at Avenstegshof

T-R

X continue across road (K7)

L along Bruckdaelweg, towards Hafen

T-R along bike path alongside roadway (K7)

L along Hanenkruitstrasse

R along bike path

X continue towards Wesel (also Route 19)

End of bike path, continue along Bislicher Strasse (also Route 19)

Road swings hard R

X continue across roadway (K7), along Am stummer Deich, on dike-top

[KM 828]; [KM 827]

[KM 826] viewpoint

[KM 825] continue past Bislich

[KM 824] X continue along dike-top

[KM 823] continue through Marwick

[KM 822] X-R along dike-top

Y-L along road parallel with Rhine, on your RHS

T-L away from river

T-R

Y-L

T-R along bike path on LHS of road (K7)

([KM 821] Mars area)

Continue along Bislicher Strasse (K7)

R-L along Deichweg

X-R along Am Jachthafen

T-R along Römerwardt

Continue along Rheinpromenade

Continue past viaduct

[KM 815]

Cross rail line, continue along Fischertorstrasse (street)

X (lights) continue along Pastor-Bölitz-Strasse

Past church (Dom)

(Info office, Verkehrsverein, immed. L behind church in Grosser Markt Mon–Fri 09h00–12h00 + 14h30–17h00, Sat 09h00–12h00)

Bear L along Brückstrasse

Bear R along Hohe Strasse

Continue along Berliner-Tor-Platz

Continue along Wilhelmstrasse

Cross road to Wesel Bahnhof (train station); route ends here.

Diversion Route 6B: Wesel to Xanten

Distance: 32 km/20 miles

Terrain: Mostly flat, some longer, easy slopes; paved bike paths and roads

Maps: Falk-Wanderkarte Niederrhein 1 (No. 1615); 1:50,000 (2 cm = 1 km)

            ADFC Radtourenkarte Münsterland Niederrhein (No. 10); 1:150,000 (1 cm = 1.5 km)

Description:

Cross the Lippe river and the Rhine before turning north along the west bank of the Rhine. Near the Rhine bridge are the remains of Fort Blücher.

Pass through the villages of Willich and Perrich through the Xanten Old Rhine bird sanctuary and nature reserve. This reserve (NSG) and other protected areas alongside the Rhine are safe havens for many birds, especially the great flocks of geese migrating southwards during late autumn (December). You will pass an information center in the reserve.

After reaching the Xanten–Bislich ferry (and restaurant) [KM 823], turn away from the river and cycle directly to Xanten.

Xanten has an enormous amount to offer, from Roman remains and ar-

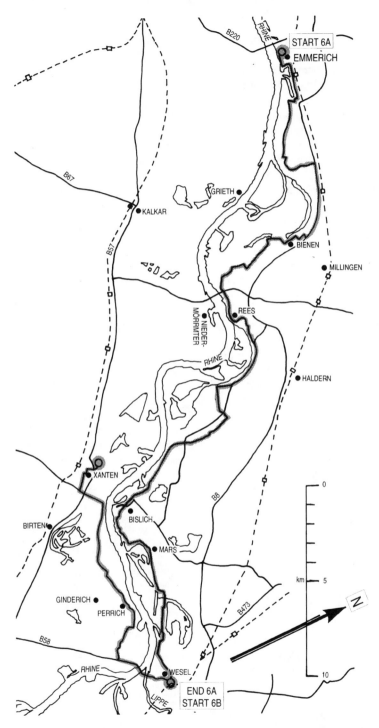

chitectural and historical art to the beginnings of the most famous of all Germanic sagas.

A Roman camp was established at Xanten in 15 BC as a base for campaigns against the Teutons across the Rhine. Near the camp the civilian town of Colonia Ulpia Traiana was built by Trajan in AD 100. It once had over ten thousand inhabitants. As this is the only early town north of the Alps which has never been built over, the archaeological value of the ruins is enormous. The foundations survived under fields and are being excavated and partially restored. The amphitheatre and other Roman remains can be seen at the park at Trajanstraße 3, daily at 09h00–16h00.

Varus led his Roman troops against the German tribes from Colonia Ulpia Traiana. However he suffered a humiliating defeat at the hands of Hermann (Arminius) in the Teutoberg forest and for a while the Romans were restricted to Europe west of the Rhine.

The present town of Xanten grew to the south of the Roman settlements around the site of a church built over two martyrs' graves. The Theban legions were faithful soldiers of the Roman army, and they were Christians. When the legions were ordered to bow to the image of Caesar, Victor (an officer of the Theban legion) and his soldiers refused and were slaughtered by the Romans in the amphitheatre. The new town was known as Ad Sanctos, from which comes the present name.

The St. Viktor Dom (1190–1516) was built on the site of the fourth century grave of two martyrs; in 1933 a double grave was uncovered in which lay the remains of two men who had died a violent death. Excavations revealed that eight successive churches

had been built on this site. The Dom is one of the most historically important churches on the Lower Rhine, specifically for its architectural features and remains of its early construction. It is a five aisled, Gothic basilica and has the oldest choir stalls in the Rhineland, dating from 1250, as well as fourteenth century glass windows. You can visit from Tuesdays to Saturdays, 10h00–12h00 and 14h00–18h00, but in winter it is closed in the morning.

The double Klever gate dates from 1393. In the town center is the Altstadt (old town), with medieval houses and town walls. There is also an eighteenth century windmill. The museum (Kurfürststraße 7) exhibits Dom treasures, including gold and ivory work from the fifth to the fifteenth century and a history of the town.

The story of the Nibelungenlied, the massive and dramatic saga immortalised by Wagner in his series of four operas, "Der Ring des Nibelungen", begins in Xanten. Siegfried, the hero of the legend was born here, son of king Sigismund and his wife, Sieglind. The action never stops from this moment, reaching a bloody climax in the court of Attila, king of the Huns.

Directions:

Start at Wesel Bahnhof (train station)

Exit the station, L through the parking area

L along Dinslakener Landstrasse

(1st) R along Roonstrasse

Continue along Schillstrasse

Continue along B58 towards Geldern on bike path on RHS of road

Exit Wesel

Cross Lippe river

Cross Rhine, along Weselerstrasse

R towards Kleve and Xanten along Xantenerstrasse (L460) on bike path

R towards Perrich along Perricherweg

Y-L, towards radio mast

T-R along Perricherweg, past radio mast, on your RHS (also Route R8)

Road turns hard L, continue along Zur Bauerschaft (road)

Through Perrich along Zur Bauerschaft

Enter Werrich

T-R (also Route R8)

X-R (also Route R8)

Road swings hard L

Exit Werrich

Info, NSG information center, on your RHS

X-L along bike path on RHS of road (L480) (R to Xanten-Bislich ferry)

X (lights) continue across freeway (B57)

X-R along Viktorstrasse

Through pedestrian area of Xanten

Bear L at town square

L immed. before archway, along Bahnhofstrasse

X (circle/roundabout) R to archaeological park, Colonia Ulpia Traiana

You can return by the same route, crossing to Bislich on the ferry and returning along the east bank of the Rhine to Wesel as a variation. Or you may prefer to return via the forest trail through Die Hees, south of Xanten. You should be able to get a route map from the Xanten Info (Verkehrsverein) office. Be aware of the dangers of straying off the forest trails, though. Check at the Information office.

Route 7: Wesel to Ruhrort (Duisburg) via Rheinberg and Orsoy

Distance: 45 km/28 miles

Terrain: Flat; paved bike paths and
             roads, compacted dirt
             roads

Maps: Falk Wanderkarte
             Niederrhein 1 (No. 1615);
             1:50,000 (2 cm = 1 km)

             Falk Stadtplan Duisburg
             (No. 142); 1:23,000 (1 cm =
             230 m)

             ADFC Radtourenkarte
             Münsterland Niederrhein
             (No. 10); 1:150,000 (1 cm =
             1.5 km)

Diversions: See suggestions at the end
             of this section.

Description:

From Wesel cross the Lippe and Rhine rivers and cycle south on the west bank of the Rhine past the nature reserve, past Büderich [KM 812], Nieder-Wallach, Wallach [KM 808] and Ossenberg to Rheinberg with its 1449 Rathaus (town hall) and Pulverturm (powder magazine).

From Rheinberg cycle through the former flood plains of the Rhine past Spanish-built fortifications to the hamlets of Milchplatz and Hasenfeld [KM 796]. Continue alongside the Rhine to Driessen [KM 795] and Orsoy [KM 793].

The legend of Gerd Wardmann, the Deichgraf (dike warden) of Walsum (across the Rhine from Orsoy) tells of Gerd rescuing a Diekmänneken (dike dwarf) who undertook to make all repairs to the dikes in Gerd's keeping, on condition that Gerd never told anybody who was doing the work.

When Gerd was an old man, and probably worried about making a bargain with the devil, he confessed the arrangement to a priest. From then on the dikes deteriorated until a section opened and the Deichgraf's farm was swept away.

From Orsoy, continue through Binsheim, past Baerl and Alt-Homberg to the Friedrich-Ebert-Brücke (bridge) and across the Rhine to Ruhrort [KM 780] at the confluence of the Rhine and Ruhr rivers.

Duisburg (say Doosburg) harbor [KM 780], situated at the confluence of the Rhine and Ruhr rivers, is the world's largest inland port, covering 919 hectares (2,270 acres) and handling over fifty million tons of goods annually. Most of the ships for the Rhine trade are built here, especially barges and tug boats. It is the main producer of iron and steel in Europe.

Duisburg was originally a Roman town and later a Merovingian palace was built here. The Merovingian army gathered here before defeating the Romans at Cambrai.

In the thirteenth century the course of the Rhine shifted west and Ruhrort developed at the new confluence of the Rhine and Ruhr rivers. The port is situated around this area.

The Flemish geometrician Gerhard Kremer (Mercator) came to Duisburg to work for the Duke of Cleves after a guarantee of freedom of worship for Protestants was given in 1552. In 1569 Mercator published his 'Map of the World' using the Mercator projection. Mercator is remembered through a monument in the town square (Burgplatz), the Mercator rooms at the Rathaus (Burgplatz), a memorial stone at the Salvatorkirche (fifteenth century tufa basilica) and the Mercator Halle (1962, exhibition hall).

The Lower Rhine Museum in Friedrich Wilhelm Strasse displays a cartographic collection as well as the history of the town. It opens Tuesday–Sunday 10h00–17h00, except it closes one hour earlier Wednesdays and opens one hour later Sundays.

The tourist information offices are at Konigstrasse 53, near the main railway station (Hauptbahnhof).

The river bottom would normally require regular scouring to remove silt to maintain the required depth of water for navigation. However the river maintains an almost constant depth due to subsidence caused by coal mining in the immediate vicinity.

The mining activity in the region has produced its own mythology, including the Kobolds, elves who assisted the miners by warning of gas pockets and rockfalls, and Nickels who played tricks on the miners and changed copper ore into Kupfernickel (bronze).

In the seventeenth century a magistrate ordered a Wesel skipper (Koch) to set up a regular weekly boat service between Duisburg and Nijmegen in the Netherlands. This accelerated development of the area and demonstrated the potential for shipping. In 1808 the Stinnes shipping empire began when a bargemaster's son working as a deck hand bought his first barge, building from these humble beginnings a huge conglomerate.

There are regular cruises around the port from the Schifferbörse in Ruhrort and from the Rheingarten in Homberg during the summer, which take about two hours.

The Museum der Deutschen Binnenschiffahrt (Museum of German Inland Shipping) is situated at Dammstrasse 11, Ruhrort. Open 10h00–17h00, except Weds and Thurs closed 16h00, closed Mondays. The Museum ship, a side-paddle steamer, is at a nearby dock.

Directions:

Start at Wesel Bahnhof (train station)

Exit the station parking area

L along Dinslakener Landstrasse

(1st) R along Roonstrasse

Continue along Schillstrasse

Continue along B58 towards Geldern on bike path on RHS of road

Exit Wesel

Cross Lippe river

Cross Rhine, along Weseler Strasse

U-turn R off bridge, towards Büderich (bicycle sign)

Continue towards river, below and alongside bridge embankment, bridge on your RHS

R through subway under road (B58)

Immed. R up slope, alongside bridge embankment

T-L along asphalt dike-top bike path, river on your LHS

[KM 813];

[KM 812] pass Büderich, on your RHS

[KM 811]

T-L along dike-top bike path

[KM 810]

Pass Niederwallach, on your RHS

[KM 809]; [KM 808]

Pass Borth and Wallach, on your RHS

[KM 807]

L immed. before railway crossing, continue along asphalt road

R (where road turns hard L), cross rail line, continue along hard sand road

Through Ossenberg, continue along Werftstrasse, rail line on your LHS

Cross rail line

X-R along bike path on RHS of road (B57), to crossing

(60 m) L across road, immed. L along bike path on RHS of road, towards Rheinberg

Enter Rheinberg, continue along bike path along Xantener Strasse

L along Kanalstrasse, to end

R along Am Kanal

L across bridge

Immed. L along asphalt road

Cross bridge

Road ends, L across parking area

* Dismount, walk bike to roadway ahead, R along road

(1st) L along Orsoyland (road), asphalt road

(1st) R along Orsoyland, to Rhine

[KM 804]

R along dike-top bike path, Rhine on your LHS

(140 m) R off dike

Road swings hard L towards dike

R alongside dike, dike on your LHS

T-L towards Milchplatz

X continue towards Milchplatz (R to Eversael)

Continue alongside dike, dike on your LHS

Enter Milchplatz

T-R

T-L towards river wall

R, dike on your LHS

Continue, bear L towards top of dike

R along dike-top on compacted dirt road, Rhine on your LHS

(Alternative; brick-paved road at base of dike, dike on your LHS)

[KM 796]; [KM 795]

R off dike-top, L along bike path alongside dike, dike on your LHS

X continue, past Orsoy harbor

Cross rail line

Continue through Orsoy

X continue (L to ferry along Fährstrasse)

Continue along Binsheimer Strasse on bike path on RHS of road

Continue along Orsoyer Strasse

Enter Binsheim, bike path ends

Y-L along Woltershofer Strasse

Up slope to dike-top, R along Dammstrasse

[KM 787] (Baerl on RHS)

U-turn L off dike, R towards Rhine, along Dollstrasse

R alongside Rhine along Leinpfad, river on your LHS

[KM 786]

Continue along Rheinstrasse

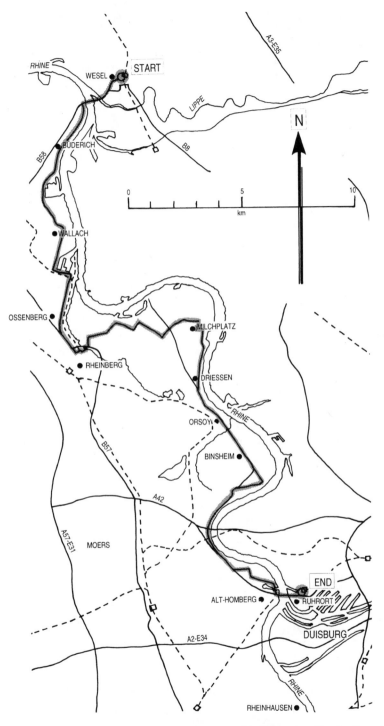

Under freeway (A42) bridge

Under railway bridge (Hans-Knipp-Brücke)

[KM 785]

T-L along RHS of Rheinstrasse

[KM 784]

(Gerdtweg on RHS; make the following L turn here)

L across roadway, up to dike-top, R along dike-top bike path

Continue along Hochwasser-Schutzdeich, on dike-top bike path

[KM 783]

Continue along Dammstrasse

[KM 782]

Cross swing-bridge over harbor entrance

[KM 781]

Continue alongside Rhine

R up ramp to top of motor bridge, L across bridge (Friedrich-Ebert-Brücke) on bike path on LHS of roadway

Continue along Homberger Strasse

L along Friedrich-Ebert-Strasse

Ends at Ruhrort train station

Diversion Suggestions:

1. You can follow the Ruhr river closely, eastwards through the Ruhr industrial region, which stretches to Dortmund. The distance to the Baldeneysee (lake) at Essen is approximately 40 kilometers, another 50 kilometers to Hagen. You could take a train to a distant point and return by road.

2. Moers Altstadt, the old town center of Moers, has enough of interest to keep you busy for a full day. The direct route is quite a busy road, but there are a number of alternatives which are not much longer, but definitely quieter traffic-wise.

3. You can take a boat trip from Ruhrort, around the Duisburg harbor area, explore Ruhrort itself and visit the museum of Rhine shipping, or just relax at the dockside cafes.

4. Duisburg inner city offers parks and forests.

Route 8: Ruhrort (Duisburg) to Düsseldorf via Uerdingen, Krefeld, and Kaiserswerth

Distance: 51 km/32 miles

Terrain: Flat; paved roads and bike paths, compacted dirt roads

Maps: ADAC Duisburg Stadtplan; 1: 20,000 (1 cm = 200 m)

ADAC Düsseldorf Stadtplan; 1:20,000 (1 cm = 200 m)

ADFC Radtourenkarte Munsterland – Niederrhein (No. 10); 1:150,000 (1 cm = 1.5 km)

Diversions: See suggestions at the end of this section

Description:

Leave Ruhrort across the Friedrich-Ebert bridge and cycle south alongside the Rhine west bank. Pass Rheinhausen, skirting its industrial site, through Friemersheim and Hohenbudbergen to Uerdingen. The Herberzhäuser (Marktplatz, Uerdingen) is a neoclassical block of houses built for the Herberz merchant family in 1832. The Rathaus and library now occupy this building. Continue through Uerdingen to Krefeld.

Krefeld is noted for its chemicals, engineering and especially its textiles industries, silk weaving having been introduced by the von der Leyen family in 1656. Haus Neuleyental (Cracauer Strasse 32) is a three winged building decorated in the Empire style, built as a summer residence for the von der Leyen family at the end of the eighteenth century.

The Deutsches Textilmuseum (Andreasmarkt 8, Linn) housed in an 1880 building, has the largest textile collection in Germany. It opens daily except Mondays, April to October, 10h00–13h00 and 15h00–18h00.

The Rathaus (Von-der-Leyen-Platz 1) is the former Schloss von der Leyen (1791–94), rebuilt in 1955 after it had been damaged in World War II.

The twelfth to seventeenth century moated Burg (castle) Linn (Albert-Steeger-Strasse, Linn) began life as a residential tower on an artificial hill. Ring walls and six corner towers were later added. In the fifteenth century it was converted into a residential castle. However the war of the Spanish Succession (1701–13) left the castle in ruins and a small hunting lodge was built in the outer works in 1740.

Nearby is the Lower Rhine History Museum which includes folklore of the region. It opens daily from April to October, 10h00–18h00, but closed for lunch 13h00–15h00. The museum Haus Lange (Wilhelmshofallee 91) designed by Mies van der Rohe, houses modern art works.

From Krefeld–Linn cycle past the village of Nierst to Langst-Kierst and take the ferry [KM 755] across the Rhine to Kaiserswerth.

Kaiserswerth (Emperor's island): In the seventh century, Suitbert, an English monk of noble birth, settled on an island in the Rhine. Suitbert met Pepin the Short and his queen and they asked him to establish a monastery. Suitbert helped the local farmers with their work and generally made himself useful. He built a beacon on the upstream end of his island to help the Rhine boatmen, which was probably the first navigation beacon on the river. Suitbert also retrieved bodies from the waters for burial and it is said that he even restored some to life. A legend has it that no bodies pass Kaiserswerth without being washed to shore. The night that Suitbert died, the river was floodlit by a luminous glow around the island. The following day the river swept gravel into a channel to connect the island with the right bank. The seventh century collegiate church of St. Suitbertus was rebuilt as a twelfth century Romanesque basilica and it houses the golden shrine of the saint.

The eleventh and twelfth century Kaiserpfalz was also originally built on an island in the Rhine. It was rebuilt by Frederick I (Barbarossa), becoming known as Barbarossapfalz, but was ruined in 1702 during the wars of Spanish Succession. Surviving today is the outer wall of the former palace wall facing the river.

Düsseldorf [KM 748] is situated on the confluence of the Rhine and Düssel rivers, where the Rhine is 300 meters (325 yards) wide. Düsseldorf is the capital of the state (Land) of Nordrhein-Westfalen. It is the richest city in Germany and, with its year-round trade fairs, congresses, and exhibitions, it is the shop window of Germany. The first fair was attended by Napoleon in 1811.

Düsseldorf was developed from the twelfth century, principally by the von Berg family. The counts (later dukes) of Berg passed Düsseldorf on to their cousins, the Electors Palatine and the Elector Palatine, Johann Wilhelm II (Jan Willem) came to live here about 1700. Jan Willem was a popular ruler; there is a statue of him near the Rathaus and he was buried in the St.

Museum ship, side-paddle steamer, Ruhrort harbor, Germany.

Andreas church (Andreasstrasse). The children turning cartwheels on the Königsallee ("Kö"), known as "Radschläger," emulate the boy who attached himself to a wheel which came off Jan Willem's wedding coach, to prevent it injuring the onlookers. The boy was rewarded with one golden ducat, but the Radschläger at the "Kö" do it for pennies.

The Königsallee is the shopping center of Düsseldorf. Built astride part of the old moat which is crossed by many bridges, it has gardens at each end and is also the city promenade.

In 1806 Napoleon made Düsseldorf capital of the Grand Duchy of Berg, first appointing his brother-in-law Joachim Murat as Grand Duke, succeeded by Jérome Bonaparte.

Germany's favorite poet, Heinrich Heine, was born here (Bolkerstrasse) in 1797. He wrote the poem about the Rhine maiden, the Loreley, as well as travel sketches of the Rhineland ("Reisebilder"). Though Heine was Jewish, his works were so popular, that the Nazis were unable to suppress them.

In the nineteenth century, Düsseldorf became a famous center for music. Mendelssohn directed the Rhine Festival, Schumann was the conductor of the municipal orchestra for four years, and Brahms lived here for a time with the Schumann family.

Along the course of the Düssel river, in a valley named after Joachim Neander, a composer of hymns, some quarrymen found some bones which turned the scientific world into turmoil. This 1856 find predated Darwin's publication *On the Origin of Species* by three years. The bones were brought to J.C. Fuhlrott, a teacher of Elberfeld, who identified them as the remains of an ancient human, an Ice Age hominid. Fuhlrott was attacked for his views, but subsequent finds, especially in caves in the south of France, confirmed that these were the bones of a primitive hominid, Neanderthal man.

The pink Jägerhof (hunter's lodge) was built in 1748–53 by Prince Elector Carl Theodor zu Pfalz as a residence for the head Bergisch huntsman. The court garden was laid out in 1769 and it was the first public municipal park in Germany. The Jägerhof houses the largest private collection of Meissen porcelain in the world.

The Altstadt (old town) escaped damage during World War II, though Düsseldorf was half destroyed. The St. Lambertus church is a gothic hall church which replaced the original Romanesque basilica in 1288–1394. The west tower is 72 meters (235 feet) high and it has a curiously twisted belfry tower. The church was the burial site of the nobility until the St. Andreas church was built.

The St. Andreas church was built by the Count Palatine Wilhelm von Neuburg in 1622–29 as a Jesuit monastery church. It was used as the court church and burial place for the Counts of Neuburg. St. Andreas is the finest seventeenth century building in the lower Rhine area and was modeled on the court church in Neuburg an der Donau (Danube) and on Roman buildings of the late Renaissance and early baroque periods. In the aisles are life sized wooden statues of the Apostles and Saints.

Some exceptional museums can be found in Düsseldorf, amongst them the Landesmuseum Volk und Wirtschaft, an economics museum unique in Germany. The Haus des Deutschen Ostens in Bismarckstrasse 90 displays customs and history of East Germany and Sudeten territories as well as a weapons collection. Few places in Germany escape the web of Goethe, and here there is the third largest Goethe museum in the country. The Schlossturm (castle tower) is all that remains of the old castle which now houses the shipping museum.

Modern architecture is a feature of this progressive city. The Kaufhof in Königsallee (1907–19) marks the end of Art Nouveau and the beginning of functionalism. Next to the Rhine is the highly functional Mannesmannhaus (1911–12), and the Ehrenhof-Anlage (1925) exhibition hall. In 1924 the first German "skyscraper" appeared, Wilhelm Marx house, eleven storeys high. The Phoenix-Ruhrort skyscraper is another modern building of exceptional merit. The St. Rochus church is a cantilever supported mushroom dome.

Festivals are part and parcel of the Düsseldorf experience. The Altstadt festivals take place on the Monday before Lent and on 10 November. Carnivals evolved from ancient mid-winter fertility rites which were adopted by the Romans as Saturnalia. Fasching (carniaval) is the festive time immediately before Lent, the name now synonymous with carnival deriving from Fastnacht, the fasting nights of Lent.

The St. Martin's day procession on 10 November has up to fifty thousand children walking through the city carrying lanterns.

About thirty kilometers (19 miles) due west, near the border of the Netherlands, is the town of Dülken. In 1450 the Count of Kleve-Berg founded the first Academy of Fools in a windmill at Dülken, starting the Rhineland carnivals. The windmill has been preserved and is now a museum of the carnival.

Among many other sights worth seeing are the Triton fountain on Königsallee, the Rheinturm (tower

234m/768ft) in Rheinpark Bilk with a restaurant at the top, the Japanese garden presented to the city by its Japanese community and the Japan-Center in Immermannstrasse.

Directions:

Start at Ruhrort Bahnhof

Along Homburger Strasse towards bridge across Rhine (Friedrich-Ebert-Brücke)

Cross over to LHS bike path, continue across bridge on LHS

Immed. L across another bridge, enter Homberg along Königstrasse

(About 400 m) U-turn L (where road curves R), to Rhine, U-turn R alongside river

Continue along bike path alongside Rhine, river on your LHS

[KM 780] (Ruhr–Rhine confluence across river)

[KM 779]

Exit Essenberg

Under freeway (A40) bridge

[KM 778]

Up slope, away from river, bike path ends, U-turn R up to roadway

L along Wilhelmallee (road)

Info on your LHS

X continue along Deichstrasse, waterworks on your LHS

Enter Hochemmerich

X-L along Deichstrasse, along dike-top road

L along Fährstrasse

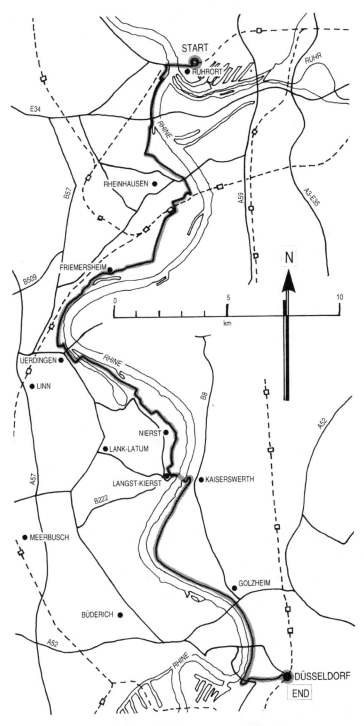

START

RUHRORT

RUHR

E34

RHINE

RHEINHAUSEN

A59

A3-E35

B57

FRIEMERSHEIM

B509

N

0   5   10

km

UERDINGEN

RHINE

LINN

B8

NIERST

LANK-LATUM

A52

LANGST-KIERST

KAISERSWERTH

A57

B222

MEERBUSCH

GOLZHEIM

BÜDERICH

DÜSSELDORF

END

RHINE

A52

Cross rail line

Immed. R along bike path, Rhine on your LHS

Under motor bridge

[KM 775]

Immed. before bridge U-turn R along Deichstrasse

L along Hochfelderstrasse

L along Ursulastrasse

T-L along Atroper Strasse

X-L along Friedrich-Alfried-Strasse

Under railway bridge

Immed. road swings hard R, past Rheinhausen Ostbahnhof (rail station)

Continue along Kruppstrasse

Continue along Bismarckstrasse

Continue along Reichstrasse, to end

T-R along Schleusenstrasse

(1st) L along Am Kuppengraben

T-R along Am Damm, on dike-top bike path

L off dike, continue alongside dike along Friemersheimer Strasse, to end

R over dike (Martinistrasse), immed. L along Roosstrasse

T (water tower ahead) R along Turmstrasse

T-L along bike path alongside Uerdingenstrasse

Continue along Rheinuferstrasse

[KM 766]

Cross to LHS bike path, continue alongside Rhine, river on your LHS

Bike path ends, continue along Hohenbudberger Strasse

Enter Uerdingen

L along Oberstrasse (pedestrian area)

X-L along Düsseldorfer Strasse to Rhine

Road swings R at Rhine, continue alongside Rhine, river on your LHS

X (lights) L, cross rail line, cross bridge, continue along Hohestrasse

Road swings R, continue along Hentrichstrasse

L along Bataverstrasse, to end

R along Heidbergsstrasse

L along An der Römerschanze (K9) towards Nierst

Enter Nierst

(1st) L along Werthstrasse

R along Am Oberen Feld (street), continue along Hosterzweg

Continue along Am Rheinblick

L along Zur Rheinfähre to ferry

Cross on ferry, Kierst-Langst – Kaiserswerth

[KM 755]

Off ferry, up slope, L across front of hotel along Fährer Weg

Immed. R along bike path (after hotel, before bridge)

Continue along Lohauser Deich, Rhine on your RHS

[KM 754]; [KM 753]

Under freeway (A44) bridge

[KM 752]; [KM 751]; [KM 750]; [KM 749]

Continue along Rotterdamer Strasse, Rhine on your RHS

[KM 748]; [KM 747]

Under freeway (A7) bridge (Theodor-Heuss-Brücke)

Immed. R towards Rhine

L along Robert-Lehr-Ufer, Rhine on your RHS

[KM 746]

Continue along Tonhallenufer

[KM 745]

Under motor bridge (Oberkasseler Brücke)

[KM 744]

Continue alongside Rhine

Under motor bridge (Rheinkniebrücke)

Immed. L away from river, continue along Hubertusstrasse, alongside bridge

L under bridge along Neusser Strasse

R along Haroldstrasse

Continue along Graf-Adolf-Strasse

R to Hauptbahnhof

Ends at Düsseldorf Hauptbahnhof.

Diversion Suggestions:

1. It's not that difficult to cycle around Düsseldorf, although admittedly the car is king. The tourist infofrmation office (close to the Hauptbahnhof, main rail station) will be able to give you some good tips and interesting routes to explore.

2. Neanderthal is about 10 kilometers (6 miles) east of Düsseldorf. The Düssel river flows through this valley, site of the discovery of the famous Neanderthal skull. There is a game park and a museum of pre-history. You can follow the Düssel through the city, but note that there are two branches of the river. One (north) ends near the airport (Nördlicher Düssel) and the other (south) near St. Martin Kirche. Sometimes the river disappears for a while, but with a good map you should have no difficulty.

3. Across the Rhine from Düsseldorf is the historically interesting city of Neuss. See Route 9 for details. There is also a water-meadow open air museum near the suburb of Helpenstein. If you travel from Düsseldorf station to the Rhine, follow the Rhine and cross the Düsseldorf–Neuss bridge, follow the Rhine west bank to the Erft confluence and then follow the Erft to the Insel Hombroich, the round trip will be about 32 kilometers (20 miles).

Route 9: Düsseldorf to Cologne (Köln) via Zons

Distance: 70 km/44 miles

Terrain: Flat; paved roads and bike paths, compacted dirt roads

Maps: ADAC Düsseldorf Stadtplan; 1:20,000 (1 cm = 200 m)

ADAC Köln Stadtplan; 1:20,000 (1 cm = 200 m)

ADFC Radtourenkarte Münsterland – Niederrhein (No. 10); 1:150,000 (1 cm = 1.5 km)

Diversion See suggestions at the end of this section

Description:

From Düsseldorf cycle south along the east bank of the Rhine, over the harbor entrance and along the riverside dike past Hamm. Across the Rhine is the city of Neuss.

Neuss [KM 738] is situated on the confluence of the Rhine and Erft rivers. The town developed from a Roman legionaries' camp called Novaesium established in AD 40. A town charter was issued in 1190 and by the Middle Ages, Neuss had become an important Rhine port and member of the Hanseatic league.

Rivalry with nearby Cologne (Köln) was constant and fierce. In the 1470s Cologne unsuccessfully stormed the town walls sixty-five times in ten months of a siege. Investing soldiers seized and ate horses belonging to Landgraf Heinrich III of Hessen. After the end of hostilities a bill was sent to Cologne, but it was refused. In 1480 merchants from Cologne were arrested

at St. Goar by the Landgrave and made to pay 7,000 guilders for his horses.

The basilica of St. Quirinus, chronologically one of the last Romanesque churches on the Rhine, has an eleventh century crypt and a baroque dome. The east crossing tower has unusual flower shaped windows.

The Obertor (upper gate) was built in the thirteenth century. Near the Obertor, part of the town fortifications, is the Clemens Sels museum, displaying Roman finds, the history of the town, local folk art and fourteenth to nineteenth century fine art.

In Gepaplatz there is a cult site of Cybele, uncovered in 1956, where priests performed animal sacrifices.

At Insel Hombroich near Helpenstein in the Holzheim district, Erft river water meadows have been made into an open air museum.

Continue alongside the Rhine past Volmerswerth and cross to the west bank over the Fleher Brücke. Follow the river through Uedesheim and St Peter to the Benrath ferry.

Benrath [KM 721]: The Elector Karl Theodor had a Rococo palace and park built by Nicolas de Pigage in 1755–73. Schloss Benrath, with cavaliers' houses either side, has a total of eighty-four rooms in the Louis XVI style.

Continue along the west bank of the Rhine to Zons [KM 719]. Zons, once Roman Sontium, must be explored. The fourteenth century walls are the best preserved medieval walls in the Rhineland. They were built by Archbishop Friedrich von Saarwerden around 1373 when he used Zons as a river toll station.

Schloss Friedeström on the Rhine is surrounded by farm and other buildings to provide self sufficiency. The Kreismuseum, the former Herrenhaus, is devoted to the history of the complex in which it is kept, giving a unique impression of life in a medieval fortress community. During July and August historical plays and children's performances are given in the open air theater in the old keep.

Cycle on alongside the Rhine, past Rheinfeld to Dormagen [KM 711]. Dormagen, Roman Durnomagus, was a strategic site where the 22nd Legion was stationed. Continue past the giant Bayer factory to Worringen [KM 709], once Roman Buruncum.

Keep on alongside the Rhine along the dike-top bike path past the villages of Langel, Rheinkassel, and Kasselberg to Merchenich. Across the Rhine is the city of Leverkusen [KM 700]. In the Opladen district of Leverkusen, is the Friedenberger Hof, a sixteenth century knight's castle.

The Bayer AG dye factories and skyscraper headquarters of Bayer Chemical industries are here and this is where aspirin is produced. There is a Japanese style garden next to the skyscraper.

The Agfa-Gevaert photo museum is here too; it opens weekdays 09h00–17h00.

From Merchenich, travel around another factory, then turn back towards the river and cycle alongside the Rhine into Cologne, the largest Rhineland city.

Cologne [KM 688] began as a native settlement called Oppidum Ubiorum by the Romans. The Romans stationed a legion here, their camp covering one square kilometer. Today's Hohestrasse (High Street) in the pedestrian precinct is in exactly the same position as it was in Roman days. In AD 50 the German born Roman Empress

Agrippina, wife of Claudius, made the camp a "Colonia," a town for retired legionary veterans. The town was renamed Colonia Claudia Ara Agrippinensium; the monogram CCAA appears on old Roman stones and inscriptions. The town became the capital of the Roman province of Lower Germany and with its toll station from AD 70, headquarters of the Prefect of the Rhine fleet.

In the fifth century, Conan, an English warrior fighting in Brittany, made a marriage agreement with the father of a Cornish maiden, Ursula. Conan's band wanted wives too, so Ursula was accompanied by her ten most beautiful girl friends, each attended by one thousand maidens. The party set out from England intending to land at Cherbourg, but were blown off course by a storm and they landed at the Hook of Holland.

Ursula led the group upriver to Cologne, at which point Conan called off the arrangement. Ursula continued with the girls on a pilgrimage to Rome. The party decided to return home by the same route, but at Cologne they stumbled upon the camp of the heathen Huns, led by Attila himself. Supposedly all the girls were killed by the Huns, but at least three of them reappear at various places in the Rhineland at later dates. Ursula, who was offered her life if she married Attila, refused and Attila shot an arrow through her heart. This slaughter is fixed at AD 451.

By AD 1200 the town was bounded by walls with gates such as the surviving Eigelsteintor (north), Hahnentor (west) and Severinstor (south). The ring streets mark the line of fortified walls dating from 1180, the time of the Hohenstaufens. Outside the rings is a green belt 500 meters (550 yards) wide and about 10 kilometers (6 miles) long. The new town grew up between the "Wall streets" and the fortress ring and when the city developed outside the rings in the nineteenth century, a new period of growth began, including the completion of the Dom in 1880.

The Hanseatic League was created by Cologne and Lübeck in the mid-thirteenth century. The League became so powerful that in 1367 it was able to declare war on Denmark.

In the twelfth and thirteenth centuries the population rose to about forty thousand. About one hundred and fifty churches were built, of which forty seven were demolished during secularization.

The church of St. Gereon (Gereon-/Christophstrasse) began as a fourth century Christian martyr church built on a Roman burial site. St. Gereon was a Theban legionary martyr. This is one of the most unusual and excellent medieval buildings in the West, comparable with Florence cathedral or Hagia Sophia in Istanbul. The crypt pavement mosaics date from 1156.

St. Kunibert church (Konrad Adenauer Ufer), the last and most lavish of the late Romanesque churches with suggestions of early Gothic, was completed in 1247. The stained glass window cycle in the choir and east transept (1220–30) are the most important late Romanesque windows in Germany.

The church of St. Maria im Kapitol (Pipinstrasse/Eichhof) was the site of the Roman temple to Jupiter, Juno and Minerva. The building has the largest crypt in Germany after Speyer. The Mourning Woman, a memorial to the Colgne war victims by G. Marks (1949) is inside the church.

The church of the Rhine Boatmen, St. Maria Lyskirchen (Am Leystapel) is a thirteenth century building placed over one of the tenth century. It was hardly damaged during World War II. You can see the Boatmen's Madonna here, over 2 meters high, in the soft style (about 1420).

St. Pantaleon's church houses the tomb of the Empress Theophano (died AD 991), wife of Otto

The Gürzenich, the city's banquet hall and ball room (1441–47) was rebuilt after World War II. In the ruins of Alt St. Alban adjoining the Gürzenich, is a copy of the Mourning Parents, a memorial to those killed in Colgne during World War II ,by Käte Kollwitz.

The most imposing building in Cologne is the Dom (Cathedral of St. Peter and St. Mary). The foundation stone was laid in August 1248. Six hundred and thirty two years later, in October 1880, the cathedral was finally consecrated. This church was built to house the shrine of the Magi, captured by Frederick Barbarossa from Milan in 1164. The relics brought so many pilgrims that the building became a necessity. It was planned to build in the high Gothic style of northern France on the site of the old cathedral. There are five naves and two towers more than 150 meters (500 feet) high. The stone (trachyte) was quarried from the Siebengebirge across the Rhine from Bonn.

When the Dom was completed it was 157 meters (515 feet) high, the tallest building in the world and one of the largest churches in all Christendom. The interior has many exceptionally important and unique furnishings such as the Gero cross, glass windows, choir stalls, the reliquary, the Lochner Dom picture, the van der Burch statue of Christophe and Rubens tapestries.

The treasury is one of the richest in Europe.

A strange legend connects the building of the cathedral with Reynaud (Reinhold), one of Charlemagne's paladins and leader of the four sons of Aymon and their magical horse Bayard. After their defeat by Charlemagne, the horse was thrown into the river at Liège with a millstone tied to his neck, but he broke free and escaped to the forests of the Ardennes. Reynaud was living as a peasant when he heard about the construction of the cathedral. He signed on to carry stone blocks from the barges to the building site but worked too hard for his workmates' liking, so they stoned him to death and threw his body into the Rhine. Reynaud's body floated to the surface and he was found to be wearing a gold embroidered belt which identified him as Reynaud of Montauban. His remains were enshrined in the cathedral and some miracles were ascribed to them. When some pilgrims from Dortmund asked for relics, Reynaud's shrine jumped towards them on three consecutive visits, despite being replaced on each occasion. The shrine was then put on a wagon and the draught animals left unguided as was the custom in these circumstances. Eventually the wagon stopped at Dortmund, where the relics were then kept.

The former Minorite church of Mariae Empfängnis is the burial place of John Duns Scotus (1260–1308), an eminent Scottish churchman of the Middle Ages. His arguments were rejected by the church and the word "dunce" then came into the English language.

During World War II, Cologne was bombed relentlessly, as it is a most important rail (nine railway lines meet here) and road junction. Of the inner city, ninety percent was destroyed, and seventy percent of the outer suburbs. By 1945 the population had reduced to forty thousand from eight hundred thousand and of over two hundred and fifty thousand accommodation units, only twenty thousand remained. A world-wide competition was held after the war for plans to rebuild the city and it was won by Fritz Schaller. Amazingly enough the cathedral, although suffering fourteen direct bomb hits, was hardly damaged.

The Altes Rathaus (old city hall, Alter Markt) with its five-storey Rathausturm (tower) was built with the confiscated assets of the Patricians after the victory of the Guilds (1407–14). During World War II it was almost totally destroyed and has since been rebuilt. Parts of the Hansasaal built circa 1330 with stone figures of the nine good heroes (1360) survived the bombing.

Notables who lived and worked in Cologne were Albertus Magnus, the thirteenth century scholar; Thomas Aquinas; Meister Eckhardt; Karl Marx; and the 1972 Nobel prizewinner for Literature, Heinrich Böll. Peter Paul Rubens was born in the parish of St. Peter in 1577 and one of Rubens' last paintings, the Crucifixion of St. Peter, is kept in a special chapel in the war damaged St. Peter church (Jabachstrasse).

The composer Carl Rosier (1640–75) was born here, as was Jacques Offenbach (1819–80) who ran the city opera. The studio for electronic music opened under the leadership of Karl-Heinz Stockhausen.

Konrad Adenauer, the first Chancellor of post-war Federal Republic of (West) Germany was born in Cologne in 1874. He became "Oberbürgermeister" (Mayor) and served 1917–33. W. Leibl, the artist, was born in Colgne in 1844.

By the fourteenth century, 1,100 barges and 200 passenger vessels were plying between Cologne and Mainz. From Cologne, ships were physically hauled upstream against the current, to Mainz. Vessels of up to one hundred tons were pulled by ten to twelve horses. The horses were tended by men known as "Halfen," each driving two or three horses. The cost of hiring each horse for the entire journey was about 10 thalers. When fodder was more expensive, the price went up. Besides the price for the horses, ships provided board, lodging and free beer for the halfen. The upstream journey took from eight to seventeen days, the return trip three days.

Stapelrechten (right of Staples) whereby passing shipmen had to offload their goods and offer them for sale for a fixed number of days, was abolished by the Congress of Vienna in 1815. Cologne was one of the river ports with this right.

Heumarkt (Haymarket) is in the old quarter of Köln and here you can find picturesque old taverns near the Rhine.

Gottestracht is a procession held at Corpus Christi which marches around the Cathedral and onto boats on the Rhine. The pre-Lenten Cologne Carnival is unrivaled in the Rhinelands for sheer exuberance, ingenuity and intensity. The Carnival begins the Thursday before Ash Wednesday and lasts the entire week.

The Kölner Stadtmuseum (Zeughausstrasse 1) in the old arsenal, a Renaissance brick building (1594), documents the City's history and has a 1571 Mercator model of Cologne.

The Wallraf-Richartz museum houses a collection of Old Masters in the Expressionist style and a wide range of other works. It also contains the Ludwig Museum (paintings) and the Agfa Foto Historama with photographs and photographic equipment since 1840.

The Römisch-Germanisches (Roman-Germanic) Museum (Roncalliplatz 4) is a new building (1970–74) covering the Dionysius Mosaic and the Poblicius tomb. It is one of the best technically conceived buildings in post-war Germany. During excavations for air raid shelters in World War II, a 2nd-century palace was uncovered. The chief hall contains a Dionysius mosaic 10.75 m x 7.7 m (35 feet x 25 feet), with thirty-one separate designs and more than one and a half million pieces of different colors.

The botanical gardens (Florapark) and Zoo are on the west bank of the Rhine, north of the Zoobrücke.

The Pantomimentheater (Aachener Strasse 24) is Western Europe's only mime theater (86 seats).

Production of Eau de Cologne "4711" in 1987 reached 10 billion (US) (or 10 milliard UK) liters. Romans made perfumed oil here in the second century. Giovanni-Maria Farina first made Eau de Cologne in 1709.

Viewpoints:

Severin bridge to Dom; Dom south tower (500 steps) over city; Telecommunications tower (Fernmeldeturm) 243 meters (797 feet) high with viewing platform at 170 meters (558 feet); cable car (Rheinseilbahn) across Zoo bridge (Zoo to Rheinpark over river). Also Bastei restaurant on an old city tower (Kaiser Friedrich Ufer).

[KM 688] Köln-Deutz: Originally the site of a Roman fort. In 1864 the

Deutz motor company came into existence and by 1987 employed 17,000 people. The motor museum is at Deutz, Mülheimer Strasse 111, open weekdays 09h00–16h00.

The fairground was built (1925–27) for the "Pressa" by A. Abel.

Directions:

Start at Düsseldorf Hauptbahnhof (train station)

Exit west, L along Graf-Adolf-Strasse

Continue along Haroldstrasse towards Rhine

Continue along Horionplatz, under bridge (Rheinkniebrücke)

R to Rhine

L alongside Rhine along Parlaments-Ufer, river on your RHS

[KM 743]

Cross bridge over harbor inlet

Continue along dike-top bike path

[KM 742]

L away from river

T-R along asphalt road, past golf course

Bear R at end of road

Continue along asphalt bike path

Continue alongside Rhine, river on your RHS

Under railway bridge, continue along Am Sandacker

[KM 738]

Continue along bike path alongside river

Continue along Auf der Böck

R along dike-top bike path, on Hammer Deich

Under freeway bridge (Südbrücke)

[KM 737]; [KM 736]; [KM 735]

Continue along Volmerswerther Deich

[KM 734]

Through Volmerswerth, alongside river, river on your RHS

[KM 733]

Continue along Fleher Deich

Immed. before bridge across Rhine, L up ramp to top of bridge

R, continue across bridge (Fleher Brücke)

U-turn R and off bridge towards Rhine (bicycle sign)

X-R towards Zons (bicycle sign + paddestoel), along asphalt road

Under (Fleher) bridge

Road swings hard R

Continue through farmyard, along asphalt road

Y-L along Altwahlscheid (road)

X-L along Am Reckberg (road), on bike path on LHS of road

L along Wahlscheider Weg

Immed. before village, L along brick-paved bike path

R alongside dike on bike path

Continue to top of dike

Info, on your LHS

R off dike, into Uedesheim, along Rheinfährstrasse

X (lights) L along Macherscheider Strasse

(Pass Jugendherberge (youth hostel) on your RHS)

Continue to Rhine

R alongside Rhine, river on your LHS

[KM 728]

T-L along bike path on RHS of road (B9 Koblenzer Strasse)

Cross bridge over inlet, Rhine on your LHS

[KM 727]

X (lights) continue along Düsseldorfer Strasse

Enter St. Peter

X (lights) L along Bahnstrasse

X (circle/roundabout) continue along bike path to end of roadway

R down bank, continue along compacted dirt road

T-R along asphalt road

(70m) L along asphalt road, continue to Rhine

[KM 721]

Past slipway, continue alongside Rhine along hard sand road, past campsite

(Benrath across river)

[KM 720]; [KM 719]

Enter Zons along Rheinau (road)

X continue (Zons–Urdenbach ferry on LHS)

(140 m) L along brick-paved bike path on dike-top

[KM 717]; [KM 715]; [KM 712]

Continue along asphalt bike path past waterworks (on your RHS)

T-L along bike path on LHS of road (B9, Neusser Landstrasse)

Continue along bike path past Bayer factory

[KM 710]

Enter Worringen

Continue along bike path on RHS of road (don't be tempted by cycle signs to turn right!)

X (lights) cross to LHS bike path and continue

Exit Worringen

(80m) L along dike-top bike path (Werthweg)

Continue along Langeller Damm, on dike-top bike path

[KM 708]; [KM 707]; [KM 706]

Enter Langel

T-L along Fährweg (slipway) towards Rhine

R alongside Rhine, along bike path, on Langeler Deich

[KM 705]

[KM 704] exit Langel

R off dike, enter Rheinkassel along Amandusstrasse

Continue through square (where main road turns R)

T-L along Kapelleweg

T-L along Kasselberger Weg

[KM 703]; [KM 702]

L immed. before freeway (E37-A1) bridge (Leverkusener Brücke) towards Rhine, alongside bridge

R alongside Rhine, under bridge, river on LHS

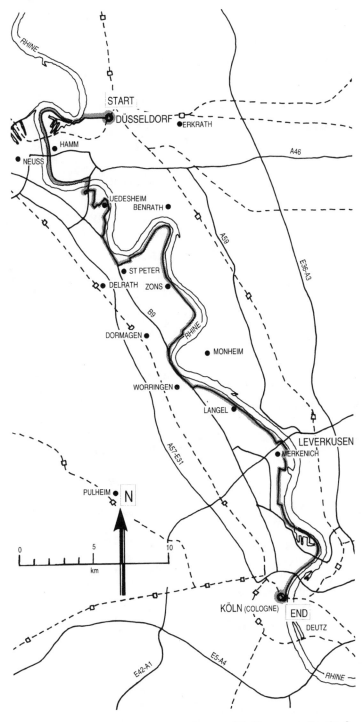

START
DÜSSELDORF
ERKRATH
A46
HAMM
NEUSS
UEDESHEIM
BENRATH
A59
E36-A3
ST PETER
DELRATH
ZONS
B9
RHINE
DORMAGEN
MONHEIM
WORRINGEN
LANGEL
LEVERKUSEN
A57-E31
MERKENICH
PULHEIM
N

0   5   10
km

KÖLN (COLOGNE)
END
DEUTZ
E42-A1
E5-A4
RHINE

RHINE

[KM 701]

R along Fährgasse, away from river

L along Merkenicher Hauptstrasse

R along Ivenshofweg

T (lights) L along Emdener Strasse

Enter Köln-Niehl

Under motor bridge

(1,75 km) X (lights) cross Geestemünder Strasse

Immed. L across Emdener Strasse at cycle crossing (lights)

Continue along Geestemünder Strasse, towards Rhine

* Caution: tram lines

T-R along Merkenicher Strasse on LHS bike path alongside Rhine, river on your LHS

[KM 697]

L along bike path alongside Rhine

Continue along Niehler Damm

[KM 696]

L up ramp, cross bridge over harbor inlet

R along Am Molenkopf, on dike-top bike path, river on your LHS

[KM 695]; [KM 693]

Continue along Niederländer Ufer

[KM 692]

Under freeway (B51) bridge (Mülheimer Brücke)

Enter Köln-Riehl

[KM 691]

Continue along bike path, Rhine on LHS, road on RHS

Info on RHS

[KM 690]

Under freeway (B55a) bridge (Zoobrücke)

Enter Köln (Cologne) Center-City area

Continue along bike path, Rhine on LHS, road on RHS (Konrad-Adenauer-Ufer)

[KM 689]

Under railway bridge (Hohenzollernbrücke)

Immed. R, up ramp to Dom (Cathedral)

Bear R to walkway from rail station

Enter gate to platform (Gleis) 1-A at rail station; gate open 06h00 to 20h00; route ends here.

Diversion Suggestion

There are countless parks and green belts in and around the city. It is possible to follow the "rings" of the city for most of the way through parks, along bike paths. The inner city is bike-friendly and there is a substantial pedestrianized area.

Route 10A: Cologne (Köln) to Linz am Rhein via Bonn

Distance: 75 km/47 miles

Terrain: Flat; compacted dirt roads, paved roads and bike paths

Maps: ADAC Köln Stadtplan; 1:20,000 (1 cm = 200 m)

           Kompass Wanderkarte Köln – Brühl – Bonn (No. 819); 1:50,000 (2 cm = 1 km)

           Kompass Wanderkarte Bonn – Ahrtal (No. 820); 1:50,000 (2 cm = 1 km)

           ADFC Radtourenkarte Rheinland – Eifel (No. 15); 1:150,000 (1 cm = 1.5 km)

Diversions: See Route 10B (Ahr Valley to Altenahr)

Description:

From Cologne, cross the Rhine to the east bank over the Hohenzollern bridge. Cycle southwards alongside the river past Porz and Langel to Lülsdorf. Across the Rhine (Lülsdorf–Wesseling ferry), 5 kilometers west, is the historic town of Brühl.

Brühl was the residence of the Archbishop Electors of Cologne after the citizens of the city took temporal power from them.

In 1724 Clemens August, Archbishop Elector of Cologne built his summer residence in Brühl. It was constructed on the foundations of a heavily fortified and moated burg which had been blown up in 1689. The lavishly decorated and furnished Schloss Augustusburg, is a magnificent example of the transitional style between late Baroque and Rococo, the finest Rococo achievement in the Rhineland. The staircase hall is by Balthasar Neumann and ceilings by Tiepolo. Nowadays the building is used by the German government for state functions.

The Falkenlust hunting lodge was built 1729–40. The former court and monastery church of St. Maria zu den Engeln (1491) was rebuilt in 1735.

South of Brühl is the Phantasialand amusement theme park with a cable way, water park and monorail. Fairy tale scenes are depicted with a wild west town, pony ranch and a Pacific Western Express section.

If you prefer, you can cross to the west bank here and continue southwards alongside the Rhine, to join the described route at Bonn.

From Lülsdorf, cycle past Niederkassel, Rheidt, Mondorf, Bergheim and Vilich to Beuel [KM 655]. Schwarzrheindorf, north of the Kennedy bridge, has the most remarkable church in Germany. It was built on the site of a Roman guardhouse on a hillock for Arnold of Wied, Archbishop of Cologne in 1151 as a Burg (castle) chapel. It is a double church, with the upper floor for the nobility and the Archbishop. The lower floor has some of the finest Romanesque frescoes in north Europe.

Cross the Kennedy bridge to the city of Bonn [KM 655]. Bonn was the federal capital of West Germany until 1999, which has since removed to Berlin, though Bonn retains its administrative function. On September 1, 1948, Konrad Adenauer formally created the Parliamentary democracy of the Federal Republic in the Bonn Museum building. The Federal Parliament sat in the Bundeshaus (Federal Building) which was a Pedagogical Academy (teachers' college).

The middle Rhine gorge extends from Bonn to Bingen, a distance of 128 kilometers (80 miles). From Bonn upstream, the Rhine route enters the Rhenish uplands from the Cologne lowlands. At this point, more than 400 kilometers (250 miles) from the North Sea coast, the river is 64 meters (210 feet) above sea level. The Siebengebirge (seven mountains) are visible near the east bank of the Rhine, south of the confluence of the Sieg and Rhine rivers.

Originally Bonn was a Roman citadel called Castra Bonensia. The Roman city which developed was supplied with drinking water from the Eifel mountains by an aqueduct, remains of which can be seen in the woods to the south.

Heinrich Heine studied law at Bonn University. Other alumni include Schlegel (Shakespearean scholar), Kekulé (organic chemist), Hertz (physicist) and Angelander (astronomer). During 1852–63, Angelander compiled a census of 324,198 stars in the northern sky. Gottfried Kirkel, the revolutionary and poet, lectured in theology at Bonn University. Prince Albert of Saxe-Coburg-Gotha, husband of Queen Victoria, attended Bonn University.

The Münster (Cathedral) of St. Martin replaced an earlier church dedicated to Cassius and Florentinus, officers of the Theban Legion, who were martyred in the third century for refusing to recognize the Roman Emperor as a god. The earlier Christian church was founded on a Roman cemetery by St. Helena, mother of the Emperor Constantine. It is one of the finest Romanesque (eleventh to thirteenth centuries) churches on the Rhine. In 1928 a votive stone of the mother goddess was found under the basilica.

In 1846 the Ramersdorfer Kapelle (Bornheimer Strasse) was rebuilt in the old Bonn cemetery to save it from demolition. This mid-thirteenth century former chapel of the Teutonic Order (of knighthood), was sited at the foot of the Siebengebirge at Ramersdorf. The cemetery was established for the burial of soldiers and foreigners. Entombed there are E.M. Arndt (patriot), A.W. Schlegel (scholar), J.L. Tieck (poet), Beethoven's mother, Schiller's wife Charlotte and their son Ernst, Adele Schopenauer, and Robert and Clara Schumann.

Beethoven was born at 515 (now number 20) Bonngasse in Bonn in December 1770. The house has been a museum since 1889 and houses the largest and most valuable Beethoven collection (20,000 volumes) in the world. Beethoven left Bonn in 1792 for Vienna and never returned to Bonn or the Rhineland. His father was employed as organist by the last Archbishop Elector, Maximilian Franz (son of Maria Theresa) in Bonn.

The Beethovenhalle was built in the gardens on the Rhine embankment for Beethoven festivals, the first being held in 1845. Important guests, including the King and Queen of Prussia and Queen Victoria and Prince Albert of Great Britain, gathered on the balcony of the Fürstenburg Palace (now the Post Office) to see the Beethoven statue unveiled. When it was observed that the statue faced away from the dignitaries, remarks were made that it was in keeping with the character of the composer. This first festival was directed by Spohr and Liszt and attended by Berlioz and Meyerbeer.

The Government Quarter is based on "millionaires row," large houses built along the Rhine. The Presidential residence is the Villa Hammerschmidt, designed in the nineteenth century for a professor. Next door is the Chancellor's residence, built in 1858 for a textile merchant and known as Schaumburg Palace, as Prince Adolf zu Schaumburg-Lippe had lived there.

On the 125 meters (410 feet) Kreuzberg, is a Franciscan friary with a Baroque church, attached to which is the staircase (Heilige Stiege) designed by Balthasar Neumann, based on the Scala Sancta in the Lateran Cathedral in Rome. The middle section can only be mounted in a kneeling position.

The Rheinisches Landesmuseum (Colmanstrasse 16) presents a survey of Rhineland Roman art, early Christian finds, Roman weapons and altars, Christian art and sixteenth century Dutch panel painting.

From Bonn, continue southwards along the west bank of the Rhine. Across the river is a range of hills called the Siebengebirge ("Seven Mountains"). The Siebengebirge are actually thirty volcanic hills, but seven of the peaks are most prominent. Legend has it that there was once a lake nearby which continually flooded the surrounding plains. Some giants were asked to cut a drainage channel, which they did, leaving seven heaps of soil.

Plittersdorf [KM 649] was once an important relay station and base for the "Halfen." The Halfen (= helps, n. pl.) provided and controlled the horses which hauled barges upstream. They wore white breeches, heavy nailed boots, a heavy jacket over a blue waistcoat, a bright neckerchief and a broad felt hat. Bargemen and Halfen fixed the terms for their services in a saloon and sealed the bargain with a round of wine paid for by the bargee. At the end of the journey the contract ended with a round of wine, bread, and cheese.

The Schaumburger Hof was built for the Guild of Halfen in 1755. The relay station was on the route between Wesseling and Kripp. The towpath followed the West (left) bank of the river only and the horses were blinkered on the left side (river side). One man handled three or four horses, riding with an open knife to cut the traces in case of emergency. When steamships began to take away their livelihood, the Halfen fired upon them with small cannons. Hussars were then sent from Bonn to patrol the river banks.

[KM 648] The Cistercian Heisterbach Abbey was dissolved by Napoleon. Buildings were blown up in 1809 and the stones sold or used for construction of the Canal du Nord. The Heisterbach Kloster (monastery) basilica begun in 1202, was consecrated in 1237. The choir of the church still survives thanks to Napoleon's timely defeat. A Cellite convent of the eighteenth century can be seen near the ruins. St. Bernard of Clairvaux banished the nightingales from Heisterbach to Nachtigallental (nightingale valley) above Königswinter.

[KM 647] The Godesberg (west bank, inland from Plittersdorf), a basalt crag, was originally a meeting place for Odin worshipers. Archbishop Dietrich of Cologne built a fortress here in 1210. The St. Michael chapel built by early Christian missionaries was included in the castle. In 1583 the building was destroyed by a mine weighing 1,500 pounds.

Hitler and Chamberlain met at Bad Godesberg in 1938. Chamberlain consequently made his "peace in our time" speech.

Königswinter [KM 645] hosts an annual Anglo-German conference to promote co-operation and understanding between the two nations. Chamberlain and Hitler had met here, which led to the Munich agreement.

Königswinter derives its name from its vineyards (vinitorium), not the season of winter. Red wine made here is called Dragon's Blood. During the annual wine festival, a local Bacchus presents medals to vintners for "quenching burning thirst."

From quarries below the Drachenfels (dragon skin) [KM 644] came the trachyte stone for Cologne Cathedral. Drachenfels castle, later bought by Emperor Friedrich Wilhelm III, was built for the Archbishops of Cologne in AD 1117.

The Nibelungenlied hero Siegfried came to Drachenfels to serve an apprenticeship with the famous armorer Minier. Because he was too strong, breaking anvils and out-wrestling his fellow apprentices, Siegfried was sent on a dangerous quest in the hope that he would never return. He completed his tasks, but angered at the danger he had faced, returned and killed Minier.

You can reach the top of the Drachenfels [viewpoint] by the oldest rack railway in Germany, horse-drawn carriage, on the back of a donkey, or you can cycle (or drive) up the road.

[KM 641] Bad Honnef was Konrad Adenauer's residence and he is buried here. His former house is now a memorial museum.

Nonnenwerth (Nuns' island) has an old convent built upon it. Edward III (of Britain) stayed here on his return down the Rhine (1338) after meeting Louis the Bavarian, King of Germany and Holy Roman Emperor and forming the alliance of Koblenz which recognized Edward's claim to the French throne.

Nonnenwerth convent and the Drachenburg (Drachenfels castle) are connected in legend by Roland and his betrothed Hildegund. After Roland's rearguard action at Roncevalles protecting Charlemagne's retreating army, Roland returned to Drachenfels. It is ordinarily accepted that Roland was killed at Roncevalles and the news of his death must have reached Hildegund, for she entered the convent and took her vows. Roland's exertions in reaching Drachenfels caused his terrible wounds to re-open and he was forced to spend time recovering in Drachenburg. Knowing that he had arrived too late to marry Hildegund, Roland had a castle built on the river bank opposite the convent, so he could watch Hildegund from a distance. When Roland saw Hildegund's funeral procession leave the gates of the convent, he too died.

Roland's castle, known as Rolandsbogen (Roland's arch), was actually built in the twelfth century, some three hundred years after the battle of Roncevalles. By 1839 the building had decayed and the archway was destroyed by a storm. The poet Freiligrath made an appeal in the Cologne newspaper for restoration work to be done and the castle was subsequently repaired [viewpoint]. The castle is built on the Roddenberg, the northernmost point of the Eifel volcanic area.

At this point you leave the State of Nordrhein-Westfalen and enter the State of Rheinland-Pfalz (Palatinate).

[KM 638] Oberwinter derives its name from its vineyards (vinitorium). A sketch by Wenceslaus Hollar shows the ship of Lord Arundel (Thomas Howard, 2nd Earl of Arundel, 1586–

1646), who was on a diplomatic mission to Emperor Ferdinand III, King of Hungary and Holy Roman Emperor, being towed by nine horses approaching Oberwinter. Hollar had been employed by Lord Arundel as an artist.

[KM 636] At Unkel the reef in the river, known as the Unkelstein (Unkel rock), was dynamited to allow the river to run more freely. There was a custom whereby a person would leap from the bow of a ship onto the Unkelstein with a bottle of wine and a glass in hand, drink a toast to the passengers and crew and leap back on the ship before it passed by. There are no records to tell how many passengers were stranded in this way.

[KM 634] Erpel is opposite Remagen and there is a seasonal ferry operating between them. A story is told of the ferryman woken one night by voices he heard at the ferry. Though he saw nobody, he pulled the chain-ferry across the river only to see little people disembark. Each paid him with a silver Cologne piece.

[KM 632] Remagen was named after the Roman fort of Ricomagus. It was originally a Celtic settlement. The river cliffs were caused by volcanic action, as were the mineral springs. A medieval wall and a Roman gateway survive.

A bargeman, Captain Jonas Jülich, was caught in a storm on the river and promised to feed the poor of Remagen if delivered. Every St. Agnes day a dole of pea soup and bacon is dished out to the poor, in compliance with his promise.

During World War II the Americans were able to seize the Remagen, bridge because of a delay in blowing it up and were thus able to establish a bridgehead on the right (east) bank of the Rhine. The bridge collapsed soon afterwards and was not replaced. The remains are now preserved as a monument to Peace (Gedenkstätte des Friedens). There is a Peace museum in the tower on the west bank.

[KM 631] Ockenfels Castle was once a seat of the Archbishop Electors of Cologne. It was destroyed in 1475 and rebuilt in 1925. It is now used as an hotel.

Take the ferry from Remagen to Linz am Rhein and enter the old walled city through the town gate.

[KM 630] Linz am Rhein is opposite the confluence of the Rhine and Ahr rivers and the town of Kripp, once a relay station for the Halfen. The twin town gates, Rheintor and Neutor are remains of the town walls and fortifications which were demolished in 1861. The old Rathaus (City Hall) was built in 1392 in late gothic style. It is the oldest town hall in daily use in the state.

In the Marktplatz and Burgplatz are well preserved half-timbered houses. The 14thcentury Burg Feith (1365) was the summer residence of the Archbishop of Cologne .

Directions:

Start at Köln (Cologne) Hauptbahnhof (train station)

From platform (Gleis) 1-A, you can leave directly through a gate (open 06h00–20h00) that leads onto a parapeted walkway

L along walkway (cathedral on your RHS)

Cycle along road to your R, away from the train station, behind the cathedral

L towards equestrian statue

L-R, continue with rail line on your LHS

Continue along bike path on railway bridge (Hohenzollernbrücke), across Rhine

X-L along bike path on LHS of road

Under railway subway

Immed. L alongside bridge, on LHS bike path

T-R along bike path, away from bridge

(50 m) L across road

Immed. L along bike path alongside Rhine, river on your RHS

Under railway bridge

Continue along quay (cobbles); Kennedyufer, river on your RHS

Under bridge (Deutzer Brücke)

Continue along Deutzer Werft

Under bridge (Severinsbrücke)

Up slope, (½) L along hard dirt track

T-R towards lift bridge

Cross rail line

Cross lift-bridge (Drehbrücke) over harbor

L along dike-top bike path (Alfred-Schutte-Allee), river on your RHS

[KM 686]

Under railway bridge (Südbrücke)

R towards river

L alongside Rhine, river on your RHS

[KM 685]; [KM 684]

Under freeway (E40-A4) bridge (Rodenkirchener-brücke)

[KM 683]

Up slope, Y-R

Bike path skirts inlet

[KM 682]

T-R along Weidenweg

T-R-L alongside Rhine, river on your RHS

[KM 681]; [KM 680]; [KM 679]

Continue along Friedrich-Ebert-Ufer

T-R-L along Leinpfad alongside Rhine, river on your RHS

[KM 678]

X continue past yacht harbor, on your RHS

R towards Rhine (at end of harbor)

L alongside Rhine, river on your RHS

[KM 677]; [KM 676]

T-R along top of dike (Rheindamm)

[KM 675]

Y-R alongside river along asphalt road (In der Aue) (Langel on LHS)

[KM 674]; [KM 673]

Road swings hard L away from river

(Some maps show a continuation of this road along the river bank, but this is private property and the right of entry is not always offered; further along the road can get extremely muddy and impassable through the nature reserve)

T-R along roadway

X-L towards dike-top bike path

Road swings L up slope to dike-top

R along dike-top bike path, river off to your RHS

Continue along Rheindamm

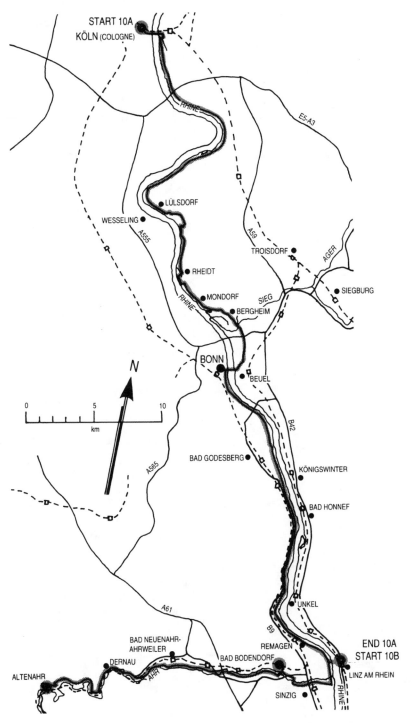

START 10A
KÖLN (COLOGNE)

RHINE

E5-A3

LÜLSDORF

WESSELING

A555

TROISDORF

A59

AGER

RHINE

RHEIDT

MONDORF

SIEG

SIEGBURG

BERGHEIM

BONN

BEUEL

N

0   5   10
km

BAD GODESBERG

B42

KÖNIGSWINTER

A565

BAD HONNEF

A61

UNKEL

B9

BAD NEUENAHR-
AHRWEILER

REMAGEN

END 10A
START 10B

DERNAU

BAD BODENDORF

ALTENAHR

AHR

LINZ AM RHEIN

SINZIG

RHINE

Continue along Uferstrasse, alongside river, river on your RHS

Enter Lülsdorf

[KM 668]

Ferry, Lülsdorf–Wesseling (seasonal)

[If you prefer, you could take the ferry to Wesseling and turn L alongside the Rhine, cycling next to the river the entire way to and through Bonn, rejoining the described route at the Kennedy bridge.[

Continue along Uferstrasse, to end

L along Burgstrasse

T-R along Auf dem Penel

T-L along Burgstrasse

X-R along Rhein-/Berliner Strasse along bike path on RHS of road

X (lights) R along Feldmühlestrasse towards Bonn (bicycle sign)

Exit Ranzel, enter Niederkassel

X-R along Hauptstrasse towards Bonn (15 km), Nieder-Kassel (1 km) (bicycle sign)

Cross rail line

R along Waldstrasse

T-R along Rathausstrasse (ignore bicycle sign)

(1st) L to Rhine

L alongside Rhine on bike path below dike wall, Rhine on your RHS

[KM 666]

Continue along Hochwasser Schutzdamm

Exit Niederkassel

[KM 665]; [KM 664]

oad swings L away from Rhine, alongside inlet

Enter Rheidt

R across causeway, along Auf dem Werfchen, to Rhine

T-L alongside river, river on your RHS

[KM 663]

L away from river

T-R

Y-R along river bike path

[KM 662]; [KM 661]

Enter Mondorf

X (circle/roundabout) R towards Rhine

L alongside Rhine, river on your RHS

Pass small boat harbor (on your RHS)

Continue along Hafenstrasse, up slope

T-R

(50 m) R along bike path towards Bonn (bicycle sign)

* Caution: sharp turn L

Continue along Nachtigallenweg towards Siegfähre (sign)

Cross bridge over motor road

X-R along Bergstrasse towards Bonn (6,2 km, bicycle sign)

T-L

Up slope, X continue towards Bonn (6 km) along Zur Siegfähre (directly across Oberstrasse and down slope)

Exit Bergheim

Immed. before bridge underpass, U-turn R, up ramp towards Bonn (5.2 km) (bicycle sign), to top of bridge

U-turn L along bike path on LHS of road (L269 - Niederkasseler Strasse)

Across Sieg river

Under freeway (565) bridge

X (lights) continue along Niederkasseler Strasse on LHS bike path

Enter Beuel

X continue, switch to RHS bike path

X continue (across Clemensstrasse)

X (lights) R along St.-Augustiner-Strasse

Continue along Konrad-Adenauer-Platz

Cross Kennedybrücke along RHS bike path

Continue along Berliner Strasse

(1st) R along Doetschstrasse on RHS bike path

X (1st) R along Josefstrasse

T continue across to Rhine

R alongside Rhine, river on your LHS

[If you crossed on the Lülsdorf–Wesseling ferry, you will rejoin the described route at this point.]

Under Kennedy bridge, continue along Brassertufer

[KM 654]; [KM 653]

Continue along Stresemannufer, past Bundeshaus (federal parliament building)

Continue alongside Rhine, river on your LHS

[KM 652]

Under motor bridge (562) (Konrad-Adenauer-Brücke)

Continue along von Sandtufer, alongside river

[KM 651]; [KM 650]; [KM 649]

Pass ferry, Bad Godesberg–Königswinter

[KM 648]

Continue along Rheinufer, alongside river

Info

[KM 647]

Continue along John-J-McCloy-Ufer, alongside Rhine, river on your LHS

[KM 646]; [KM 645]

(Mehlem on RHS)

[KM 644]

[Across river are Drachenfels and Drachenburg castles; the mountains are the Siebengebirge.]

[KM 643]

(Across river is Bad Honnef.)

X continue towards Koblenz (bicycle sign)

T-L along Bonner Strasse (B9 roadway)

Continue along bike path alongside river (where road swings away to R)

[On RHS is Rolandswerth; Rhine island is Nonnenwerth.]

Pass ferry, to Nonnenwerth

Continue up very steep slope past ferry, continue along bike path alongside Rhine

Continue along bike path below embankment alongside Rhine, river on your LHS

Pass ferry, Rolandseck–Bad Honnef

[KM 640]

R away from river, (20 m) L, (20 m) R

T-L along bike path on roadway, past harbor and boatyard

Exit Rolandseck, enter Oberwinter

Continue along bike path through Oberwinter

L away from roadway, down dike, to bike path alongside river

[Across river is Unkel]

[KM 637]

Continue along LHS of roadway

R towards bridge

Immed. L under bridge, along asphalt bike path

Continue along Am Unkelstein

Continue under canopy of bridge, Rhine on your LHS

Cross small bridge, continue along brick-paved bike path alongside river, rail line on your RHS

[KM 636]; [KM 635]

Enter Remagen

[KM 634]

(100 m) Info, bike map on RHS

Continue along bike path alongside river

[KM 633]

(Remagen Peace Bridge and museum)

[KM 632]; [KM 631]; [KM 630]

Ferry, Kripp–Linz am Rhein (DM 1.50)

Cross Rhine on ferry

L-R through subway

Enter the town square through the old town gate

* Pedestrian area

Bear L through the square, past the dolphin fountain and Burg Linz

Bear L and pass under archway

T-R along roadway

L through subway under rail line

Immed. R through parking area

Continue along road, Info board at station

Linz am Rhein Bahnhof; end of route.

Diversion Route 10B: The Ahr Valley to Altenahr

Distance:	39 km/24 miles (excludes train journey; equivalent by road is 25 km/16 miles)	Map/s:	Kompass Wanderkarte Bonn – Ahrtal (No. 820); 1:50,000 (2 cm = 1 km)
Terrain:	Flat to Bad Bodendorf (take the train to Altenahr); mostly down-hill or flat on the return journey; along paved roads and bike paths, some compacted dirt roads		ADFC Radtourenkarte Rheinland – Eifel (No. 15); 1:150,000 (1 cm = 1.5 km)

Description:

The Ahr river valley is considered to be one of the most beautiful of the Rhine tributary valleys. The source of the Ahr is near Blankenheim in the Eifel mountains and the river winds down the 89 kilometers (56 miles) to its confluence at Kripp, descending nearly 400 meters (1,300 feet).

The fertile mouth of the Ahr was settled by the Celts and later fortified by the Romans. The Romans introduced the wine culture here from about AD 260. This is supposedly the northernmost red-wine-producing area in Germany, though red wine is also produced at Radebeuel in the State of Saxony.

The red wines produced here are generally late Burgundies (Spätburgunder). The features which allow the successful growing of vines are the steeply sloping mostly south-facing slate cliffs, which incline at the same angle as the sun's rays at that latitude, and the high shale content of the soil. This maximizes the warming effect of the sun as the rays are direct during the growing season, as well as storing the heat in the shale itself.

From Altenahr, a procession of wine-producing towns, villages and hamlets follow down the valley towards the Rhine; Reimerzhoven, Laach, Mayschoss, Rech, Dernau, Marienthal, and Walporzheim lead to the lovely town of Ahrweiler, now coupled with the spa town of Bad Neuenahr.

Altenahr is well worth exploring. At every turn you'll find some unexpected, quaint and sometimes even breath-taking sight. Perhaps a market, a festival, a marching brass band or an old-fashioned wedding coach pulled by magnificent horses. In winter too, it's a veritable fairyland.

Along the road to the Rhine, the valley is lined with vineyards, with castle ruins topping the heights above. There is a marked walking trail — the Red Wine Route — from Lohrsdorf (east of Bad Neuenahr) to Altenahr, a distance of about 32 kilometers (20 miles). From Altenahr there are any number of walking trails into the Eifel, as well as cycling routes.

The train branch line travels up the Ahr valley as far as Dümpelfeld, about 12 kilometers past Altenahr.

Walporzheim hosts the provincial school of viticulture and fruit growing.

Ahrweiler is the main center of the red wine trade. Bad Neuenahr boasts the only alkaline hot springs in Germany. The ruins of Burg Neuenahr, with a look-out tower [viewpoint] are on the 340 meter Neuenahrer Berg.

Sinzig is near the confluence of the Rhine and Ahr rivers. Originally a Celtic settlement, it later became the Roman Sentiacum. It is connected with the Frankish and the later Imperial palatinate. It was the Imperial residence of Pepin, Heinrich III and Frederick Barbarossa.

The St. Peter church (Im Zehnthof) built 1220–50 is an important link in the development of late Romanesque churches on the Rhine. The seemingly small building is surprisingly extensive inside, with lavish interior painting.

The Heimatsmuseum is in the nineteenth century neo-gothic schloss (castle). It displays fifteenth to nineteenth century sculpture, seventeenth to nineteenth century paintings, and historic finds amongst others.

Note:
During the main tourist season, the valley roads and towns can get very crowded, especially on weekends and on holidays. There may be many tourist buses (coaches) on the roads. Where there is no bike path, use sidewalks between towns freely, but give way to walkers.

Directions:

Start at Linz am Rhein Bahnhof (train station). With the station building on your LHS, cycle towards the parking area ahead, with the rail line on your LHS. Through the parking area, L through subway under rail line

Immed. R along road

L before rail bridge underpass

Bear L and pass under archway into the pedestrian area

Bear R through the square, past the dolphin fountain and Burg Linz

Exit the square through the old town gate

Continue through subway

R to ferry (Linz–Kripp)

Cross Rhine on ferry

Up ramp, L across road and continue along bike path alongside Rhine towards Koblenz (bicycle sign), river on your LHS

Cross Ahr river on covered wooden bridge

[KM 629]

R towards Bad Bodendorf (large bicycle sign), along asphalt road

Y-R towards Ahr river (L to Sinzig)

Under freeway (B9) and railway bridge

Road swings away from river to top of dike, then R parallel with Ahr

Y-R along top of dike, along hard sand bike path

X continue (bridge across river on RHS)

Continue along dike-top asphalt bike path, river on your RHS

Under motor bridge

Cross drain, pass playground (on your LHS)

R across bridge

Immed. L alongside Ahr river, river on your LHS

Pass aviary and animal park, picnic area, on your RHS, river LHS

X continue (bridge on LHS, tennis courts RHS)

X (at road bridge) R away from river along road

Road swings R

L along Bader Strasse

X (lights) continue along Bahnhofstrasse

Cross rail line

Immed. L to Bad Bodendorf Bahnhof (train station)

[From here, take the train to Altenahr. Bicycle ticket not required. The train time-table is easily interpreted and against the name and time of your train you will see a bicycle symbol with either an "h" or a "v" alongside; "h" (hinter) means the bicycle carriage is at the end of the train; "v" (vor) indicates the bike carriage will be at the front of the train, immediately behind the driver's cab. The platform is low, so expect to lift your bike up into the carriage — and down again at Altenahr. Trains run on the right-hand side track as a general rule.

At Bad Bodendorf you board from the center platform onto a train on the RHS track as you look towards the mountains up the valley. At Altenahr you disembark on the opposite side. If necessary, ask somebody on the train to help you with your bike; a smile works wonders. At the time of writing (1999), the train leaves Bad Bodendorf at 13 minutes past every hour and an adult one-way ticket costs DM 7.30 (less than US $4)]

* Note: Bicycle signs here are generally red background with white lettering.

Off train at Altenahr Bahnhof (train station)

Through parking area towards road bridge

Info, far side of parking area, near exit

R across bridge (note: town to L)

R along road (B 267) towards Sinzig (27 km)

Through tunnel

Exit Altenahr along road (B267)

Under bridge, river Ahr on RHS, sidewalk either side

Info, on RHS in parking area

Through Reimerzhoven, along roadway

Through Laach

Through Mayschoss

Enter Rech along Rotweinstrasse

Info, in parking area

Exit Rech

Through Dernau

Exit Dernau along bike path, rail line on RHS, road LHS

Cross river along bike path, rail line on RHS

Marienthal on LHS

Cross river along bike path, rail line on RHS

Continue along asphalt bike path alongside road

(About 10 m) R (bicycle sign painted on bike path)

Immed. L across bridge alongside rail line, across river Ahr

Continue alongside rail line, cross river

Continue along bike path alongside roadway

(About 220 m) U-turn R towards Ehlingen (bicycle sign)

Immed. under rail line through subway

(About 10 m) L at bicycle sign

Enter Ahrweiler

Swing hard L along road (Ahruferstrasse)

X continue along bike path (bicycle sign) (bridge on RHS)

X continue along Herrestorfstrasse between allotments (bridge on RHS)

X continue (bridge on RHS)

X cross road and L along bike path on RHS of road

(About 50 m) opp. Ahrtor (on your LHS) R along alley, cemetery on your LHS

L alongside Ahr river, river on your RHS

X continue

Under bridge

Through subway

X continue, bridge on RHS

Y-L

L across bridge

Immed. R along bike path

X continue, bridge on RHS

X continue, bridge on RHS

X continue, bridge on RHS

X continue, pedestrian bridge on RHS

Under freeway (B266) bridge

Under freeway (E31-A61) bridge

T-R across motor bridge along bike path

Immed. L along asphalt bike path, river on your LHS

Enter Heimersheim

Under pedestrian bridge

Under motor bridge

X continue along hard sand bike path towards Ehlingen (bicycle sign) alongside river (Lohrsdorf L across bridge)

Cross small bridge and L

Continue along asphalt road

Y-L along compacted dirt road, river on LHS (or, alternatively, R along asphalt road)

L under bridge

T-L across bridge over river Ahr

[At this point you join your incoming route, retracing your tracks to Linz]

Immed. R along asphalt bike path, river on your RHS

Pass aviary, on your LHS

R across bridge (end of road)

Immed. L

Y-L alongside river

Under motor bridge

Y-L

Under freeway (B9) and railway bridge

T-L

T (at Rhine) L along bike path

[KM 629]

Cross Ahr river on covered wooden bridge

R to ferry (Linz–Kripp)

Cross Rhine on ferry

L through subway

Enter the town square through the old town gate

* Pedestrian area

Bear L through the square

Bear L and pass under archway

T-R along roadway

L through subway under rail line

Immed. R through parking area

Ends at Linz am Rhein Bahnhof

Route 11: Linz am Rhein to Koblenz via Bad Breisig and Andernach

Distance: 51 km/32 miles

Terrain: Flat, alongside the Rhine; paved roads and bike paths

Maps: ADAC Koblenz Stadtplan; 1: 20,000 (1 cm = 200 m)

Kompass Wanderkarte Der Rhein: Köln – Mainz (No. 829); 1:50,000 (2 cm = 1 km)

ADFC Radtourenkarte Rheinland – Eifel (No. 15); 1:150,000 (1 cm = 1.5 km)

Diversions: See suggestions at the end of this section

Description:

Continuing through the middle Rhine gorge and the Rhenish uplands, cross the Rhine from Linz to the west bank of the river and turn southwards. Cycle alongside the river to Bad Breisig.

[KM 624] Bad Breisig has an old customs house, a Baroque church and an even older church with medieval frescoes. It was a Roman settlement, Brisiacum, popular for its mineral springs. There is a sixteenth century hall of the Knights of St John.

[KM 624] Bad Hönningen: Arenfels castle with its thirteenth century foundations was rebuilt in the nineteenth century. Called the "castle with uncountable windows" it has an estimated 365 windows. It's possible to visit the park.

[KM 622] The Limes come down to the Rhine opposite Rheineck castle. The Limes is the Roman earth rampart and series of blockhouses and strong-points from the Rhine to the Danube, constructed to keep Germanic tribes out of Roman territory.

[KM 622] There is a chairlift to Rheineck castle. Built about 1080 and rebuilt in 1832, the castle is open to the public [viewpoint].

[KM 620] Brohl-Lützing is opposite Rheinbrohl. Nearby is Brohleck castle. The harbor is a loading point for stone such as tuffa. Here you can turn west to Maria Laach and the Laacher See (lake) past Schweppenburg castle. It's a stiff ride of about 12 kilometers (7.5 miles) along a scenic and popular route.

Across the river are the ruins of Hammerstein castle.

[KM 617] Hammerstein, a former Imperial stronghold, dates back to the tenth century. The castle, said to have been built by Charles Martel, was destroyed in the seventeenth century and the ruins can be visited.

[KM 616] Timber rafts were assembled at Namedy for floating down to the Netherlands. Voyage took from seven days to six weeks. Trees felled along the Neckar and Main rivers were bundled at the rivers' confluences with the Rhine and added to as they floated downstream, especially at the mouth of the Mosel.

Rafts were of extraordinary size; they could be over 300 meters (1,000 feet) long and 30 to 60 meters (100–200 feet) wide. There might be up to eight hundred oarsmen who lived on the rafts in wooden huts, sometimes with their families. Often there were upwards of one thousand people on a raft. There were butchers to deal with the live cattle on board. A typical store of food would include 22,000 kilograms (50,000 pounds) of bread, 440 kilograms (1,000 pounds) of smoked beef, 5,400 kilograms (12,000 pounds) of cheese, fifty sacks of vegetables, five hundred barrels of beer and eight barrels of wine.

This occurred regularly from the sixteenth to the nineteenth centuries. In 1900 more than three hundred rafts supplied the Ruhr mines with pit props.

[KM 615] Leutesdorf, on the east bank of the Rhine, has picturesque buildings and a pilgrimage church. Wine has supposedly been produced here continuously for more than fifteen hundred years.

[KM 613] Andernach, originally a Celtic settlement, was later a Roman fort called Autunnacum. In 12 BC Drusus built a fortified citadel where the Rhine crossed the Eifel road; it still serves as a good access point to the Eifel region. It was an important trad-

ing post, especially during the middle ages. In the old quarter, medieval towers and walls can be seen.

The local black basalt volcanic rocks were quarried to provide building materials for the dikes of the Netherlands.

The Schuldturm (debtors' tower) dates from before 1340. The Round tower (1448–52), which is octagonal at the top, is 56 meters (184 feet) high, has a diameter of 15 meters (49 feet) with walls 5 meters (16 feet) thick. It withstood all attempts by the French to blow it apart in 1689 and is now used as a youth hostel.

The reason given for the carvings on the town gates is that they determined the credentials of craftsmen who said they'd served their apprenticeships there. They were asked to describe the city gate by prospective employers. The Rhine Gate has carved romanesque figures.

Ehrenbreitstein and fortress, across the Rhine from Koblenz, Germany.

The late gothic Rathaus (Town Hall), dating from (1572, is on the Markt (market). There is a town museum (Stadtmuseum, Hochstrasse 97).

During a siege a nun was seized, stripped, covered in honey and feathers and paraded through the streets. The commander of the troops had those guilty of the deed dropped into a cauldron of boiling water; then proceeded to burn the town, the church, and the convent.

[KM 608] Weissenthurm is at the confluence of the Rhine and Nette rivers and opposite Neuwied. There is a monument to General Hoch of the French Revolutionary Army who commanded the occupying troops and who was well-liked and respected. This is a fruit producing area.

[KM 608] Neuwied is at the confluence of the Rhine and Wied rivers. The present town replaced the former village of Langendorf which was completely destroyed during the Thirty Years' War. Count Friedrich III of Wied planned his Schloss (castle) and the town together. Building plots were given to those who agreed to build houses to a prescribed plan, for architectural unity. The 1648 Schloss was destroyed by the French in 1689 and rebuilt 1706–56.

Further inland (due north upriver near Altwied across the Limes) is Mon Repos, the country residence of the Counts of Wied. Ruins of the castle of the Counts of Wied are nearby on a peninsula. The principality was ended by the French in 1806 and given to Nassau, but restored at the Congress of Vienna (1815). Princess Elizabeth of Neuwied, wife of King Carol I of Romania, lived at Mon Repos as a child. She wrote under the pen-name of Carmen Sylva and was a friend of Sarah Bernhardt, Queen Victoria, and Tennyson.

After the Thirty Years' War, Neuwied provided refuge for dissenting sects, particularly the Moravian Brethren. George Meredith, the English poet and novelist, attended the Moravian school 1843–44.

The Kreismuseum (Raiffeisenplatz 1a) has prehistoric and early Frankish grave artefacts.

[KM 591] Koblenz is at the confluence of the Rhine and Mosel rivers. It was originally a Roman camp, established under Tiberius AD 14–37, named Castrum ad Confluentes (castle at the confluence), from which Koblenz' name is derived. A Roman trading town quickly developed but was destroyed during the barbarian invasions. Roman remains are found in the presbytery of the Liebfrauenkirche and below the choir at St. Florin church. Later the Franks took over the settlement.

On the site now occupied by the Church of St. Castor, the Treaty of Verdun was agreed. This 843 AD treaty divided up the Holy Roman Empire amongst Charlemagne's three grandsons. It was drafted in French and German because the eastern and western Franks could no longer understand each other's languages. Charles the Bald inherited France (the west), Ludwig the German, Germany (the east) and Emperor Lothar I, the rest.

Deutscher Eck (German corner) was so named because the order of Teutonic Knights (Deutschordenskommende) was supposedly established here in 1216. The Eck is the spit of land formed by the confluence of the Rhine and Mosel rivers. The spit is called the Hundschwanz (dog's tail), being at the end of the range of hills called the Hunsrück (dog's back).

An equestrian statue of Kaiser Wilhelm I of Prussia was raised here, with a hundred steps to the pedestal and observation platform [viewpoint]. The statue is 14 meters (45 feet) high and the platform 40 meters (130 feet). During World War II the complex was badly damaged. The statue was shot down and it disappeared into storage. A legend came about after the partition of Germany that when the country was re-united the statue would reappear here, which it did. The Renaissance building of the Komturswohnung with a floral courtyard behind was rebuilt in its old form. It is now a monument to a united Germany. The inscription by Max von Schenkendorf reads, "Nimmer wird das Reich zerstöret wenn ihr einig seid und treu" (Never will the Empire be destroyed if you remain united and obedient).

Balduin, Archbishop of Trier, had local basalt quarried for the Mosel bridge now known as the Balduin bridge. It had fourteen arches and is 308 meters (1,000 feet) long. It was built 1332–38 and withstood the 1830 floods. Some of the arches were removed to regulate the flow of the Mosel.

At the city end of the Balduin bridge is the thirteenth century Old Castle. It was built on the site of a Roman fort in 1276–89 and later extended as the Elector's castle. It has a sandstone spiral staircase and is now the City Library.

Behind the old castle is the twelfth century Romanesque church, the Liebfraukirche (Am Plan), with ornate spires. It was built on Roman and Carolingian foundations from 1180 and completed in the early thirteenth century. It has been the principal parish church of Koblenz since the Middle Ages. Later additions were in Gothic and Baroque styles.

The baroque city hall, formerly a Jesuit college has a courtyard with a "Schlängel" fountain topped by a gamin (street urchin) spouting water.

Koblenz prospered in the twelfth to fourteenth centuries when its great religious buildings were constructed. This remains its most striking feature.

The palace with a pink and yellow façade (Clementsplatz), a neo-classical building completed in 1791, was erected for the last Elector, Clemens Wenzeslaus.

Ehrenbreitstein is the second largest fortress in Europe after Gibraltar. It is situated on a bluff 150 meters (500 feet) above the river and was owned by the Archbishops of Trier for over eight hundred years. The first fortifications were built in the eleventh century, the bastions started in the sixteenth century and extended in the seventeenth and eighteenth centuries. The forts and batteries were added in the style of Baroque buildings. The fortress church is a gigantic barrack-like building, with galleries and barrel vaulting.

Ehrenbreitstein was never taken by force but the garrison was sometimes starved out. The fortress held out against Louis XIV (1688) but was taken by the French in 1799. It was blown up in 1801. During the siege by Louis XIV, the Germans noticed that some of their shells weren't exploding and it was found that a master gunner was sending information in empty shells to the French. The gunner's head was sent to the French in an empty shell.

After the Congress of Vienna (1815) Ehrenbreitstein was given to Prussia and rebuilt over ten years. Nowadays it is used as a museum of prehistory and ethnography and a youth hostel (the largest one in Germany). There is a chair lift from Pfaffendorf at the end of the new Rhine road bridge [viewpoint]. After World War II the fortress was not destroyed as were all German military installations because its size made it unique.

The floods of 1784 caused by the sudden break up of the ice dams were disastrous at Koblenz. In 1830 ice from the Mosel blocked the Rhine and the artillery was called in to break up the ice dam. The floods reached back up the Mosel to the village of Lay, 9 kilometers (5.5 miles) from Koblenz, where the entire village was crushed under the weight of the ice.

Karl Baedeker who was born in Essen, began his guide book business here in 1827. His first guide book was about the Rhine.

During summer, operettas are staged on a floating platform off the promenade. The "Rhine in Flames" is a spectacle with illuminations and fireworks that is staged a few times a year.

Directions:

Start at Linz am Rhein Bahnhof (train station). With the station building on your LHS, cycle towards the parking area ahead, with the rail line on your LHS.

Through the parking area, L through subway under rail line

Immed. R along road

L before rail bridge underpass

Bear L and pass under archway

* Pedestrian Area

Bear R through the square, past the dolphin fountain and Burg Linz

Exit the square through the old town gate

Continue through subway

R to ferry (Linz–Kripp)

Cross Rhine on ferry

Up ramp, L across road and continue along bike path alongside Rhine towards Koblenz (bicycle sign), river on your LHS

Cross Ahr river on covered wooden bridge

[KM 629]; [KM 628]

Continue through parking area/slipway

Info, on LHS

(Leubsdorf across river)

[KM 627]; [KM 626]

Continue along bike path alongside river, river on your LHS

[KM 625] Ahrenfels castle across river

[KM 624] Enter Bad Breisig

Continue along waterfront

Info

[KM 623]

Pass ferry, Bad Breisig–Bad Hönningen

Info at ferry

Continue along bike path alongside Rhine

R away from river, through subway, under road (B9), under railway

Immed L along road, rail line on your LHS

[The alternative route on the B9 freeway, along the contra-flow hard shoulder is not recommended; it is a tense 8 km and you will have to be constantly on your guard, so won't be able to enjoy the scenery.]

Exit Bad Breisig

Enter Brohl-Lützing

T-R-L

R immed. before rail line

T-R (continue) along road

L under rail line, where road swings hard R away from rail line

Immed. R along bike path between rail line and freeway (B9)

Down ramp, R under rail line

Immed. L along asphalt bike path, away from rail line, into countryside

Pass Namedy Schloss, on your RHS

Enter Namedy along Hauptstrasse (bicycle signs)

X continue along Hauptstrasse

X continue along Hauptstrasse on bike path on LHS of road

Bike path ends, continue along roadway

Continue under canopy of freeway bridge

[Across Rhine is Leutesdorf]

[KM 614]

Down ramp, R, swing L, through subway under train line

L towards Koblenz (bicycle sign)

Enter Andernach

X, cross road, down ramp towards Rhine, past old crane (bicycle signs)

R along Rhine bike path, river on your LHS

[Ignore bicycle signs pointing R]

Continue alongside river, as close as possible

Info

[KM 613]

Through gate in old town wall

R away from river at harbor

T-L along bike path on LHS of road

X continue

Cross rail line, continue along Koblenzer Strasse

X (lights) continue along bike path on LHS of road

Pass cemetery

Immed. L along bike path on LHS of road

T cross rail lines then R along bike path on RHS of road

Swing L at end of road

Cross rail line, continue towards Rhine

T-R along bike path, river on your LHS

Down bank, continue alongside Rhine

[KM 610]; [KM 609]

Weissenthurm on RHS, Neuwied across river

[KM 608]

Under freeway (B42) bridge

[KM 607]

Continue along roadway alongside Rhine

Continue along bike path alongside river

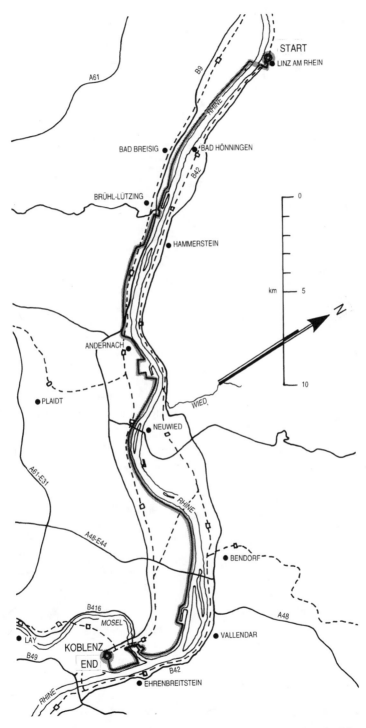

START
LINZ AM RHEIN

A61

B9

RHINE

BAD BREISIG
BAD HÖNNINGEN

B42

BRÜHL-LÜTZING

HAMMERSTEIN

0

km   5

N

ANDERNACH

PLAIDT

WIED

10

NEUWIED

RHINE

A61-E31

A48-E44

BENDORF

B416

MOSEL

A48

LAY

VALLENDAR

KOBLENZ
END

B49

B42

RHINE

EHRENBREITSTEIN

[KM 606]; [KM 605]; [KM 604]; [KM 603]

Urmitz on RHS

Under rail bridge

[KM 602]

Engers across river

Enter Kaltenengers, continue along Obermark to end

L to bike path, continue alongside river

[KM 599]

St Sebastian on RHS, Bendorf across river

Under freeway (E44-A48) bridge

[KM 598]; [KM 597]

Bear R away from river, past harbor

T-L

X-L along Carl-Spaeter-Strasse, on bike path on RHS of road

Continue along Hans-Böckler-Strasse

Cross rail line

Immed. L along Fritz-Ludwig-Strasse (bicycle sign "Zentrum")

Cross rail line

Continue towards Rhine

R along bike path alongside river (bicycle sign "Zentrum")

[KM 595]

Wallersheim on RHS

[KM 594]; [KM 593]; [KM 592]

L along Schartweiserweg

Road swings R

T-L along Neuendorfer Strasse towards "Zentrum"

T-R along Strasburger Strasse

T-L along Brender Weg

X (lights) continue along bike path on RHS of Brender Weg

Cross Mosel river bridge on bike path on RHS, enter Koblenz

Down off-ramp, U-turn R to bottom, continue towards Mosel river

X cross road, immed. R, under bridge

Continue along Peter-Altmeier-Strasse

Pass Deutscher Eck monument, on your LHS

Continue to Rhine

R alongside Rhine, river on your LHS

[KM 592]

Continue along promenade

Down ramp to riverside bike path

Past Schloss

[KM 591] under freeway (B9) bridge

[KM 590,1] ferry, R towards Koblenz Hauptbahnhof along Jan-Zick-Strasse and Markenbildchenweg

Route ends at Hauptbahnhof (train station)

Diversion Suggestions:

1. Around Koblenz: Koblenz is not a large city and is easy to get around. It's very bicycle-friendly and there are a disproportionate number of interesting places to visit. The markets along the Mosel near Deutscher Eck, as well as the other seasonal activities are fascinating.

2. Mosel–Rhens–Koblenz: There is a bicycle route which cuts across the Rhine–Mosel divide from Rhens.

It's a pretty tough climb at times and the entire circuit is about 40 kilometers (25 miles) long. It's possible to do the circuit in either direction. You could also take the train to or from Rhens and spend some time in this lovely old walled town.

3. Along the Lahn (+ train/boat): The Lahn is a pretty river with interesting towns en route, and you can cycle up or down the valley quite easily. You could take the train as far along as you please and cycle back to Koblenz — or travel up by boat and back by train. Or do parts by bike, others by boat or train. There are endless options. Some sections of the road can get very busy during the height of the season.

Route 12: Koblenz to Bacharach via Boppard and St. Goar

Distance: 55 km / 34 miles

Terrain: Flat; alongside river, mostly paved bike paths and roads (about 2 km hard sand), narrow bike path sections for short distances alongside busy roadway, near Loreley

Maps: ADAC Koblenz Stadtplan; 1: 20,000 (1 cm = 200 m)

               Kompass Wanderkarte Der Rhein Köln – Mainz (No. 829); 1:50,000 (2 cm = 1 km)

               ADFC Radtourenkarte Rheinland – Eifel (No. 15); 1:150,000 (1 cm = 1.5 km)

Diversions: See suggestions at the end of this section

Description:

The Rhine Gorge from Koblenz to Bingen is 65 kilometers (40 miles) long. From Koblenz to Mainz there are no bridges across the Rhine.

From Koblenz cycle south alongside the west bank of the Rhine. Across the river from Stolzenfels is the town of Lahnstein.

[KM 586] Lahnstein is at the confluence of the Rhine and Lahn rivers and was formed by joining Oberlahnstein (town charter 1324) and Niederlahnstein (1332). Niederlahnstein was a fourth century Roman "burgus" (town).

One of the earliest tolls on the Rhine belonged to the Archbishop of Mainz. The round tower with a pentagonal top at Niederlahnstein was incorporated into the Martinsburg which was designed as a moated castle in 1244. The building is mainly fourteenth to fifteenth and eighteenth century. There is a five storey tower at the south corner and a chapel in the north wing, as well as a fourteenth century residential tower.

Castle Lahneck at the mouth of the river Lahn was built in the thirteenth century to protect shipments of silver from the mine belonging to Mainz. The Knights Templars were excommunicated by Pope Clement V in 1313 and were expelled from France. Twelve Templars forced entry to Lahneck castle seizing it from the Archbishop of Mainz. The Archbishop's army besieged the castle and when an assault was mounted, the Templars came out fighting. When only one old knight remained standing, a messenger arrived with a pardon for the Templars from the Pope and the Archbishop, guaranteed by the Emperor. Earlier offers from the church alone had been rejected. The old knight then fought his way to the leader of the besiegers, grappled with him and wrestled them both over the cliff to their deaths.

The Electors met here during the visit of Edward III (of England) to offer him the Imperial crown (1338) and again in 1400 to depose the Emperor Wenceslas IV (of Bohemia), brother- in-law of Richard II (of England). Wenceslas was declared to be "useless, idle and thoroughly inept..." The following day a meeting across the river at Rhens elected Ruprecht of the Palatinate as the new Emperor.

In 1633 the Swedes and Imperial troops damaged the castle and in 1688 it was destroyed by the French. From 1850 to 1860 the castle was owned by a

Briton called Moriarty who restored the castle in the English Gothic Revival style. Restoration was completed in 1871 by subsequent German owners. A description of the building was written by the American Bailey Willis who spent time there as a boy (1871). In 1871 Friedrich III and his wife Victoria, daughter of Queen Victoria (of Britain) visited the castle and presented a portrait (Winterhalter 1840) of Queen Victoria.

In 1852 Miss Idilia Dubb of Edinburgh climbed one of the Lahneck towers. After she reached a viewing platform the staircase collapsed behind her. She wrote a diary of her last four days before she died of exposure. Her remains and the diary were found during renovations in 1863.

Formerly, fish from certain waters had first to be offered to the customs clerk and the castle cellarer at fixed prices. Salmon and lamprey were given free to the lord of the castle. The fishermen of Niederlahnstein were not permitted to fish the Oberlahnstein side of the stream. When the river was frozen both sides could be fished by chopping fish from the ice. One quarter of the fish removed from the ice on the Oberlahnstein side was given to the customs clerk.

[KM 585] Stolzenfels castle was built opposite the Lahn mouth in 1242 by Arnold, Archbishop of Trier to control the Lahn–Rhine traffic. It was destroyed by the French in 1688. In 1836 it was rebuilt in neo-Gothic style for Friedrich Wilhelm IV of Prussia. There is a museum in the castle.

A fourteenth century legend says that Stolzenfels conceals a hoard of gold, made in an alchemist's laboratory. Leonardo, an Italian adventurer, persuaded the castle keeper and toll collector, Frundsberg, that he was about to discover the philosopher's stone, but that the process would be expensive. When Frundsberg ran out of money he falsified the accounts and when the Archbishop Elector of Mainz announced his intention to collect his money, Leonardo persuaded Frundsberg's daughter Gertraud to save her father by offering herself in sacrifice for the final gold-making process. The captain of the guard saved Gertraud, Leonardo fell off the cliff and Gertraud married the captain.

[KM 582] The lovely medieval walled city of Rhens is mentioned in 874. Most of its medieval fortifications including town gates and some half timbered late Gothic houses have survived (Markt 7–9 and Hochstrasse 20). It has a beautifully kept medieval town hall dated about 1560 and a medieval Deutschherrenhaus (house of Knights of the Teutonic Order).

The Königstuhl was where the Electors (four of whom had castles nearby) deliberated over their options for the position of Emperor. A modern reconstruction of the Königstuhl replaces the fourteenth century coronation stone which was broken by French revolutionary troops. The modern construction consists of seven pillars and arches supporting an octagonal platform.

[KM 581] Braubach opposite Rhens is a wine town. In the Middle Ages silver and lead were mined nearby. Marksburg castle [viewpoint] was built to protect the mines.

Marksburg castle stands 170 meters (560 feet) above the Rhine. It was considered impregnable and never stormed or captured and is the only Burg on the Rhine still intact. The first owner in 1135 was Count von Gröningen. The counts of Eppstein took over and the castle passed to the counts of Katzenelnbogen in 1283 through marriage. The Katzenelnbogens held the castle for two hundred years when it passed on to the Landgraves of Hesse. The castle was damaged by fire in 1705 and it withstood two earthquakes in 1780. In the eighteenth century prisoners of state were interned here. In 1803 the castle was acquired by the house of Nassau and in 1866 Nassau was absorbed by Prussia. Nassau used the building to house disabled soldiers and the Prussians used it as common housing. In 1900 Marksburg castle was acquired by the association for the preservation of German castles.

In 1437 the chapel of St. Mark the Evangelist, from which the castle gets its name, was built. There is a Gothic Knights' hall (Rittersaal). The library of books and archives on medieval castles is the biggest in Europe.

The most important part of the castle is the Gothic residence in the inner bailey and the Kaiser Heinrich tower. There are three twelfth to fourteenth century wings around a triangular courtyard in which is a thirteenth century keep. The ring walls

Old half-timbered house in Rhens, Germany.

date from the thirteenth century and other walls from the fifteenth to seventeenth centuries, as do the battlements, round towers, and bastions.

[KM 574] Osterspai is the halfway point of the navigable length of the Rhine.

[KM 571] Boppard was a Roman citadel, Bodobriga, built by Drusus in 20 BC. Gedeonseck [Viewpoint] is reached by a chairlift. The castle built by Archbishop Balduin of Trier is now a museum, the Städtisches Heimatmuseum (Alte Kurfürstliche Burg). A monastery was founded here by St. Bernard of Siena. The ferryman refused to carry him free across the river, so Bernard threw his cloak on the water and sailed across in that. The building was destroyed by the Swedes during the Thirty Years' War.

In the tenth century relics of St. Severus were brought from Trier. The St. Severus church is a Romanesque building of the early twelfth century. The towers were incorporated into the new buildings about 1200 and the church dedicated in 1225. Immediately new extensions were begun, the nave was raised and in 1236 the apse was extended. The spires were added in 1605.

The Wald- und Holzmuseum/ Thonetmuseum (Burgstrasse) has displays of woodwork and forestry. There is a butterfly collection.

Cross over the Rhine on the Boppard–Filsen ferry and continue southwards alongside the east bank of the river to Kamp-Bornhofen.

[KM 568] At Kamp-Bornhofen there is a Franciscan monastery and a 1224 pilgrimage church. In the 1594 Von der Leynsche Hof is the museum of rafts and navigation. Nearby are remains of the thirteenth century twin castles called the "Hostile Brothers,"

Sternberg (also Sterrenberg) and Liebenstein. The story tells of two brothers who cheated their blind sister of her inheritance. The brothers had decided to go hunting, so Sternberg shot a bolt at the shuttered window of Liebenstein to wake him up. Liebenstein opened his window at that moment and was killed. Sterrenberg went on a crusade in atonement and the blind sister, who had founded a convent at Bornhofen, inherited the estates and used the money to complete the convent buildings.

[KM 566] Bad Salzig on the west bank of the Rhine is a spa town. Behind the town, to the west, the cliffs of the heights of Fleckert mark the abrupt end of the middle Rhine uplands. Tugs split their barge loads here due to the strong currents up to Bingen.

[KM 559] Thurnberg (Deuernburg) castle at Wellmich was built by an Archbishop of Trier to rival Katz castle near St. Goarshausen. The Count of Katzenellenbogen abusively called it castle Maus (mouse). The castle ruins are not open to the public.

[KM 556] St. Goarshausen is a wine center. Nearby is Katz castle (Neu-Katzenelnbogen) built in 1393. A salvo shot at French troops from here made Napoleon's horse shy, so the castle was blown up by his troops in 1804. The castle has since been restored. It is in private ownership and permission can be had to visit it.

In the river opposite Katz castle was a whirlpool off the shoal known as the "Bank." According to Victor Hugo, pilots of log rafts had a tree trunk (a "dog") attached by a rope to their raft thrown into the whirlpool. This caused the raft to be swung away into midstream, the rope was cut and the raft continued down river, while the "dog" was sacrificed to the whirlpool. Before passing the Bank, a three bell signal would call raftsmen to prayers. The Bank dropped 4 feet in 150 yards, creating a fast passage for rafts at a steep angle and for some time afterwards the angle was maintained so that the forward raftsmen were up to their waists in water.

Cross the Rhine on the St. Goarshausen–St Goar ferry.

[KM 556] St. Goar has a harbor where goods are trans-shipped to shallow draft vessels because of the up-river shoals and shallows.

The hermit St. Goar came here about AD 611; he was either Irish or from Aquitaine. Some historians doubt the existence of St. Goar and say the name comes from a corruption of "sand gewer," the dangerous swirl by the sandbank at the upper edge of the town, but there is an early medieval biography of the man. It's believed that Goar made a study of the river and worked as a pilot. Bishop Rusticus of Trier tested Goar by challenging him to name the parents of a three-day old abandoned child. Goar named a local woman, Flavia, and the bishop himself (a monk Wandalbert says the child spoke the names) and the Bishop was removed by King Sigburt, who offered the Bishopric to Goar, but he refused it.

Rheinfels castle at St. Goar is almost as big as Ehrenbreitstein (Koblenz) [viewpoint] and was built on the site of a monastery by Count Dieter III von Katzenelnbogen in 1245 to collect tolls from the river traffic. In 1255 twenty-six members of the League of Rhine Towns raised a force of eight thousand foot soldiers, one thousand horsemen and fifty armed barges to besiege the stronghold. In sixty-six weeks they made forty assaults but the castle held out and the League withdrew.

The castle was reconstructed in 1568 by Philip, Landgrave of Hesse, and withstood Louis XIV (who lost four thousand men in two weeks) but in 1758 it was taken by the Marquis de Castries who entered with a small force during a ball and disarmed the officers. The ball was allowed to continue and the French officers joined the dance. In 1797 the castle was blown up by the French Revolutionary army.

During the Thirty Years' War the Swedes left the town untouched, except when Gustavus Adolphus entered the protestant church and, seeing the damage done by the Spaniards, he banged his mailed fist on a corner of the altar and broke a piece off.

The local Hansa (Guild) had some strange customs up to a hundred years ago. On arrival strangers had a metal collar put on them and attached to a bracket on the wall of the customs house. They were then given a choice of "baptism" with water or wine. If water, they were soaked with a bucket of Rhine water and released. If wine, they were taken to the local tavern, crowned with a tin crown and given a large jug of Rhine wine to empty. Then they were told of their "privileges,"' which included being allowed to fish from the Loreley cliff and to hunt on the mid-stream shoals. They were then required to make a donation to the poor of the community and to stand drinks all round. An Edict of the Landgrave of Hesse-Darmstadt forbade any merchant to trade at St. Goar's Fair until he had been "hansed."

In the Krone Inn is a sketch by Edward Browne (1688), personal physician of King Charles II which shows a merchant having a bucket of water inverted over his head. Browne was also "hansed."

[KM 554] The Loreley was supposedly a beautiful maiden who lured boats onto rocks below the cliff named for her.

In 1802 Clemens von Brentano first popularized the story of Lore the enchantress. Heine wrote the words for the Loreley Lied (song) and Silcher the music. Baring-Gould (British writer and collector of folklore) said that the Loreley was a deliberate invention of Heine and Brentano. The Nazis listed the poem as "author unknown" because Heine was a Jew, but the song was too popular to ban outright.

At the Loreley rock the Rhine is 90–150 meters (100–165 yards) wide. The rock itself is a slate crag 132 meters (433 feet) high and 120 meters (400 feet) across. The area at the top is flat and Hitler Youth rallies were held here. Now there is a car park and a restaurant. A railway tunnel was cut through the hill and a road blasted from the face alongside the river.

In earlier years passenger steamers would stop at the signal station opposite the Loreley cliff and toot their horns and fire guns to get the echo effect.

[KM 550] You won't fail to be impressed by your first sight, nor subsequent ones, of the medieval city of Oberwesel. It is a wine center and was once an Imperial free city. A large number of towers (between 14 and 21, depending on your sources at whichever Weinstube) on the medieval walls survive.

The Liebfrauenkirche (Collegiate church of Our Lady) dates from the early fourteenth century. It is known as the Rote Kirche (red church). The west tower is 71 meters (235 feet) high and the building has a helm roof with eight gables. There is a triptych showing fifteen catastrophes ending the world.

The 1506 Nikolausalter has a central picture depicting St. Nicholas liberating and protecting various groups of people.

The St. Martin church (auf dem Martinsberg) on a hill north of the town is from the fourteenth and fifteenth centuries. It looks like a fortress and the bright colors of the nave painted in the fifteenth century and the chancel give it the name Weisse Kirche (white church).

[KM 549] Nearby are the ruins of the twelfth century Schönburg castle. It is of huge dimensions and stands on a peak 318 meters (1,050 feet) high. The castle was mostly destroyed in 1689 but the gatehouse tower and curtain wall survive. Restoration work began in 1885. A Schönburg fell at the battle of the Boyne fighting for William III (of England) and is buried at St. Patrick's church in Dublin. The castle is now a youth hostel (Oberwesel), hotel and restaurant.

[KM 547] Kaub is one of the leading wine towns in the middle Rhine. Some of the town walls still survive, on top of which are paths to allow residents to escape floods. It connected upper floor buildings built against the wall and is called the "Notgang" (emergency path).

[KM 546] On an island, Ludwig of Bavaria built the Castle Pfalz in 1327 with a five sided keep to collect customs duties. In Gothic times it had a three storey defense wall. Pfalzgrafenstein castle (Pfalz) has walls 2.4 meters (8 feet) thick. A bastion was added in 1607 and from a picture it seems to have had interior courtyard galleries and wooden bannisters.

The tower protected Kaub during the Thirty Years' War when it was besieged by the Spaniards. After the capture of the town, the tower held out.

The Spanish offered a truce to the defenders but it wasn't accepted and further unsuccessful attacks were made on the tower. After four weeks the garrison surrendered. A goat was lowered by rope (it had lived on vegetation growing on the tower and provided milk) then the occupants emerged—an elderly retired trooper and his wife. The Spanish left them unmolested.

[KM 546] Gutenfels castle dates from the thirteenth century and is 120 meters (400 feet) above the river. It is now a youth hostel.

When Napoleon stayed at Gutenfels in 1802, he ordered that the castle be dismantled. He obviously had a bad night. Gutenfels was rebuilt during the nineteenth century into a stately complex with two long parallel wings, battlements, gatehouse, keep and wooden arbors in the courtyard.

[KM 546] Marshal Blücher and the Silesian army crossed here on 1 and 2 January 1814 to oppose Napoleon. There is a Blücher museum in his former headquarters and a statue where the river was crossed. The Germans made a big display of celebrating the New Year, when their intention was to fool the French into thinking they weren't going to move that night. Bands continued to play at Kaub while the German army crossed unopposed, catching the French unawares.

[KM 543] Bacharach was an ancient Celtic settlement. The Romans named it Baccaracum. There was a rock in the river called Bacchi Ara (altar of Bacchus) which was dynamited in 1850. When low water exposes the rock, it is said there will be a vintage year for the local wines.

Bacharach is a wine depot and local wine has some reputation. Pope Pius II had a 250 gallon cask shipped to Rome every year and Emperor Wenceslas chose four barrels of

Rhine waterside and bicycle route at the ancient walled city of Rhens, Germany.

Bacharach wine rather than the 10,000 florins offered by the city of Nürnburg to redeem their privileges.

Bacharach is surrounded by a ring wall with a covered parapet walk and a fortified gateway. In the market and along Blücherstrasse are half-timbered houses.

The 1220–69 four-storey church of St. Peter (Marktplatz) with a late Romanesque nave and a massive tower is unusual in Germany. The tower has castellations and a spire in the Gothic upper storey and looks like a castle.

The town features in more songs than any other Rhine town, some written by Heine, Ricardo Huch, and Victor Hugo.

[KM 543] Stahleck castle [Viewpoint] dates from 1135. The towers are shaped like chess pieces, bishop, pawns, rook. Old prints of the castle give the only original impression.

Blanche, daughter of Emperor Henry IV, came here in 1402. She married Ludwig of Bavaria when she was ten years old and died in childbirth at the age of seventeen. There has been a youth hostel (Bacharach) in the castle since the 1920s.

Hermann von Stahleck, nephew of Emperor Conrad III, was appointed Count Palatine. During Conrad's absence on a crusade, Hermann abused his authority and pillaged the area. He raised an army and attacked the domains of the Archbishop of Trier who defeated him. During the reign and absence of Frederick Barbarossa, Hermann attacked the Mainz territories, Worms and Speyer. At a Diet of Worms called by Frederick Barbarossa, Hermann was sentenced to the ultimate humiliation; he had to carry a dog on his back for a specified period. Hermann returned to Stahleck, gave everything he owned to his retainers and retired to the forest to live as a hermit.

Below Stahleck castle the ruined Gothic chapel of St. Werner [viewpoint] was begun 1289 and the choir consecrated in 1337. Building continued until 1426. It was built of red sandstone with a trefoil ground plan, but the windows were never glazed and the building never completed.

Directions:

Start at Koblenz Hauptbahnhof (train station). Cycle east, directly to the Rhine, along Markenbildchenweg

R at Rhine along bike path alongside river, river on your LHS

[KM 590]

Bike path swings R alongside harbor

Bike path turns hard R

T-L

Immed. U-turn L up ramp, immed. before bridge underpass

To top of bridge

U-turn L along Mozartstrasse

X (circle/roundabout) (Mozartplatz) Continue along Beethovenstrasse

X (Beethovenplatz) R along Rheinau, to end of street

Immed. L and under bridge, along hard dirt track

L through parking lot

Continue along bike path alongside river, river on your LHS

[KM 587]; [KM 586]

(Lahnstein across river)

Pass Stolzenfels castle turning (on RHS)

[KM 585]

R away from river, up steep ramp

T-L along Grunnenstrasse (cobbles), rail line on RHS

Bear R to bike path alongside rail line (at end of factory)

Continue along asphalt road between allotments

Continue along brick-paved bike path, Rhine on your LHS

Enter Rhens

Pass entrance to Rhens (St Josef gate)

[KM 582]

(Braubach across river)

[KM 581]; [KM 580]

(Marksburg castle across river)

Enter Spay

[KM 579]

bike path swings R away from river

L along Holgertsweg through harbor area

Y-L along Rheinufer

Continue along brick-paved bike path

Continue along asphalt road, through allotments

[KM 577]

Road swings R away from river, up slope, through farm, towards church

T-L along Mainzer Strasse (bicycle sign)

Exit Spay

Continue along bike path on LHS of roadway

Continue past campsites (on your LHS)

[KM 576]

Continue alongside Rhine, river on your LHS

[KM 575]; [KM 574]; [KM 573]; [KM 572]

Enter Boppard

Continue along bike path alongside road

L along bike path towards Rhine, canalized river on your RHS

R across canalized river

Continue alongside Rhine along paved bike path, Rhine on your LHS

Continue along asphalt road, on Boppard waterfront

[KM 571]

Info, on RHS, opp. ferry

Ferry, Boppard–Filsen

Cross on ferry to Filsen (DM 2.50)

Off ferry, continue to roadway

T-R along bike path on RHS of road, Rhine to your RHS

[KM 569]

Enter Kamp-Bornhofen, bike path ends

Continue along main road (B42) (or cycle alongside the river; asphalt path)

Info, in Rathaus (Town Hall) on LHS

Immed. R to waterside, L alongside Rhine, river on your RHS

[KM 568]

Continue along bike path on RHS of road, river on your RHS

[KM 567]

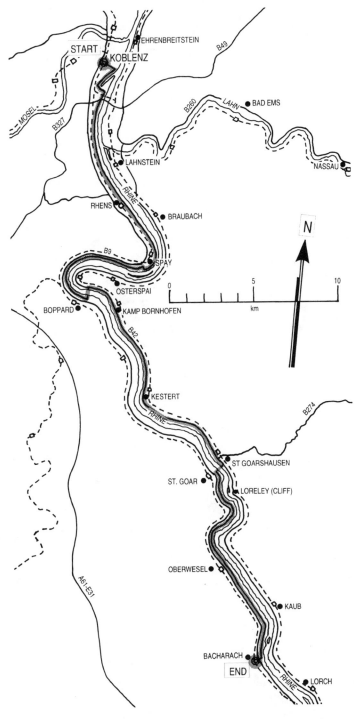

Exit Kamp-Bornhofen along road (B42) (or along RHS sidewalk)

[Sterrenberg and Liebenstein castles on your LHS]

[KM 566; across river is Bad Salzig]

[KM 565]; [KM 564]

Through Kestert village

[KM 563]

Continue along sidewalk bike path, alongside Rhine, river on your RHS

(Across river is Hirzenach)

[KM 562]; [KM 561]

Through Ehrenthal hamlet

[KM 560]

Through Wellmich

[KM 559]

(Burg Maus on LHS)

Sidewalk ends, continue along road (B42)

(1 km) R along bike path alongside Rhine, river on your RHS

[KM 558]

Enter St. Goarshausen

Continue along bike path on RHS of road

[KM 557]

[KM 556] ferry, St. Goarshausen–St Goar (06h00–21h00 work days, other days 07h00–21h00; fare DM 2.50)

Cross ferry to St. Goar

Through parking area, bear R towards roadway, L along bike path on LHS of road, river on your LHS

Pass fire station, road swings R, continue along bike path towards

Rhine traffic signal house, river on your LHS, road on RHS

Pass campsite, on your LHS

[KM 555]

Pass Loreley restaurant, on your LHS

Exit St. Goar

[Loreley rock across Rhine, on your LHS]

Continue along bike path on LHS of road, river on your LHS

[KM 554]

* Caution: For the next 3 kilometers (2 miles), the sidewalk bike path narrows considerably at times for short (10 to 100 m = 11 to 110 yds) distances; also, the surface of the bike path is in imperfect condition and it requires care and concentration to negotiate it. Under no circumstances should you use the roadway. If in doubt, walk.

[KM 552]; [KM 551]

Continue along concrete bike path on LHS of road (B9)

Enter Oberwesel

[KM 550]

Under bridge

Pass harbor entrance (on your LHS)

L towards Rhine (at ED gas station)

R along concrete bike path, river on your LHS

[KM 549]; [KM 548]; [KM 547]

[Across river is Kaub]

Pass ferry to Kaub

[On RHS is Engelsburg castle]

[Marshall Blücher monument on LHS]

[Across Rhine is Gutenfels castle, on the island in the river is the Pfalz]

[KM 546]; [KM 545]; [KM 544]

Enter Bacharach along bike path on LHS of road (B9)

Cross stream

R towards Bahnhof

Ends at Bacharach Bahnhof (train station).

Diversion suggestions:

1. If you like walking in the mountains and forests, you will be well-catered for here. The same terrain awaits cyclists who care to cycle up and down steep slopes and around switchbacks. Routes away from both banks of the river offer the same challenges.

2. There is a circular cycling route up the Wisper and Tiefenbach river valleys from Lorch to Sauerthal, then to Weisel, returning along the Dürscheid road (turning before Dürscheid) and along the Bluchertal to Kaub. Ferry crossings are at Lorch as well as at Kaub. In peak holiday season you will find the roads exceptionally busy.

Route 13: Bacharach to Mainz via Bingen and Ingelheim

Distance: 59 km/37 miles

Terrain: Flat; compacted dirt roads, paved roads (some narrow paved bike paths alongside busy roadways)

Maps: Kompass Wanderkarte Der Rhein Köln – Mainz (No. 829); 1:50,000 (2 cm = 1 km)

ADFC Radtourenkarte Rheinland – Eifel (No. 15); 1:150,000 (1 cm = 1.5 km) (Bacharach – Bingerbrück)

ADFC Radtourenkarte Rhein – Neckar (No. 20); 1:150,000 (1 cm = 1.5 km) (Lorch – Bingerbrück – Mainz)

ADAC Mainz Stadtplan; 1:20,000 (1 cm = 200 m)

Diversions: See suggestions at the end of this section

Description:

From Bacharach cycle south alongside the Rhine along the west bank. The east bank of the river is now in Hessen (State).

[KM 540] Lorch am Rhein (Hessen), the former Roman Laureacum, is at the confluence of the Wisper and Rhine rivers. In medieval times goods were offloaded from boats traveling upriver to be transported overland to avoid the Binger Loch. Remains of the town fortifications are at the Wisper mouth in Weseler Weg and the Obertor.

The thirteenth century St. Martin church (Am Markt) on a terrace above the Rhine is one of the most significant Gothic churches in the Rheingau. It has the most lavish altarpiece in the Middle Rhine, a gothic high altar of 1483. Choir stalls show animal figures and mysterious fabulous beings.

Near the St. Martin church is a gabled Renaissance dwelling, the Hilchenhaus of 1573. There are numerous half-timbered houses and a late Gothic tithe hall. The Heimatmuseum in the former monastery displays local history including the Roman past of the town. Above Lorch is Nollig castle.

[KM 541] Opposite Lorch is the Fürstenberg castle. Originally it was a toll castle of the Electors Palatine. Nowadays it's a vineyard property and cannot be visited.

[KM 535] Trechtingshausen has tugs on standby to assist ships over the Bingen rock sill. Formerly, extra horses were attached to ships for the upstream haul past Bingen.

Reichenstein (Falkenburg) castle was built from the eleventh to the thirteenth centuries for Mainz. The Hanseatic League and Emperor Rudolph of Habsburg destroyed it in 1282. The castle was subsequently rebuilt but destroyed again in the seventeenth century. It was restored for Prince Friedrich of Prussia from 1825. It is now a hotel and museum.

[KM 534] The Clemenskirche (south of Trechtingshausen on the banks of the Rhine), built in the twelfth century, has all the characteristics of a Romanesque basilica, surviving almost unchanged. The pillars are the dominant feature. Emperor Rudolph of Habsburg burnt out the toll lords of Rheinstein, Sooneck, Heimberg, and others and hanged them. The chapel was built from the gibbets and castle stones.

[KM 533] Assmannshausen produces red hock from late Burgundy grapes from vines brought from France by Cistercian monks. There is a chairlift to the Niederwald Monument (see Bingerbrück and Rüdesheim).

Rheinstein castle opposite Assmannshausen [viewpoint] had its heyday between 1280 and 1450. Prince Friedrich of Prussia restored it in neo-Gothic style in the nineteenth century. He changed its name to Faytsberg and dressed in medieval fashion when he was here. There are guided tours and a restaurant.

Bingerbrück is on the north side of the confluence of the Nahe and Rhine rivers. The "Brück" (bridge) was built here across the Nahe river by Drusus (about 20 BC). It was destroyed during World War II. The tenth century bridge chapel was partially renewed in 1946.

Opposite is the thirteenth century Ehrenfels castle, which was completely destroyed by the French in 1689.

The Mäuseturm (Mouse tower), built on a shingle shoal in the river in the thirteenth century, was a lookout for Ehrenfels castle. Presently it is used as a shipping signal station. During the Thirty Years' War (1618–48) it was destroyed, being rebuilt in neo-Gothic style in 1855. The untrue legend of Bishop Hatto was spread by the Southey (1774–1843) rhymed verse taught to children in England. In truth, the bishop lived before the tower was built and was popular and well thought of according to records of the time. The legend was merely popular anti-catholic propaganda. The "mouse" appellation of the tower is a corruption of "Maut" (toll). The tower acted as a toll point for the See of Mainz.

The Binger Loch (Bingen Hole) is the name given to the channel which dropped across sills and reefs in the river. From the time of Charlemagne attempts were made to improve the channel. In 1832 Prussian engineers enlarged the channel and in the 1890s the reefs were carefully dynamited to provide two separate channels, each 91 meters (100 yards) wide. The reefs hold back the water, helping to regulate its flow and depth, so they cannot be arbitrarily removed.

[Viewpoint] Across the Rhine is the Niederwald Denkmal (monument), the German National monument completed in 1883. It celebrates the foundation of the Prusso-German Empire in 1871. The figure of Germania is 10.5 meters (34 feet) high, holding aloft the imperial crown and a sword 7.25 meters (24 feet) long. The statue itself weighs about 32 tons and is 7 meters (23 feet) around the hips. One of the bronze reliefs shows about two hundred people life-sized. There is a cabin cable lift from Rüdesheim.

Bingen is south of the Nahe–Rhine confluence. The town is of Gallo-Roman origin. In the Middle Ages it was an imperial free city and member of the Rhenish League.

Bingen is situated at the southern end of the Rhine gorge on the outside of the bend known as the "Bingen knee." Here the river swings almost ninety degrees east. Once there were eighty reefs in the river.

Klopp castle was built on Roman foundations in the thirteenth century. In 1420 it was acquired by Mainz, and a Canon of Mainz lived here as lord of Bingen from 1438. Destroyed in 1689 by the French, Mainz blew up the remains in 1711, but in 1875–79 the castle was restored. It is now the seat of the city's administration. In the tower the museum specializes in ancient exhibits from prehistory to the Franks. The collection includes a set of Roman doctor's instruments from the second century.

In the seventeenth century the town escaped the plague. Credit is given to St. Rochus, averter of pestilence. There is a pilgrimage chapel built in 1666. During the Napoleonic wars the chapel was destroyed by artillery fire in 1814 and rebuilt in 1895. Opposite Bingen was a major Celtic settlement. An ancient track leads over the Niederwald hills from Rüdesheim towards Assmannshausen. The poem "Mosella," written by Ausonius of Bordeaux, tutor to the imperial family of Valentinian (364–375), tells about a journey from Bingen to the Mosel across the Hunsrück mountains.

Before, and for a short time after World War II, paddle steamer tugs were used on the Rhine. From below Bingen ten stokers were needed in each boat to provide enough power to travel upstream.

The Brömserburg (also called Niederburg) was built in the twelfth century and fell into decay, to be restored and enlarged in the nineteenth century. The Brömser family also owned the towers of the Ober- and Vorderburg castle. There is a wine museum (Rheingau- und Weinmuseum, Rheinstrasse 2) in the ruined Brömserburg. It is the largest specialist museum of its kind with collections relating to the history of the Rheingau and pre- and early history.

Rüdesheim is a famous brandy center and half the German export brandy, Asbach Uralt, comes from here. Brandy (Brandtwein) production was encouraged and taught by immigrants from the Spanish Netherlands.

Previously it had been the sole preserve of apothecaries, by decree.

In the Adlerturm (eagle tower) cellars, special wines are "buried" (set aside) and vintages are "exhumed" after thirty, fifty, and one hundred years. There are no guarantees, however, and the city of Bremen has a 1653 vintage Rüdesheimer which is said to be unpalatable.

Geisenheim has the biggest German training center for viticulture, fruit growing and horticulture. In the past all customs duties on pepper was collected here. In the center of Geisenheim is a 600 year old lime tree (Linde).

The Rheingau cathedral (Holy Cross church, 1510–20; Kirchplatz) has two open-work Gothic towers. The bells so impressed the American poet Longfellow, that he wrote about them at the end of his poem "The Golden Legend." The fountain on Bishop Blum Platz near the cathedral was constructed from marble from the Nassau valley and erected in honor of HW Longfellow.

Johann Philipp von Schönborn, Prince Elector of Mainz, drafted the peace treaty to conclude the Thirty Years' War (1618–48) in the former Stockheim Hof. The Prince also met here with the philosopher Leibnitz and others to consider proposals to unite the Evangelical and Catholic churches. The Stockheim Hof (Winkeler Strasse 62) is a three storey stone building from 1550, with an open plan hall.

Johannisburg is inland behind Geisenheim. It has one of the greatest names amongst Rhine wines. In 1106 the Archbishop of Mainz founded the first Benedictine monastery in the Rheingau at Bischofsberg (now Johannisberg). The monastery was secularized in 1801. Prince William of

Orange temporarily owned Johannisberg hill in 1801. Napoleon gave the hill and chateau to Marshal Kellerman, who had distinguished himself at Valmy. The 1811 harvest was an exceptional vintage and Kellerman sold the lot. The Treaty of Vienna (1815) gave Johannisberg to the Emperor of Austria, who then (1816) gave it to Prince Metternich in exchange for one-tenth of the annual yield. The Metternich family still owns the estate. Tours are possible. The terrace of the chateau affords an excellent view of the Rheingau [viewpoint]. The Palace of Johannisberg dates from the ninth century.

Winkel has the oldest house in Germany, the Grey House of Winkel built in 850 by Archbishop Rhabanus Maurus of Mainz. Later occupants of the house were the Counts Matuschka-Greiffenclau who also owned the Schloss Vollrads, a thirteenth century moated castle with a vineyard (behind Winkel) that rivals Johannisberg.

Oestrich: The church of St. Martin is Gothic except for the Romanesque tower. It is reputed to be the most ancient church in the Rheingau. The Town Hall dates from 1504. An ancient crane on the river juts out from a conical tiled roof. The town is full of interesting nooks and crannies.

Ingelheim is considered to be the birthplace of Charlemagne. At the Städtisches Museum (Rathausplatz) is a reconstruction of the Kaiserspfalz (imperial palace) complex.

Red wine is produced here. It is also an important wholesale fruit market with the biggest supply of cherries in Europe. Asparagus is grown extensively.

Sebastian Münster the cartographer was born in Ingelheim in 1489. He became Professor of Hebrew at Basel University and in 1540 produced the first accurate map of the Rhine.

Hattenheim (east bank) produces one of the best Rheingau wines called Markobrunnen. It has its own spring and is the only community in the Rheingau which owns vineyards, the others being the property of monasteries, institutions, schools and private owners.

Erbach am Rhein also produces Markobrunnen wine. Fruits, especially strawberries are grown here, with a relevant festival in mid to late June. When Thomas Jefferson toured the Rhineland in 1788, he showed a preference for Markobrunnen wines.

Eberbach (wild boar stream) is inland from Erbach and Eltville. The monastery once had a large vineyard on the Rhine which is marked by the Ebertor on the river. Its cellars still exist.

In 1135 the Cistercians took over the abbey from the Augustinians. The monks had their own ships for transporting the wine. The Steinberg vineyard, part of the Eberbach vineyards, produces the highly regarded Steinberger wine. The monastery buildings are considered a classic specimen of a reformed monastery in the High Middle Ages. The church was built 1145–86. There were up to three hundred monks and lay brothers in its heyday. The hospital was built 1215–20. In 1200 they built a wall around the settlement. Much of the 1,100 meters of the 5 meters high wall still stands (1,200 yards x 16 feet high) but the gates and the doors have gone. The monastery was suppressed in 1803 and it became a state possession of Hesse. It was used as a lunatic asylum from 1813 until 1912. Nowadays the estate and buildings are used and maintained by the State wine authorities of the Rheingau. There are guided tours at weekends by arrangement.

Eltville (east bank) is opposite Budenheim. It has the most extensive vineyards in the Rheingau and the economy is based on the sparkling "Sekt" wine. There is a Sekt festival in July with bands and a procession with Biedermeier style costumes from the 1830s.

It is the oldest town in the Rheingau and its name derives from Alta Villa. The old Alemannic settlement became the core of the town at the time of the barbarian invasions and saw many battles. In 1332 Eltville was granted town status.

Eltville castle was the summer residence of the Archbishops of Mainz. It is a fourteenth century moated "Burg" with a square ground plan. One side is directly on the Rhine and the other sides were previously defended by barbicans (projecting watch towers). Gutenberg (father of printing) lived in a room in the castle for some time and there are exhibits to commemorate this. The only honor received by Gutenberg was the title of courtier bestowed upon him by the Archbishop of Mainz, Elector Adolf of Nassau, at Eltville in 1465. In the keep is a monument to Gutenberg.

There are numerous old houses in a good state of repair. The Hauptstrasse especially gives a clear picture of the history of the town. Baroque madonnas and statues of saints on the houses is typical.

Schierstein (east bank) next to Nieder Walluf, is a river port and fishing village. Note the nets out to dry. It is also a rose-growing center and has cherry orchards.

Wiesbaden lies between the Taunus and Rheingau regions. It is the capital city of Hesse. The State Parliament sits in the former palace of the Dukes of Nassau. Wiesbaden is a spa resort with many parks and gardens, and nearly thirty hot springs. The Romans patronized the thermal springs, the Aquae Mattiacum (Mainz waters), noting too that many of the local girls had red hair; this was caused by a type of brick dust sediment in the waters.

In the eighteenth century the Dukes of Nassau developed the resort. In 1837–42 a" Schloss" (castle) was built for the Dukes Wilhelm and Adolf of Nassau. The Duke of Nassau supported Austria against Prussia and was deposed after the Six Weeks' War. Prussia took Nassau, and the Duke became the Archduke of Luxembourg. The Schloss was taken over by the Prussian Emperors in 1866.

The oldest cable car in Germany [viewpoint] travels up to the 245 meter (800 feet) Neroberg. Half-way up the mountain there is a stop at the nineteenth century Orthodox chapel memorial to the Russian princess Elizabeth Michailovna, who married a Duke of Nassau and died after a year. The chapel has five gilded onion towers and it is built entirely in the Byzantine-Russian style.

Biebrich: The palace residence of the Dukes of Nassau built in Baroque style between 1698 and 1744 faces the Rhine. Moosburg castle was built on an island in the lake in the great park in 1807.

[For a description of Mainz, see route 14]

Directions:

Start at Bacharach Bahnhof (train station). Cycle east towards the Rhine, under the subway and across the roadway.

R along asphalt bike path on LHS of road, Rhine to LHS (about 80 m away)

Exit Bacharach

Up slope to campsite entrance on LHS of road

L away from B9 (NOT towards campsite entrance), down slope and continue along asphalt road, alongside Rhine, river on your LHS

[KM 542]

* Beware of numerous cross-drains

[KM 541]

Continue under railway, alongside river, river on your LHS

Cross bridge, ON towards Bingen (bicycle sign)(on RHS is Niederheimbach)

(E bank now Hessen State)

Pass ferry (Niederheimbach–Lorch)

Continue along brick-paved bike path alongside river

[KM 539]; [KM 538]

Continue under conveyor

[KM 537]; [KM 536]

Continue past landing stage (Trechtingshausen on RHS)

Continue between allotments

Cross river, campsite on your LHS, rail line on RHS

L away from rail line towards Rhine, cemetery on your RHS, camp LHS

R alongside river, river on your LHS, church RHS (Clemenskapelle)

[KM 534]

(Across Rhine is Assmannshausen)

Continue along asphalt road, rail line on your RHS, river LHS

[KM 533]; [KM 532]

R towards Bingen (bicycle sign), towards rail line

Cross rail line

Cross another rail line

immed. L up ramp, continue along bike path on LHS of road

* Caution: sometimes very narrow, often bad surface, about 1.4 km (0.9 miles) before Bingen

Enter Bingen, continue along LHS bike path

L along Carl-Wolf-Strasse, swing R with roadway

* Caution: the next turning takes you down a very steep hill to an intersection; check your brakes

T cross over road to RHS bike path and L along Bingerbrücker Strasse

T-R over bridge across Nahe river and along Bingerbrücker Strasse (bike shop on RHS)

X (lights) L (immed. after station parking lot on LHS)

Cross rail lines

X-R along Hindenberg Anlage, with rail line on your RHS

X (circle/roundabout) continue

Pass Zollamt on your LHS (harbor on your LHS)

Pass Bingen Bahnhof (train station) on your RHS

Pass ferry, Bingen–Rüdesheim

L immed. before road bridge, towards Kempten (bicycle sign)

L over rail lines (at harbor), continue to Rhine

R along asphalt bike path, under canopy of motor bridge, harbor on LHS

Continue along hard sand bike path, rail line on your RHS

Pass small boat harbor, on your LHS

Continue along asphalt road, pass oil depot, pass sports fields

T-L along asphalt road

Cross small bridge (Sometimes it is possible to turn L here and take the river route, but the river road can get extremely muddy, especially after floods or heavy rains)

Continue under bridge

Immed. road swings R and up slope

T-L towards Gaulsheim (bicycle sign)

Enter Gaulsheim along Mainzer Strasse, rail line on your RHS

Pass train station, on your RHS

X (lights) continue

L towards Ingelheim along bike path (immed. past Ford auto dealers)

Continue along asphalt bike path, alongside autobahn embankment, on your RHS

T-L towards Ingelheim along asphalt agricultural road (bicycle sign)

Road swings L and R through vineyards and orchards

X continue along asphalt road (Sporkenheim on your RHS over freeway)

X-L towards Ingelheim-Nord (bicycle sign)

T-L along asphalt road

T-L-R towards Heidenfahrt (bicycle sign) (L to Mittelheim ferry)

Continue along brick-paved road, to end of street

Bear L and continue along bike path next to dike, dike on your LHS

Y-L towards Heidenfahrt (bicycle sign)

T-L along dike-top bike path towards Heidenfahrt

Off dike, continue along asphalt road, dike on your LHS

X-L immed. before small stone bridge (entrance to Heidenfahrt), along asphalt bike path next to dike, dike on your LHS

X (slipway to L) continue along asphalt bike path, dike on your LHS

Through orchards

T-L along brick-paved road, lake/campsite on your RHS

X continue towards Budenheim (bicycle sign)

Through allotments

Enter Budenheim

T-R along Ernst-Ludwig-Strasse

T-R along Rheinstrasse (L to seasonal ferry to Walluf)

L along Mainzer Strasse towards Mainz (bicycle sign)

Under freeway up ramp

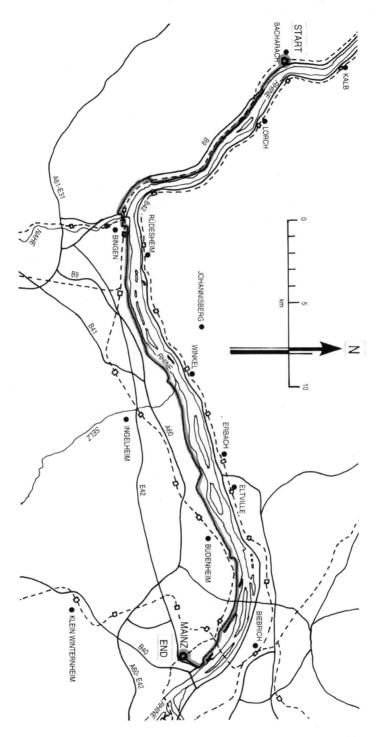

[You can turn L along Poststrasse to the Rhine, then R alongside the river, for the river route if you prefer — sometimes very muddy]

Cross rail line

T-L along Steinweg towards Mainz (bicycle sign)

T-R towards Mainz (bicycle sign), between allotments on asphalt road

T-L towards Mainz (bicycle sign), dike on your RHS, allotments LHS

T-R (before dike)

[Riverside route joins here]

Continue along hard dirt road, to freeway junction (overhead)

X-L along hard dirt road

Under bridge, continue alongside freeway on-off ramps

[KM 504]

Into parking area, continue along RHS demarcated bike path on asphalt

Continue along red brick-paved bike path

X (circle/roundabout) continue across roadway (Mombacher Kreisel)

Immed. R along red brick-paved bike path on LHS of road

R across road (at BAHR entrance, on LHS)

X (lights) L along LHS bike path towards Innenstadt (bicycle sign), alongside service road next to freeway feeder road (Rheinallee)

Cross rail line

Under railway bridge

Immed. R across road on bike path

Immed. L along bike path on RHS of road (Rheinallee)

Immed. under railway bridge

L along Illstrasse (immed. before overhead bridge)

Swing R, then L, cross rail lines, to Rhine

R along Adenauerufer, on broad cycle road in avenue, river on your LHS

[KM 499]

X-R along Kaiserstrasse

To Hauptbahnhof (train station); route ends here.

Diversion Suggestions:

1. Mainz and Wiesbaden are not large cities and are easily explored by bicycle. There is an enormous variety of interesting places and activities to enjoy. The pre-Lenten festival at Mainz rivals that of Cologne, with summer wine festivals on the Rhine bridges and promenades.

2. A trip up the river Main to Frankfurt am Main has much to recommend it. You can cycle there and back, or take a train or boat in one or both directions.

3. The Taunus mountains offer many opportunities to cycle roller-coaster roads for those with energy and stamina to spare.

Route 14: Mainz to Gernsheim via Nierstein and Guntersblum

Distance: 51 km/32 miles

Terrain: Mostly flat, some easy hills; compacted dirt roads, paved roads

Maps: Top-Stern Radwanderkarte (No. 1) Kreis Gross-Gerau; 1:50,000 (2 cm = 1 km) [Mainz – Gernsheim – Worms]

ADAC Mainz Stadtplan; 1:2,000 (1 cm = 200 m)

ADFC Radtourenkarte Rhein-Neckar (No. 20); 1:150,000 (1 cm = 1.5 km)

Diversions: See suggestions at the end of this chapter

Description:

[KM 500] Mainz is the capital city of the Rheinland-Pfalz and the Rheinhessen wine area. Opposite is the confluence of the Rhine and Main rivers. Mainz is at the north end of the Rhine Rift Valley (Rheingraben). Once this area was 150 meters (500 feet) below sea level and the site of Bingen was 150 meters (500 feet) higher. This is the point of the north-south divide.

Mainz (Mogontiacum) was the most important town founded by the Romans in the Rhine Rift Valley, and they made it the capital of the Roman province of Germania superior. It is a natural bridging site, having solid ground on both banks of the river. The 22nd Legion (Primigenia), which had conquered Jerusalem, was stationed at Mainz in the second century. Until 38 BC Mainz was a Celtic settlement.

Mainz is one of the oldest towns on the Rhine and celebrated its two thousandth anniversary in 1962. The town became a center of the Franks under Dagobert and his successors who dominated the other German tribes and later founded the Holy Roman Empire under the Carolingians.

The town lost importance on the decline of Rome but was restored in the Middle Ages as a center of the missionary effort conducted by its Archbishops to the territories beyond the Rhine. The first (746) Archbishop of Mainz, St. Boniface (formerly Wynfrith) an English wheelwright's son, is remembered in the city's coat of arms represented by a pair of wheels.

In 1254 Mainz and Worms founded a league of the Rhineland towns between Basel and Cologne, which included about eighty towns and lasted for two hundred years. Mainz prospered and became known as the Golden City. In 1462 the Archbishops of Mainz re-established the power of the church by force and the city lost its commercial edge.

Gutenberg was born at Mainz around 1400. He is credited with inventing moveable metal type (which allowed re-use of type) and with printing the Mazarin and Bamberg bibles. The former Gutenberg Museum is now called the World Museum of Printing.

Napoleon abolished this seat of the Prince-Elector and Primate Archbishop of Germany. Mainz had been a Bishopric since the third century. The Archbishops of Mainz were also Lords Chancellor of the Holy Roman Empire of the German nation since the time of Willigis (around 975 AD).

Mainz is the center of the German wine trade. In 1958 the "Haus des

Deutscher Weines" (House of German Wine) was established, with a sampling of any of the two hundred growths of the German wines.

The death mask of William Shakespeare is kept in Mainz — Germany has some of the world's foremost Shakespearean scholars.

In 975 AD Archbishop Willigis began building the Dom St. Martin und St. Stephan (Markt 10–12). With Speyer and Worms cathedrals, it is one of the most outstanding examples of Romanesque architecture in Germany. It has six towers whose decoration and size make the building exceptional. The west tower is 85 meters (275 feet) high, the other towers 56 meters (182 feet).

The cathedral is 114 meters (371 feet) long. It has more monuments than any other church in Germany.

The Kurfürstliche Schloss (Rheinstrasse) was erected from 1627 on the site of buildings which had been destroyed in the Thirty Years' War. It was the last important Renaissance building constructed in Germany. The interior of the palace was destroyed during World War II. The exterior was repaired and the east wing contains the Römisch-Germanisches Nationalmuseum. The oldest depiction of a Rhine barge is found in the museum, shown on the tomb of Blussus.

Walkers' signpost in the vineyards near Nierstein, Germany.

A copy of a Roman relic, the Jupiter column, is at the head of Grosse Bleichstrasse. The original is in the Museum of Antiquities.

On the river, south of the cathedral (Rheinstrasse) are the Holz Turm (wooden tower) and the Eiserne Turm (iron tower). On the citadel is a monument to Drusus.

The Old Quarter of Mainz, at the center of which is the Kirschgarten square, was not damaged during World War II. The St. Stephan church (Stephansplatz) has choir windows by Marc Chagall, installed in 1975. The Rathaus (Rheinstrasse) is a modern building (1971–74) clad in Norwegian marble. The Dativius Victorbogen is an arch which has survived from Roman times. Osteiner Hof (Schillerplatz) is rococo, almost neo-classical. Dalberger Hof (Klarastrasse 2) is a Baroque house of a nobleman, built 1715–18.

Heinrich von Meissen, known as "Frauenlob," was a troubadour who sang about women. His funeral was attended by hundreds of women, and vintage wine was poured into his vault in such quantities that it overflowed and flooded the cloisters.

[KM 487] Nackenheim produces wines which are highly prized. The playwright Karl Zuckmayer was born here in 1896.

[KM 482] Nierstein has a worldwide reputation for producing good wines. They have my unreserved vote too. The city received its charter in 742 AD. There is a medieval watch tower with a view of the Odenwald [Viewpoint]. In Goethe's Faust, there is mention of Niersteiner wine and Auerbach's cellar.

[KM 478] Oppenheim was a free Imperial town in 1220. There is an old gateway and a Gothic town hall. The Gothic church of St. Catherine built from the thirteenth century in red sandstone has two rose windows.

Oppenheim is the source of some sought after Rheinhessen wines, amongst them Oppenheimer Kröterbrunnen (toad's well).

The thirteenth century castle of Landskron provides a [viewpoint].

Guntersblum was once on the Rhine but is now some distance inland. The name means Gunther's garden, as Gunther, King of the Burgundians and one of the main protagonists in the story of the Nibelungen, was supposed to have had a garden here. The town is in the Rheinhessen wine region, on the Liebfrauenstrasse wine route. There are two seventeenth century castles here.

[KM 462] Gernsheim began as a Roman fortress in the first century AD. Celto-Germanic tribes settled in the area and a royal Carolingian residence was built here. The name Gernsheim is first recorded in 852 AD as being a Frankish settlement. In 908 AD the settlement belonged to the Lorsch monastery.

The town charter was given in 1356. The most famous son of Gernsheim was Peter Schöffer, who was born here in 1430. He was Gutenberg's first pupil and made his name as a great printer.

Gernsheim suffered badly in the seventeenth century, from both the plague and the Thirty Years' War, after which General Mélac's troops plundered the town in 1689. A new Rathaus (Town hall) was built in 1700, and in 1753 the St. Magdalena church, with its onion-dome spire was begun.

When Gernsheim became part of Hesse in 1803, it signaled a period of expansion and prosperity. In 1830 Gernsheim was the main port for Rhine steam shipping. The steam age brought steam-driven mills, sugar, malt, and chemical industries.

On the first Sunday in August, the town celebrates its annual "Fischerfest" (fisherman's festival).

Directions:

Start at Mainz Hauptbahnhof. Exit east and continue directly down Kaiserstrasse to the Rhine.

[KM 499]

R alongside Rhine along Adenauerufer, river on your LHS

Continue under bridge, along Adenauerufer

Bear L past fountain, continue along Adenauerufer alongside river

Info, on your LHS at Rheingoldterasse

[KM 498]

Continue along Stresemannufer

Cross Malakoffterasse

L over pedestrian bridge across harbor inlet towards Laubenheim (bicycle sign)

R along Viktor-Hugo-Ufer, Rhine on your LHS, harbor on RHS

[KM 497]

Under railway bridge

[KM 496]; [KM 495]

Bike path swings R to skirt cement works

Under bridge

Swing L, cross rail line

Immed. R

L across rail line

Immed. R

X continue (L-R) across intersection along bike path on LHS of road

Under bridge

L towards river and Bodenheim (bicycle sign) along asphalt bike path, bridge on your LHS

-R at Rhine, towards Bodenheim (bi - cycle sign)

Through parking area/slipway, bear R to roadway, continue past play area

T-L towards Bodenheim (bicycle sign)

Skirt camp site, camp site on your LHS, freeway on your RHS

Continue alongside river, along hard dirt road, river on your LHS

[KM 492]; [KM 491]; [KM 490]

Continue towards Nierstein (bicycle sign)

[KM 489]

Continue along brick-paved bike path, harbor on your LHS, road on RHS

[Subways on your RHS access Nackenheim]

[KM 487]

R towards Nierstein (bicycle sign)

Through subway, U-turn L towards Nackenheim train station (bicycle sign Nierstein)

Continue past Nackenheim train station, along hard sand bike path, with rail line on your RHS, road on LHS

T (bike path ends) R across rail line

U-turn L towards Nierstein 2 km, Worms 38 km (bicycle sign)

Continue along asphalt road, rail line on your LHS, vineyards RHS

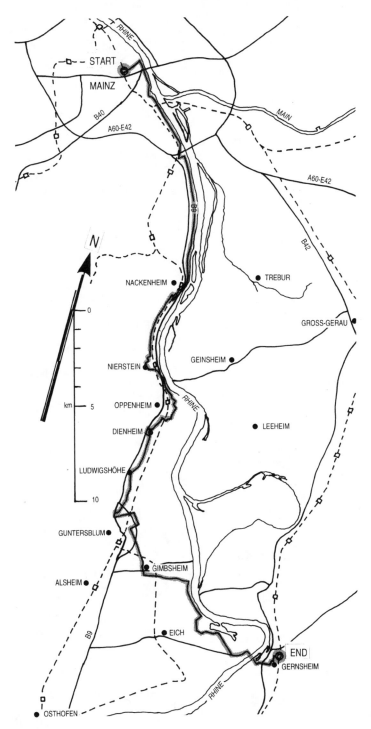

START

MAINZ

RHINE

MAIN

B40

A60-E42

A60-E42

B42

N

NACKENHEIM

TREBUR

0

GROSS-GERAU

NIERSTEIN

GEINSHEIM

km 5

OPPENHEIM

RHINE

DIENHEIM

LEEHEIM

LUDWIGSHÖHE

10

GUNTERSBLUM

GIMBSHEIM

ALSHEIM

B9

EICH

END

GERNSHEIM

RHINE

OSTHOFEN

R away from rail line

T-L along asphalt roadway amongst vineyards

[KM 484]

Enter Nierstein, next to rail line (on your LHS), along Kiliansweg

R along Breitgasse

L along Aptsgasse

T-L along Rheinstrasse

Under railway subway

T-R along Mainzer Strasse

L across roadway to Rhine

[KM 482]

R along Rheinpromenade

Up to roadway, along LHS of road on bike path

Info, on your LHS

Continue alongside Mainzer Strasse/ Rheinallee

L to waterfront on hard dirt road, some cobbles

Continue along asphalt bike path alongside Rhine, river on your LHS

Continue alongside roadway towards Oppenheim/Worms (bicycle sign)

[KM 481]

Y-L along asphalt road alongside river

Pass ferry (Nierstein–Kornsand)

Continue along LHS of Hafenstrasse to LHS bike path

Continue past harbor entrance, along brick-paved bike path on LHS of road

Enter Oppenheim

L along bike path alongside harbor (as road swings R)

T-L along bike path towards Worms 27 km, Dienheim 3 km (bicycle signs)

Continue along Fährstrasse

R along Dammstrasse (bicycle arrows)

X-L

R along In den Weingärten

T-R across rail line (bicycle signs)

X-L towards Dienheim (bicycle sign) on bike path on LHS of road

X (circle/roundabout) continue, along LHS bike path

L along Jahnstrasse

L (at end of vineyards) towards Worms 24 km/Ludwigshöhe 3 km (bicycle signs)

Enter Dienheim

T-R-L along Am Sportsplatz

R along Berliner Strasse (bicycle signs)

L along Am Ehrenmal

Swings L along roadway, continue along Kirchstrasse

Before underpass, R along Traminer Strasse (bicycle signs) to end

R along Schifferstrasse

L along In der Beune

Continue along concrete road in vineyards

Road swings R uphill

T-L along concrete road in vineyards

Enter Ludwigshöhe, continue towards Guntersblum 2.5 km/Worms 23 km (bicycle signs) along In den Pflänzeren

T-L along In den Pflänzeren

X-L along Kirchstrasse (bike shop on LHS)

R (towards Weingut Lambertushof, business sign) along concrete road between buildings (bicycle arrows), into vineyards

Exit Ludwigshöhe

Continue along main road as it swings L and R through vineyards

Enter Guntersblum

T-R along agricultural road

T (opp. cemetery) L along Hauptstrasse on RHS of road

(300 m) (1st) L along asphalt road (R to Weinolsheim/Eimsheim)

Cross bridge over B9 freeway and railway line

Immed. R across canal

T-R (towards waterworks) along K43

T-L towards Gimbsheim along bike path on LHS of road (K53/K51)

X continue along agricultural road on LHS of road (K53) towards Gimbsheim

Bike path ends, cross rail line, enter Gimbsheim

X (lights) continue through village

L along path marked "Zum Schwimbad" (at far end of town square)

Cross rail line, continue along road

Cross bridge

X continue over dike, along hard sand road to Rhine

R alongside river, river on your LHS

[KM 469]

Through parking area/slipway, continue alongside river on hard sand road

[KM 468]; [KM 467]

Immed. continue along asphalt road

R away from river (bicycle sign)

Continue over dike [dike-top path L not always reliable, but use if clear]

Road swings L

T-L towards Steinswörth (bicycle sign) along asphalt road (K47)

Road swings hard R

Continue up slope along Schwalbenweg to dike top

[Meet up with dike-top bike path from LHS here]

Info

Immed. R along dike-top on hard sand bike path

X-L (NOT U-turn L) towards Gernsheim ferry along asphalt road (L440)

Ferry (costs about DM 3.00) [military area, no photography allowed]

Cross Rhine on ferry, continue along road

X continue across major road (B44)

T-L, along road towards church

L along Heiligenstrasse

L along Schöfferstrasse to end of street

R along Schafstrasse

X-L along Darmstädter Strasse

X-R (at Postamp/post office) along Schillerstrasse

To Gernsheim Bahnhof (train station); route ends here.

Diversion Suggestions:

1. About 12 kilometers to the east of Gernsheim the heights of the Odenwald plunge down to the upper Rhine plain. The Odenwald is criss-crossed by scenic, challengingly graded roads leading to hamlets and villages with breathtaking views. For the seriously energetic.

2. Between the Rhine at Gernsheim and the Odenwald heights, there are a great many opportunities to cycle in the countryside, across water meadows and plains or through shady forests. A circular route via Hahnlein, Crumstadt, and Biebesheim for instance, would be an option. It's a trip of roughly 32 kilometers (20 miles).

3. Darmstadt is the former capital of the Grand Duchy of Hesse. As such the splendor of its palaces and chapels reflect the richness and artistry of its rulers and their patronage. The city is 15 kilometers from Gernsheim in a direct line, further by road, rail, or bicycle. You could take the train there, via Gross-Gerau. Besides the wonderful architecture, there is a zoo-park, many museums with fascinating collections and exhibitions, and entertainment for all ages. Wixhausen nearby has a village museum of country life.

Route 15: Gernsheim to Mannheim via Worms

Distance: 57 km/36 miles

Terrain: Flat; compacted dirt roads and asphalt roads; steps to climb and descend to cross the A6-E50 Rhine bridge (about 60 up and 40 down); alternative seasonal ferry

Maps: Top-Stern Radwanderkarte (No. 1) Kreis Gross-Gerau; 1:50,000 (2 cm = 1 km) [Mainz – Gernsheim – Worms]

Top-Stern Radwanderkarte (No. 4) Rhein – Neckar – Pfalz; 1:50,000 (2 cm = 1 km) [Worms – Mannhein – Germersheim]

ADAC Mannheim – Ludwigshafen Stadtplan; 1:20,000 (1 cm = 200 m)

ADFC Radtourenkarte Rhein – Neckar (No. 20); 1:150,000 (1cm = 1.5 km)

Diversions: See suggestions at the end of this section

Description:

From Gernsheim, cycle south alongside the Rhine on its east bank. Follow the dike-top bike path around the mulberry island to Worms.

[KM 444] Worms was originally a Stone Age settlement, whose inhabitants were displaced by the Celts, followed by the Romans, Franks, Burgundians, Huns, and Alemanni. The town's name evolved from Borbetomagus through Vangiones to Wormatia. On the decline of the Romans, Worms gained pre-eminence at the expense of Mainz.

Worms was a Roman garrison town and the capital of Civitas Vangionum. The Vangiones were a German tribe settled in the vicinity. The Romans invited the Burgundians to settle here after the legions were withdrawn. The Franks imposed Christianity and central government in the region.

The Burgundians were a powerful nation from the Oder–Vistula region. They were of the same race as the Goths and Vandals and came to the Rhine–Main area after being driven out of their territory. They were defeated by the Huns in 437 and moved to Gaul (Savoy and later to modern Burgundy) where they created the powerful kingdom of Burgundy around Geneva and Lyons.

The saga of the Nibelungen is largely concerned with the Burgundians, their king Gunther and his relationship with Siegfried the hero of the tale. Gunther and his brothers Germot and Giselher had a sister Kriemhild, the "most beautiful woman in the world." In order to gain favor with Gunther and to marry Kriemhild, Siegfried resorted to deception to vanquish Brunhilde to make her the bride of Gunther. The Burgundians inherited the treasure of the Nibelungen. Hagen cast the hoard into the Rhine and a statue of him doing just this is on the Rhine wall in Worms. The story ends with a bloody slaughter at the court of Attila (Etzel) King of the Huns. The basis for the legend of the Rheingold (treasure of the Nibelungen) may be attributed to the Celts having extracted gold from the Rhine shoals between Basel and Mainz. It was mostly of a purity of 22.4 to 24 carats. Rhine water carries on average 0.003 milligrams of gold per cubic meter, giving an annual discharge figure of about 113 kilograms (250 pounds).

In the ninth century the Vikings raided up the Rhine, reaching as far a Worms.

The oldest and most important synagogue in Western Europe can be found in Worms (Martinsplatz). It dates from the eleventh century and has a famous mikve (women's ceremonial bath). It also has the biggest and oldest Jewish cemetery in Europe, dating from the Middle Ages. These were destroyed during the pogrom in 1938 but have since been fully restored.

Worms is the Mother of Diets and the City of the Reformation. The Imperial Diet (national assembly) was summonsed to meet here more than a hundred times. At the Diet of Worms in 1521 Martin Luther was sentenced by Edict to be exiled, and his works to be burnt.

Worms cathedral, as seen from the steps of the youth hostel in Worms, Germany.

Worms is a wine trade center, situated in the Rheinhessen wine region. Near Worms is the convent church of Liebfrauenstift. The vineyards here produce the real Liebfrauenmilch wine grapes. Nowadays any Rheinhessen wine that is sour enough to have to be sugared is called Liebfrauenmilch.

In the fifteenth century, Worms had city walls with twelve gates. There were five castles, thirty palaces, twelve monasteries, five abbeys, fifty churches, a Romanesque cathedral, and residences of the Emperor and the Bishop. During World War II it was heavily bombed.

The Andreaskirche (Weckelingsplatz) was built by Bishop Burkhard from the stones of the Roman city wall. It is now a museum and contains Luther's parchment bible.

The cathedral, Dom St. Peter (Domplatz 1) is one of the most important examples of high and late Romanesque architecture in Germany. It was preceded by other buildings including the cathedral built by Bishop Burkhard in 1018. The present building was started in 1171 on the old site of the former Roman forum and completed in 1230. Modifications were made in high Gothic style. The cathedral is 111 meters (361 feet) long and the height under the domes is 40 meters (131 feet). It has ornate three-dimensional decoration and great doorways, some of which are inside and are unique in size and number.

Schloss Hernsheim (Hauptstrasse 1) was the Empire Schloss of the Dukes of Dalberg. It has a round tower of a fifteenth century Burg and an English park.

In the Thirty Years' War the Swedish Chancellor made his headquarters in the Bishop's residence near the cathedral. He destroyed the city walls and other defenses. Louis XIV of France destroyed Worms almost completely in 1689. Within two generations the city was rebuilt in Baroque style.

Napoleon used the Bishop's residence and the cathedral as stables. More than twenty churches were sold and the bishopric was dissolved. The town was deprived of its privileges, and the population declined to four thousand.

Since 1968 the Bischofshof has contained the Lobdengau Museum, which displays finds from the Roman towns of Lopodunum and Odenwald folk painting.

There is an impressive Siegfried fountain in the Marketplace. The Luther Monument (Lutherring) was created by Rietschel in 1868.

The Backfish festival takes place in late August which includes jousting from boats in the river.

The monster of the Rhine at Worms from which the original (Celtic) name was supposedly taken has possible middle-Eastern origins. It was a giant worm or dragon with a worm-like tai and two legs, which breathed flames from its mouth. Lots were drawn to determine who of the townsfolk would be devoured by the monster. When the queen was chosen for the sacrifice, a local cutler offered to take her place. He and his two brothers made a special suit of armor with knives projecting from it. When the monster swallowed the cutler in the armor it cut itself to pieces and perished. The queen was grateful enough to marry the cutler.

From Worms, continue southwards along the west bank of the Rhine to the Petersau ferry (or the Theodor Heuss freeway bridge).

[KM 437] About 7 kilometers south of Worms, the border between

Hesse and Baden-Württemberg reaches the east bank of the Rhine; the west bank remains Rheinland-Pfalz State.

[KM 426] Ludwigshafen is a large river port and center for the chemical industry. The BASF factories moved here from across the river at Mannheim.

In 1868, seventy thousand tons of vegetable alizarin (the red coloring matter of the madder root) was used in Europe. Plantations of madder in Alsace and elsewhere were put out of business when synthetic dye was produced simultaneously in Germany by a calico printer Heinrich Caro and in England by W.H. Perkin.

At the BASF laboratories Indigotin (blue dye) was produced by accident when a hot mixture was stirred with a thermometer which broke in the heat, the mercury acting as a catalyst to produce the dye. Two hundred thousand acres of indigo plantations in India alone went out of business.

Museums include the Wilhelm Hack Museum (Berliner Strasse 23), Stadtmuseum (Rathaus Center), K.O. Braun Heimatmuseum (in Oppau suburb, Rathaus) and Schillerhaus (in Oggersheim suburb, Schillerstrasse 6), which depicts the life and works of the poet Friedrich Schiller.

[KM 425] Mannheim, opposite Ludwigshafen, is 600 kilometers from the sea, yet sea-going ships navigate the Rhine to here. Mannheim was once the largest inland port in the world. There are 48 kilometers (30 miles) of docks. The Neckar river flows into the Rhine here. Until 1840 Rhine barges could not travel upstream as the marshlands of the Upper Rhine valley made towing almost impossible.

The town is laid out in square patterns with streets numbered in one direction and bearing letters in the cross-streets parallel with the Rhine. In 1622 during the Thirty Years' War, Tilly ravaged the town. In 1689 the forces of Louis XIV systematically destroyed the town, house by house. In 1795–99 French Revolutionary troops demolished the town and it was almost abandoned by its inhabitants. After bomb attacks during World War II, especially in 1944, the town was restored.

From 1720 to 1760 the largest baroque palace in Germany was built here for the Electors Palatine. The

View towards Ludwigshafen, Germany, with riverside industry on the other bank.

Schloss was damaged during World War II and completely restored by 1962. It is now used by the University. It has more than four hundred rooms and two thousand windows. It is south of the city and its ninety-four acre park stretches to the Rhine.

The Jugendstil square (Friedrichs-platz) was built to commemorate the three-hundredth anniversary of the town's foundation. The square has water towers, cascades and fountains which are illuminated on weekend and holiday evenings.

The Mannheim Open Air Theater (Im Waldhof) caters to amateur theater groups who put on mainly historical dramas from July to August every Saturday. Mannheim hosts an International Film week. The annual fair is held in May. Mannheim has a famous symphony orchestra and a music school. Mozart played with the court orchestra in the Knights' hall of the palace in 1777.

In the museum of Fine Arts (Städtische Kunsthalle, Moltkestrasse 9) you can see Cezanne's "pipe smoker" and Manet's "Execution of Emperor Maximilian in Mexico." It has one of the most important collections of nineteenth and twentieth century painting and sculpture in Germany.

Karl Benz made the first automobile here in 1885 and showed it in 1886. Doctor Huber built the first "Bulldog" tractor here in 1921.

Directions:

Start at Gernsheim Bahnhof (train station), with the station building on your LHS, cycle on along the roadway.

Info

Bear L with railway on your LHS

Over motor subway

Immed. R along Bleichstrasse

Stop, continue along Bleichstrasse

(bike shop on RHS)

X (lights) continue along Bleichstrasse

X continue along Bleichstrasse (across A44)

Continue along Pfälzer Strasse

Cross bridge, continue along brick-paved road, towards Rhine

L to Gross-Rohrheim and Biblis along hard sand road, 100 m before river (bicycle sign) [This road can be very muddy after river flooding; about 3 km]

[KM 459]; [KM 458]; [KM 457]; [KM 456]

T-R along hard sand road below dike, dike on your LHS

Continue past power station

[KM 455]

L over dike, R along concrete roadway, dike on your RHS

[KM 454]

Up slope to top of dike

R across bridge over Weschnitz river

Immed. R along hard sand road

Continue along dike-top (or road below dike) [The road alongside the river here is paved in a way that is a danger to cyclists]

Down slope, off dike-top, continue along concrete road next to dike, dike on your RHS

Info, birds

L away from dike (skirting a coppice), R towards dike

To dike-top, L along dike-top

T-R along brick-paved bike path on dike-top

Under railway bridge

Continue along asphalt road on dike-top

Off dike, along roadway next to dike

L away from dike, along asphalt road

T-R along asphalt agricultural road, L3261 on your LHS

Up to L3261 (road) and R along bike path on RHS of road, through Wehrzollhaus

L3261 swings L, parallel with Rhine

L3261 swings L away from Rhine

Immed. R along asphalt road on dike-top, past camp-site, on RHS

T-R along bike path on RHS of road, towards Rhine bridge

Enter Worms

X-R

X-R, towards Rhine, with Rhine bridge off-ramp on your RHS

Cross rail line

R under Rhine bridge, along asphalt road, rail line on your RHS and small harbor on your LHS

Cross rail line

[KM 443]

Continue to end of harbor area

Continue towards Eisbachweg/ Eisbachthal 3.15 km (bicycle signs), along compacted dirt road

R off dike, continue along asphalt road, dike on your LHS

Cross small bridge

Through parking area, continue past restaurant

Continue along hard sand dike-top bike path

X continue along asphalt road, dike off to your LHS

X continue along asphalt road

L immed. before bridge over highway (bicycle sign)

Cross small bridge

Continue towards Petersau along asphalt road on dike-top

X-L to Rhine, at parking area [If this ferry is operational, cross here to avoid the A6-E50 Rhine bridge, then turn R alongside the river bank and rejoin the described route under the Rhine bridge]

Continue alongside river along hard dirt road, river on your LHS, dike RHS

[KM 435]; [KM 434] (Some cobbles — alternative road on your RHS)

[KM 433]

R immed. before freeway bridge (Theodor-Heuss-Brücke), away from river, bridge on your LHS

L under bridge to bridge tower with stairs (inside) to top

[The alternate route through Ludwigshafen is best described as following the B9 freeway extension (Brunckstrasse and Rheinuferstrasse); rejoin the described route at the Kurt-Schumacher-Brücke]

At top of stairs, walk across the bridge down its center; do not under any

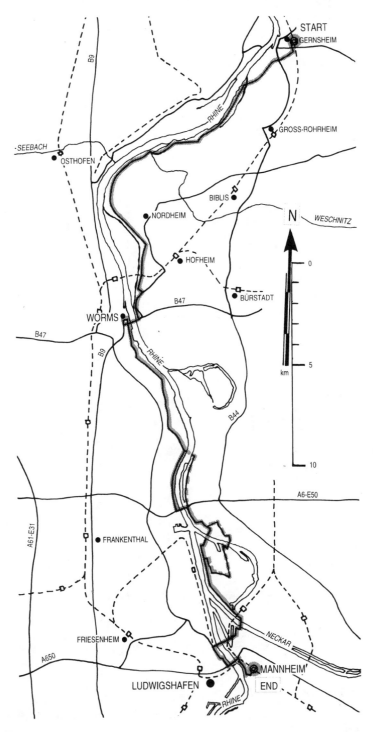

circumstances attempt to cross or use the roadways

Enter stair tower on E bank and descend to roadway at its base

Facing the Rhine, R down slope

Immed. L towards river, alongside bridge (on your LHS)

L through second-last arch before river along asphalt road

[KM 432]

T-L along asphalt road, away from river, towards dike

Through gate (gap) in dike

Immed. R along asphalt road, dike on your RHS

T-R across small bridge

X continue towards ferry

Cross Altrhein on ferry (Mannheim–Sandhofen; 16 March to 14 November, 10h00–19h00, every hour)

[Alternative route when ferry not operating: when you cycle through the dike wall, continue straight]

Swing R with road, through another dike gate

Road swings L, then R

Continue along Kalthorststrasse

R along Leinpfad (road)

Road swings L

Stop, R along asphalt track towards bridge, rail line on your LHS

Up spiral ramp to top of motor bridge

R along bi-directional bike path across bridge

Bike path ends, R off bridge

Continue alongside freeway embankment (on your LHS)

T-L along bike path on RHS of asphalt roadway

X-R along bike path alongside Diffenestrasse

X-R along Max-Planck-Strasse on bike path on RHS of road

T-R along Max-Planck-Strasse on bike path on LHS of road

L along asphalt road towards Rhine

[At Rhine, join route from Sandhofen ferry]

Continue away from Rhine along Max-Planck-Strasse

Viewpoint

Road swings L

Immed. R towards the Rhine

[KM 431]

L alongside river, river on your RHS

[KM 430]

(Meet alternate route at restaurant, opp. BASF sign across river)

Continue along asphalt road alongside river

Road swings L alongside Neckar (Neckar–Rhine confluence)

Road swings L alongside Kammerschleuse canal

* Dismount (step) R across lock

Continue along roadway

T-L along Inselstrasse alongside river, river on your RHS

Continue along Bursenstrasse

Under railway bridge, continue along bike path on RHS of road

Immed. before motor bridge, L across road, up ramp to top of bridge

R across bridge, along bike path on RHS

Bike path swings R off bridge, continue along Hellingstrasse

T-L along Hafenstrasse, on bike path on LHS of road

Immed. before motor bridge, L along Academiestrasse

Continue along up-ramp towards Ludwigshafen (bicycle sign)

Cross (Kurt Schumacher) bridge along bike path on RHS

Enter Ludwigshafen

R towards Stadt-Nord/Stadt-Mitte (near bottom of off-ramp)

Complete R U-turn

Under bridge

T-L (in center of circling on-ramp)

Across railway

Under bridge

Up ramp

Under 2 bridges

Continue along red brick-paved bike path

Continue at cycle signs

Down ramp, motor up-ramp on your RHS

Continue along Rheinuferstrasse, on red brick-paved bike path

[Alternate route through Ludwigshafen from A6-E50 (Theodor- Heuss-Brücke) joins described route here]

Continue along Zollhofstrasse on LHS bike path

Up bridge (Konrad-Adenauer-Brücke) ramp and swing L onto motor bridge LHS bi-directional bike path

Follow cycle signs to Jugendherberge (youth hostel), along bike paths

L off bridge, full circle, under bridge

Under another bridge

L towards Jugendherberge/Lindenhof

U-turn, under 4 bridges, towards Jugendherberge/Lindenhof

Continue towards Promenade (bicycle sign)

T (at Rhine) L along Rhein Promenade

[KM 424]

L towards Centrum (bicycle sign) along Schnicken Loch (street)

Continue along Tunnelstrasse

To Mannheim Hauptbahnhof (train station); route ends here.

Diversion Suggestions

1. Around Mannheim: Mannheim has miles of bike paths and is very bicycle-friendly. For its size it offers a great number of places to see and things to do. Ludwigshafen and the old medieval city of Altrip also have much to offer.

2. It is possible to cycle alongside the lovely Neckar river for most of the way to Heidelberg, the beautiful and exciting university city. Heidelberg is on the edge of the Odenwald and is an old Imperial city. You could also take a train to Heidelberg and cycle back to Mannheim.

3. You can get to Bad Dürkheim by bike, train, or car; it's about 25 kilometers east of Mannheim. Bad Dürkheim is in the wine producing region of the Palatinate (Pfalz) and on the German wine route (Deutsche Weinstrasse). It hosts the world's biggest wine festival which is held annually in September and lasts a week. An enormous volume of wine, in the region of 200,000 liters (52,840 US gallons/44,000 Imperial gallons) is consumed. This festival, known as the Sausage Fair (Dürkheimer Wurstmarkt) was first referred to in 1417, when wine, bread and sausage was doled out to pilgrims. Germany's Wine Queen opens the festival. She is chosen and crowned at the nearby wine town of Neustadt and paraded in Germany's largest wine festival procession.

   The settlement dates back to the Iron Age and remains of the grave of an Iron Age chief containing an Etruscan tripod was found here. On the Kästenberg are the remains of a Celtic ring (stone circle), the Heidenmauer (heather wall). There are ancient rock drawings on the Krimhildenstuhl and evidence of a Roman quarry.

4. If you are a Frankenstein fan — and even if you're not — you can get a train from Mannheim to the village of Frankenstein (and its ruined castle) west of Bad Dürkheim. There is a beautiful scenic route along the valleys from Frankenstein to Bad Dürkheim (17 km, first 5 km some steep grades up hills).

Route 16A: Mannheim to Wörth am Rhein via Germersheim

Distance: 88 km / 55 miles

Terrain: Flat; compacted dirt roads, paved roads

Map/s: Top-Stern Radwanderkarte (No. 4) Rhein – Neckar – Pfalz; 1:50,000 (2 cm = 1 km) [Worms – Mannheim – Germersheim]

ADAC Mannheim – Ludwigshafen Stadtplan; 1:20,000 (1 cm = 200 m)

ADFC-Radtourenkarte Rhein-Neckar (No. 20); 1:150,000 (1 cm = 1.5 km)

Diversion: See Route 16B (Karlsruhe), as well as suggestions at the end of this section.

Description:

From Mannheim cycle along the east bank of the Rhine and through the woods of the Neckarau nature reserve. Cross the Rhine to the ancient town of Altrip.

[KM 414] Altrip was already a town by AD 369. The Abbey of Prüm (Eifel), which became distinguished for its production of manuscripts, had a dependency at Altrip in the early Middle Ages. In the tenth century, Abbot Regino was the author of a history of the world for the previous thousand years.

Cycle along the west bank dike-top bike paths, around the Old Rhine meanders to Otterstadt and on to Speyer.

Otterstadt has a number of well-preserved half-timbered houses. Its position between Mannheim and Speyer, with a tremendous choice of cycling routes in the area, makes it a good base from which to explore, without city prices.

[KM 400] Speyer was settled in prehistoric times and later by Celts, Romans, Huns and Franks. The Celtic name of the town, Noviomagus was changed by the Franks to Spira. Speyer was a Free Imperial Town from 1294.

About 1030 the Salian Emperor Konrad II laid the foundation stone of Speyer cathedral (Kaiserdom). Konrad, who was crowned in 1027, built the cathedral in thanksgiving and to provide a burial place for the Emperors. The consecration in 1061 was attended by Emperor Henry IV. Extensive reconstructions were carried out later. With a length of 131 meters (433 feet) it is the largest and finest cathedral in Europe. The stonework was probably carried out by masons from Lombardy and there are superb examples of plastic art. The cathedral was built on the site of a seventh century church built by the Merovingian king Dagobert. It has two domes and four towers with pink and white limestone archways supporting a network of vaulting. Inside are the tombs of four Emperors, four Kings, three Empresses and five Bishops. In 1961 the nine hundredth anniversary celebrations were held. There is a Dom museum.

The Domnapf is a huge sandstone bowl in front of the west portal of the Dom. At the installation of a new Bishop it was the custom to fill it with wine for those who wanted to drink. It also corresponds with the altar in terms of sanctuary.

At the other end of the high street from the cathedral (Maximilianstrasse), is the Altpörtel, the most beautiful town gate in Germany. It was built in 1230 and added to in the sixteenth century. Behind the cathedral in the Domgarten is the Pagan tower (Heidentürmchen), part of the old city walls.

There are the remains of a medieval ghetto. In the twelfth century synagogue is an underground mikve (mikwa, female ritual bath) with twenty steps to the changing room, built in Romanesque style as a groined vault.

The Dreifattigkeitskirche (Grosse Himmelsgasse) was built in 1717 and is one of the most important Baroque churches in the Rheinland-Pfalz.

By 1570 more than fifty Diets (Parliaments) had been convened here, the most famous of which was in 1529 confirming the Edict of Worms (1521) which condemned Luther and his works. The Protestation Memorial church (Landauer Strasse) built in 1904 in neo-Gothic style commemorates the stand taken against the 1529 Diet by six Protestant Princes and fourteen Free Towns.

The Old Quarter is called Hasenpfuhl (hares' pool). It is bounded by Eseldamm (donkey dike) and contains the old fish market and timber market. Fishermen and shipmen used to live here. The front of the Half Moon Inn (zum Halbmond) was rebuilt in the seventeenth century in the original German Renaissance style and can be read almost like a comic book (picaresque novel). Some of the old houses have domestic statues, as in Haus zum Grossen Senfgarten (the house of the large mustard garden). On the Schustergasse is a sandstone statue of St. Jost, protector of pilgrims. The market is held in Königsplatz, where there is the Brezel (pretzel) fountain, a monument to bread. Every summer there is a pretzel festival (Brezelfest).

Near the cathedral is the Palatinate Historical Museum (Grosse Pfaffergasse 7) which displays the head of a centaur with silver "following" eyes in a bronze face and the 1200 BC Golden Hat of Schifferstadt. The wine museum is in the same building. A bottle of wine from the third century is said to be the oldest wine in the world.

River view with compacted dirt road near Mechtersheim, Germany.

Hockenheim: The motor racing circuit and test track is across the Rhine, 10 kilometers (6 miles) to the east of Speyer.

From Speyer, this route takes you around the Old Rhine, meandering past little towns and villages such as Berghausen, Heiligenstein, Römerberg, Mechtersheim and Lingenfeld to Germersheim.

From Germersheim the route follows the Rhine proper along its west bank past Sondenheim and Leimersheim to Wörth am Rhein, across the river from Karlsruhe.

Directions:

Start at Mannheim Hauptbahnhof (main train station). Exit towards the Rhine and the youth hostel (Jugendherberge, bicycle sign), along Pennershofstrasse.

T-L along Stephanienufer

Road swings R

T-R, with Rhine park on your RHS

Y-R, continue along asphalt roadway

Y-R

Y-R

T-R along asphalt road

T (at parking area) L away from river, along Französicher Weg

(About 140 m) R along asphalt bike path through woods

Continue up to dike-top path, R along asphalt bike path, river on your RHS

L away from river, skirting factory, along dike-top asphalt bike path

Down slope, off dike-top, between allotments

T-R along Aufeldweg-IV (street)

Continue along road as it swings L (Rheinbadweg)

X-R along Marguerrestrasse (also on maps as Aufeldstrasse)

Continue along Plinaustrasse (bike path on LHS of road)

Road swings L

Immed. before rail line, R along Altriper Strasse, along brick paved bike path on RHS of road

Over rail line

Ferry

Cross Rhine on ferry [Altrip-Neckarau: 05h00–22h30, every 15 mins]

L along An der Fähre (street)

Continue along Rheinstrasse

Swing R along roadway

L along asphalt dike-top bike path

([KM 414] at river)

Immed. before entering Altrip town (buildings), down dike and L along asphalt roadway, with dike on your LHS

Pass small boat harbor (on your LHS)

T-L along roadway

(About 50 m) R off road onto bike path, dike on your LHS

([KM 411] at river)

Pass parking lot/restaurant

Up slope to top of dike

R along asphalt dike-top bike path

Bike path swings L off dike-top (at Otterstadt)

X-R (at Zum Alt Rhein restaurant)

L along asphalt bike path

X-R along roadway, towards Speyer (bicycle sign)

Road swings R, immed. L along bike path, alongside dike

Up ramp, onto sidewalk bike path alongside road

Under freeway (A61-A31) bridge

Continue along asphalt agricultural road, on RHS of roadway

At Rhine, continue along sidewalk bike path on RHS of road ([KM 402.5])

L across roadway, across dike to Rhine

R alongside river on compacted dirt road, river on your LHS

[KM 402]

Continue past slipway, along gravel road

[KM 401]

Continue with river on your LHS, buildings on your RHS

Continue along asphalt roadway

Y-L alongside harbor inlet

Continue along hard sand road

Immed. before harbor buildings, R

T-L along red brick paved bike path on RHS of road (Hafenstrasse)

Cross rail line

Cross river

Under pedestrian bridge

Continue along hard sand bike path in park

L across road, along Rheinallee (opp. mini golf)

Cross rail line

At Rhine, R alongside river towards bridge, river on your LHS

[KM 400]

Under road bridge (B39)

Continue along compacted dirt road

Immed. before old Rhine ship (on land), R-L onto roadway

Continue along asphalt road, rail line on your RHS

X continue along RHS bike path on roadway

X (at end of harbor) L towards river (ignore cycle sign indicating R)

X-R along asphalt bike path below dike towards Germersheim 22 km (bicycle sign)

Y-L along asphalt bike path, dike on your LHS

Info, on LHS (top of dike)

L to dike-top, continue along dike-top on compacted dirt road

X (ferry to R) continue along bike path, descending R off dike, road on your RHS, dike on your LHS

When road turns away to R, continue along lower dike bike path, dike on your LHS, towards Germersheim (bicycle sign R52)

T-L to dike-top and continue

Pass turning to Berghausen

Pass turning to Heiligenstein

Pass turning to Mechtersheim

Bike path turns hard R

[Continue along this bike path if you do not want to take the next turn to the river and cycle alongside on a

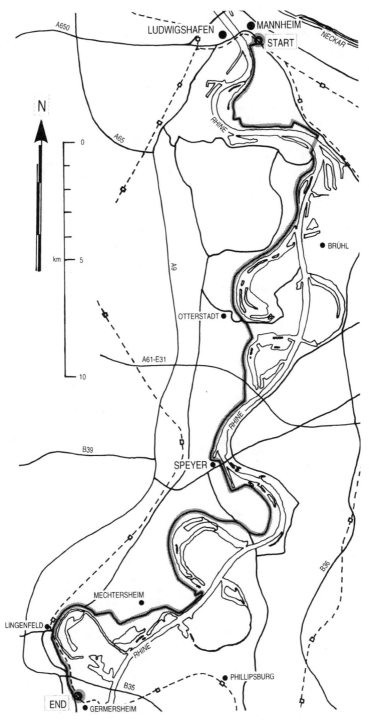

compacted dirt road; the two routes join 2.3 km further along]

L up dike, U-turn L over dike, R along tar road then hard dirt track towards river

At Rhine, R alongside river on hard sand road, river on your LHS

[KM 389]

Across parking area/slipway, R away from river on brick paved road

[Meet up with alternate route]

Continue along roadway

L along dike-top towards Lingenfeld 5.3 km (bike sign), past pump house

R down dike and alongside on bike path

L to top of dike, continue along asphalt bike path

Bike path swings L, lake and caravan camp on your RHS

Up slope, cross to LHS of road before intersection

X (at Katzenbuckel) L along agricultural road on RHS of roadway

Enter Lingenfeld along Speyerer Strasse

Cross rail line

Immed. L along Kolpingstrasse, rail line on your LHS

At end of road, continue across pedestrian bridge

L along Berliner Strasse

Road swings R into Bismarckstrasse

Immed. L along Friedrich-Ebert-Strasse, to end

Swing R along Kirchenallee

L along Erlenweg

Y-R

X continue along asphalt road, rail line on your LHS

Continue along Im Alter Zoll, on LHS sidewalk bike path

T-L along sidewalk bike path on LHS of road

Under freeway (A35) bridge, railway on your LHS

Info at Germersheim Bahnhof (train station)

Continue alongside K31 on sidewalk bike path

Y (K31) L along Lingenfelder Strasse

Continue along Bahnhofstrasse, on bike path, road swings L

Continue along Rudolf von Habsburgstrasse

Over rail line, under railway bridge, continue along bike path on LHS of road, towards river

At Rhine, R along fenced-off track

[KM 384]

Immed. before bridge, L towards river

R under railway bridge, along asphalt bike path, alongside river, river on your LHS, dike on your RHS

[KM 383]; [KM 382]; [KM 381]

Pass turning to Sondernheim

Continue along asphalt bike path, low dike on your LHS

R up slope to dike-top, continue along asphalt bike path

Cross sluice

Pass turning to Hördt

X-R towards Leimersheim (ferry to L), along bike path on RHS of road

L immed. before entrance to Leimersheim

Cross bridge

Up slope and R before dike-top (ferry on LHS)

Continue along asphalt bike path, dike on your LHS

Pass turning to Neupotz

Pass turning to Jockgrim

Up slope to L and across bridge

Up slope to dike-top, continue along dike-top along asphalt bike path

X continue along bike path below dike

Immed. before pump house, bike path swings hard R away from dike

Across bridge

Pass factory fence corner (Mobil refinery)

Continue along asphalt roadway

T-L to end of freeway overpass

R across road (K25), along asphalt agricultural road towards Wörth (bicycle sign)

Up ramp towards bridge over autobahn (A9)

T-R over bridge

Immed. L off bridge

T-L at bottom of bridge ramp, continue along asphalt roadway

Enter Wörth, continue along Friedrichstrasse

T-R along Forlachstrasse

T-L along Ludwigstrasse

Road swings R

L along Bahnhofstrasse

Through pedestrian area to subway

L through subway

L before next subway

T-R along bike path on RHS of road (L555/Hans-Martin-Schleier-Strasse)

Wörth Mitte Bahnhof (Central train station) on RHS; route ends here.

Diversion Route 16B: Wörth am Rhein to Karlsruhe

Distance: 11 km/7 miles (from Wörth Mitte Bahnhof to the Landesmuseum)

Terrain: Undulating, with easy hills

Map: ADAC Karlsruhe Stadtplan; 1:18,500 (1 cm = 185 m)

Description:

Karlsruhe (Karl's rest) was built from 1715 around the site of the ruins of Durlach Burg which was destroyed by the French in 1689. The focal point was the palace, a scaled down version of Versailles. Thirty-two streets radiate outwards from the palace, nine to the town and twenty-three to the woods. Legend has it that Margrave Karl Wilhelm of Baden rested in the Hardt forest here and liked the place so much,

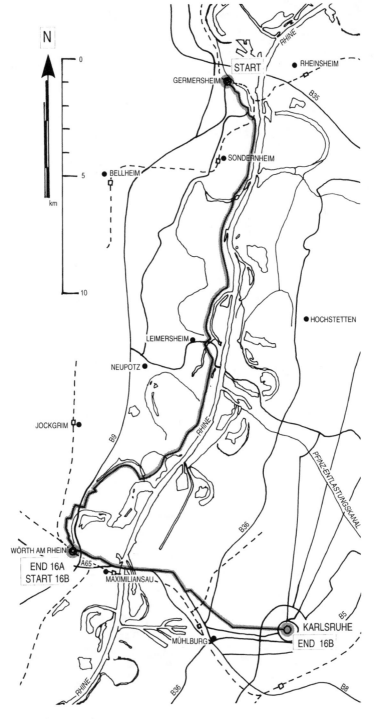

he decided to build a town. People of all denominations were invited to settle at Karlsruhe.

The Margrave's ashes are enclosed in a red sandstone pyramid monument in the city center at the edge of the Forum. Originally the monument was made of wood. Karl Friedrich of Baden enlarged Karlsruhe. In 1800 the architect Weinbrenner laid out the Kaiserstrasse, parallel to the palace. Only the palace tower survives as the other buildings were replaced 1749–81, following the original ground plans. The palace was badly damaged during World War II and restored to the original design. The palace museum displays some works by Grünewald.

Directions:

Start at Wörth am Rhein Bahnhof (train station), with the station building on your RHS and the roadway on your LHS.

Continue along Hans-Martin-Schleier-Strasse (L555) on RHS bike path

Under freeway bridge (A9)

Take bike path route up bridge on RHS (not on maps)

Bridge crosses rail line

U-turn L down ramp and off bridge

U-turn R away from bridge (between two rail lines)

Continue towards Maximilianstrasse, rail line on your LHS

Continue along bike path on LHS of road (Maximilianstrasse)

R towards bridge underpass

Immed. before bridge, L up bike path ramp to top of freeway (A10) bridge

L along bike path on LHS of bridge

L off freeway at Kirchtal (immed. before motor off-ramp to Rheinbrückenstrasse)

Along Am Kirchtal

Immed. U-turn R alongside LHS of motor off-ramp

X continue along bike path on RHS of Rheinbrückenstrasse

L along Sudetenstrasse

X-R along Siemensallee

Continue along Moltkestrasse

Pass Schlossgartenbahn, on your LHS

Arrive at Landesmuseum, on your RHS

[Return by the same route]

Diversion Suggestions

1. Landau: You could cycle via Kandel and Herxheim (50 km/31 miles) to the lovely little city of Landau, or take a train there and cycle around the district. Annweiler with its Trifels castle is another great destination.

2. Closer by, the Blenwald (forest) offers good cycling, through little villages such as Büchelberg.

France 17

Although part of the following routes pass through Germany, much of the route runs though the French Departments of Haut Rhin and Bas Rhin

Route 17: Wörth am Rhein to Kehl/Strasbourg via Drusenheim and Seltz

Distance: 92 km/58 miles

Terrain: Flat; compacted dirt roads, paved roads and bike paths, short sections over cobbles

Maps: ADFC Radtourenkarte Rhein – Neckar (No. 20) and Schwarzwald – Oberrhein (No. 24); 1:150,000 (1 cm = 1.5 km)

IGN Serie Verte (No. 12) Strasbourg – Forbach; 1:100,000 (1 cm = 1 km)

ADAC Stadtplan Strasbourg; 1:15,000 (1 cm = 150 m)

Diversions: See suggestions at end of this section

Description:

From Wörth am Rhein cycle to the Rhine at Maximiliansau, and continue alongside the river on its west bank.

Skirt Neuburg harbor and return to the Rhine bank to cross the border into France over the Alte Lauter river sluice.

Lauterbourg is situated near the confluence of the Lauter and Rhine rivers. It is one of the towns fortified by Vauban, and previously by the Romans. A gate with Louis XIV's emblem and some of the ramparts are still standing. Its church has a polygon choir dating from 1467. Lauterbourg is a center of the Alsatian tobacco industry, which has been grown since the sixteenth century.

Continue past Lauterbourg through the Sauer river lakeland with its waterfowl and flat-bottomed fishing boats. Travel alongside the Rhine, passing by Mothern and Münchhausen, two villages typical of the Ried region (wetlands) which have preserved their Alsatian character. They are connected with former forestry and rafting industries

Continue around the wetlands to Seltz, Roman Saletio. Cross the Rhine to Germany on the Seltz ferry.

Cycle on to the friendly town of Plittersdorf. A dedicated bike path follows the old Rhine waterways past former eel-fishing waters, to rejoin the Rhine at Iffezheim. Keep on alongside the Rhine past Sollingen and Greffern, to cross the Rhine to France on the Drusenheim ferry.

Cycle along the top of the river wall where possible (or on the road below) past Offendorf and cross back to Germany on the Gambsheim bridge. From here, continue alongside the Rhine on its east bank to Kehl.

[KM 293] Kehl is the principal town of South Baden and an important Rhine port. As the bridgehead for Strasbourg it has played its part in the history and development of the upper Rhine. The Kinzig river joins the Rhine here, flowing from the Black Forest.

[KM 293] Strasbourg was a settlement of the Nordgau (north people), a Germanic tribe under domination of the Alemanni, the Romans called it Argentoratum and later Strateburgum.

The Rhine Rift valley is 32 kilometers (20 miles) wide here. The Rhine falls 120 meters (400 feet) from Basel to Strasbourg, a distance of 110 kilometers (70 miles). Fruit orchards and vineyards abound and corn (maize), hops and tobacco are also grown. Alsace comprises the departments of Haut-Rhin and Bas-Rhin. Alsatian beers and wines are equally famous, and most of the beer produced in France comes from this region.

Strasbourg is the fourth largest port in France and one of the largest inland ports in the world, with wonderfully picturesque waterfronts.

The river Ill flows through Strasbourg, running almost parallel with the Rhine from the southern uplands.

Seltz ferry, crossing from France to Germany.

Punishments were once carried out by ducking or drowning in the river. Those condemned to death were dropped from the Pont du Corbeau (formerly the Pont des Supplices) with weights attached to them. The night before their execution, the condemned were entertained at public expense in a house left by the parents of a condemned murderer for that purpose.

Boat trips on the Ill start from the Place du Marché aux Poissons behind the Rohan Palace.

The French national anthem was written by Rouget de L'Isle in 1792 at Strasbourg. The name "Marseillaise" was given the song when the Marseilles contingent sang it as they entered Paris during the Revolution.

Strasbourg hosts the Council of Europe, the European Court of Human Rights and the Central Commission for the Navigation of the Rhine. The Rhine Commission represents the riparian states as well as the UK, Belgium, and others. Italy sat on the Commission until 1945 when it was replaced by the USA. The USA later dropped out. It was founded at the Treaty of Vienna in 1815. After World War II the Commission was responsible for clearing the Rhine for traffic. Every bridge from Switzerland to the Netherlands had been felled and more than two hundred thousand tons of steel and concrete had to be cleared away.

The Council of Europe, the European Union Parliament, sits in a building called the Palais de l'Europe. It is open to visitors weekday mornings and afternoons, except November to March, public holidays and during sittings of Parliament.

The Notre Dame Cathedral has a famous clock of moving figures which can be seen from the Cathedral square. The first clock made in the fourteenth century eventually failed and a new clock was ordered in 1547. It was designed by three leading mathematicians of Alsace and after twenty years it was handed over but it was still incomplete. Another professor of mathematics was brought in to finish the design and two mechanics built the machinery, which ran for two hundred years, stopping in 1789. Fifty years later a skilled mechanic was called in and after four years he had modified and rebuilt the entire works, adding motion to formerly fixed figures.

The 142 meter (461 feet) cathedral spire was completed in 1439 and until the nineteenth century it was the tallest building in Christendom. There is a magnificent sculpture adorning the doorways and a thirteenth century pillar of angels in the transept.

In 1576 there was unrest in Strasbourg and the magistrate held an arquebus shooting contest. Fifty-four marksmen from the Guilds of Zürich decided to do the four day trip downriver in only one day. They placed a large iron pot (porringer) filled with hot gruel in the center of the boat and when they reached Strasbourg the porridge was still hot. Johann Fischart, who witnessed the arrival of the Swiss, tells the story in a poem which was printed in 1577 and there is a copy in the Rhine Shipping museum in Basel harbor. The Zürichers promised that if Strasbourg was ever in need, they would respond sooner than "it takes a pot of porridge to cool." The original pot is in the museum by the Ill in Strasbourg. In 1870 the Zürichers sent US $1,600 (£1,000) to Strasbourg after a great bombardment of the city during the Franco-Prussian war. Thirty men from Basel who attended the contest brought a live deer and four live salmon in containers in their boat as part of their food supplies.

The Château de Rohan (palace) is built of white sand stone in the eighteenth century French style. Four Rohan princes were Cardinals and Bishops 1704–90. Musée Alsacien with the Historical museum display crafts of the area and folklore. In the Place de la Cathedral is a decoratively carved restaurant, Maison Kammerzell.

Directions:

Start at Wörth am Rhein Bahnhof (train station), station on your RHS, roadway on your LHS.

Continue along Hans-Martin-Schleier-Strasse (L555) on RHS bike path

Under freeway bridge (A9)

Take bike path route up bridge on RHS (not on maps)

Bridge crosses rail line

U-turn L down ramp and off bridge

U-turn R away from bridge (between two rail lines)

Continue towards Maximilianstrasse, rail line on your LHS

Continue along bike path on LHS of road (Maximilianstrasse)

Old cobbled tow-path near Maximiliansau, Germany.

Continue along Rheinstrasse (when Maximilianstrasse turns R under bridge), to Rhine

R alongside Rhine, river on your LHS, along asphalt track

Under freeway bridge (A10)

Under railway bridge

[KM 362]; [KM 361]

Bear R through slipway area and continue (do not turn R away from river)

L down concrete slipway

Cross small bridge

Continue along compacted dirt road

Cross bridge

To Rhine, continue alongside river, river on your LHS

[KM 359]

Continue through slipway area to water's edge

* Dismount and walk your bike over the cobbles for 750 meters (810 yards) alongside the river

[KM 358]

Cobbles end

Continue alongside river on hard dirt track

[KM 357]

* Dismount, cobbles for 50 meters (54 yards)

[KM 356]

[KM 355,6] R away from river

Continue along asphalt roadway, past Neuburg Boat Club

Up to dike-top, L along asphalt bike path

Cross sluice

Continue along asphalt bike path, dike on your LHS

Pass Dike Warden hut Neuburg I

To dike-top, continue along bike path

T-L across bridge and along road (L545)

Road swings R away from Rhine

L along compacted dirt road, towards Lauterbourg 5.2 km and Beinheim 18.2 km (bicycle signs), dike on your LHS

To dike-top at sluice [this waterway is the border between France and Germany]

Cross sluice bridge, continue along dike-top on asphalt road

Info on your RHS

Road swings L down dike, towards river

T-R alongside river

[KM 350]

Enter Lauterbourg

Info, map

Bear R out of car park [Viewpoint on LHS]

Continue along roadway, away from river

Cross rail line

X-L towards Mothern and Beinheim, along asphalt road

Cross rail line

L through crushing plant grounds (bicycle sign)

Under conveyor

Past slipway, continue along asphalt road on dike-top

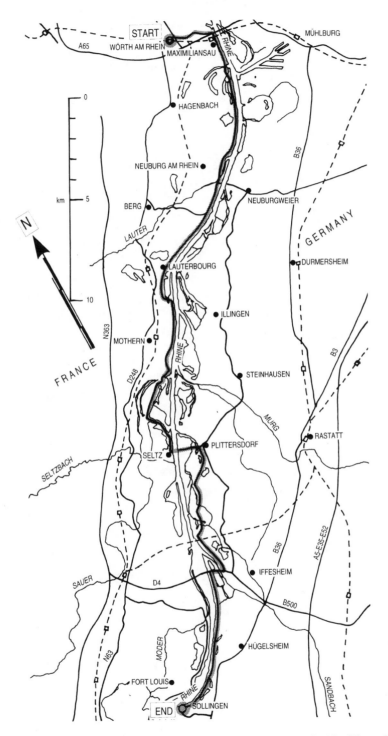

Road swings L over sluice

Y continue towards river

L towards river, along asphalt road on dike

At Rhine, R alongside river, river on your LHS

[KM 347]; [KM 346]

Road skirts inlet, up to (red-colored) asphalt dike-top bike path

Bike path swings away from river, briefly along roadway

L along dike-top asphalt bike path

Off dike, T-L

Cross bridge (la Sauer river)

Continue along asphalt road, swings R

Continue along (red) asphalt bike path, dike on your LHS

Cross bridge (stream)

Y-L along (red) asphalt bike path

Continue along cycle-marked asphalt bike path

Continue along demarcated bike lane (solid white line) on RHS of roadway

At Rhine, R on asphalt road alongside river, river on your LHS

T-L towards Seltz ferry

Cross Rhine on ferry

Continue along paved agricultural road on LHS of road (L77)

Bike path ends, continue along roadway

Immed. cross bridge

Enter Plittersdorf along Fahrstrasse

(1st) R, up slope to dike-top (bicycle sign)

L along compacted dirt dike-top bike path

Info, on LHS (birds)

Cross sluice

X continue along dike-top bike path

Info, on sluice bridge (eel fishing)

R off dike, L under motor road bridge (L786)

Continue along asphalt road

Info, on your LHS (Rhine Plains Route)

Continue towards Iffezheim 3.2 km (bicycle sign)

Continue along asphalt road (K3760)

Immed. before gate (gap) in dike, R up slope to dike-top, R along dike-top bike path

Y-L up to road (B500) bridge

R along B500 roadway

Cross 2 waterways (Sandbach river and a lake, but **not** the Rhine)

L along K3758 road (traffic signs)

Road swings L away from river wall (on your RHS)

Immed. before waterway, R towards river

Up ramp to top of river wall

L alongside Rhine, river on your RHS

[KM 332]; [KM 331]; [KM 330]

Continue through parking lot/slipway

[KM 329]; [KM 328]; [KM 327]

Continue through parking lot/slipway

[KM 326]

Continue through quarry harbor area, under conveyor

[KM 325]; [KM 324]; [KM 323]; [KM 322]

Skirt factory area

Continue through parking lot

Skirt Greffern small boat harbor

X continue along dike-top bike path

Under conveyor

At Rhine, L alongside river, river on your RHS

Cross sluice

[KM 320]; [KM 319]

Cross on ferry (free) Greffern–Drusenheim (March through Oct.: Mon–Fri 06h20–20h00, Sun + hols 06h40–22h00; Nov. through Feb.: Mon–Fri 06h20–20h00, Sun + hols 07h00–20h00; until 22h00, evenings before 1 May, 14 July, and 3 Oct.)

[The intention from here is to cycle alongside the Rhine, on top of the river wall, as much as possible. However, this is sometimes not possible, with only parts of this route accessible, although a full width asphalt road running alongside the bottom of the river wall, is the alternative.]

Continue away from river

X U-turn L back towards river along RHS roadway (of 3)

At Rhine, R along dike-top compacted dirt road, river on your LHS

(Alternatively, take the asphalt road below the river wall, running in the same direction)

[KM 317] (distance boards on river wall can be seen from road)

[KM 316]; [KM 315]; [KM 314]

River wall swings R around an inlet, continue

X-L towards river

Y-R to Rhine, R along dike-top, river on your LHS

[KM 311]

R down dike, away from river

X-L towards river

Continue along asphalt road, past quarry

Under conveyors

Immed. before X (circle/roundabout) cross to LHS bike path

Cross road at bike crossing

Immed. L along bike path towards bridge (Gambsheim barrage)

Continue along sidewalk, over waterway

Info, tourist office behind restaurant

[KM 309]

Continue along roadway across waterway

Info, in picnic area

Continue along roadway

X-R along L87 towards Kehl and Freistett

L towards Schiffswerf and Kehl (bicycle sign)

Continue towards Schiffswerf (road swings away to L)

Cross bridge

L across compacted dirt parking area towards ramp up river wall

Up ramp to top of river wall

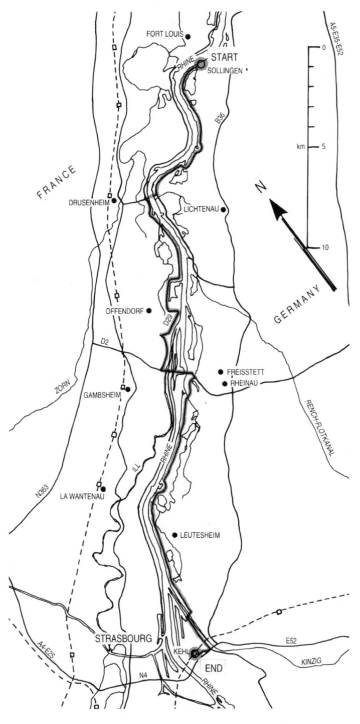

At Rhine, L alongside river on compacted dirt road, river on your RHS

[KM 307]; [KM 306]

Under conveyor

[KM 305]; [KM 304]

Road skirts harbor and quarry, under conveyor

[KM 303]; [KM 302]; [KM 301]; [KM 300]; [KM 299]

L alongside Kinzig river ([KM 298] at confluence)

Bike path ends

T-R across one-way bridge

Immed. L along hard sand dike-top bike path

Under road bridge (Hafenzufahrt Ost)

Under railway bridge

Up ramp to top of road bridge (A28-N4-E52)

R along bike path on RHS of road (Strassburger Strasse)

X (lights) R along Königsberger Strasse

Continue along road as it swings L

Continue along Bahnhofstrasse

To Kehl Bahnhof (train station); route ends here

Diversion Suggestions

1. Strasbourg has much to offer in the way of sights and activities. Festivals, exhibitions, recitals and concerts are daily fare, but the everyday life around the streets and canals can be just as entertaining and enlightening. Even in

Waterfowl along the banks of the Rhine on a misty autumn day.

wintertime the mood is equally magical, especially around the old quarter.

2. Offenburg lies on the Kinzig river where it emerges from the Black Forest. It is an important town in the Ortenau wine producing region. It has many 18th century buildings and some older architecture. You can reach Offenburg by train, or cycle the 18 kilometers (11 miles) zigzagging across the Rhine plain through wetlands, woods and little villages. You could also follow the European cycleroute alongside the Kinzig river, from Sundheim-Neumühl. There are numerous walking and cycling trails into the Black Forest and the views are stunning.

Route 18A: Kehl/Strasbourg to Breisach am Rhein via Rhinau

Distance: 105 km/65 miles

Terrain: Flat; paved surfaces, compacted dirt roads

Maps: IGN Serie Verte (No. 12) Strasbourg – Forbach; 1:100,000 (1 cm = 1 km)

IGN Serie Verte (#31) St-Dié – Bâle; 1:100 000 (1cm = 1 km)

ADFC Radtourenkarte Schwarzwald-Oberrhein (No. 24); 1:150,000 (1 cm = 1.5 km)

ADAC Strasbourg Stadtplan; 1:15,000 (1 cm = 150 m) (relevant sections of Kehl included)

Diversion: See Route 18B (Colmar)

Also suggestions at the end of this section

Description:

From Kehl, cycle southwards alongside the east bank of the Rhine. Cross the Rhine wall to the riverside at Segelhafen, continuing through leafy woodlands and wetlands to the Schwanau region. Along the way, pass by the villages of Marlen, Goldscheuer, Altenheim, Meissenheim, and Ottenheim.

[KM 271] In the fourteenth century Walter von Geroldseck established a fortress on Schwanau island. The outer defense of swamps surrounded a system of deep moats. In 1333 the Basel and Strasbourg townsfolk organized an attack on the robber occupants. A bridge of boats brought catapults to hurl garbage and other missiles. When the garrison of sixty capitulated they were executed; three tradesmen were catapulted against the walls and only a very old man and a young boy were spared.

Cross the Rhine barrage and the Grand Canal d'Alsace locks and hydro-electric installation here. Turn south alongside the wall of the canal, then away from the waterway to the floral village of Gerstheim, which boasts an eighteenth century castle.

Cycle through villages with well-preserved half-timbered houses, old barns and agricultural relics, all emblazoned with a great variety of flowers and plants; Obenheim, Daubensand, Rhinau.

Rhinau typifies the Ried (wetlands) countryside near the Rhine. The specialized plants of the area are strictly protected, as is the wildlife.

Cycle on through Friesenheim, Diebolsheim, Saasenheim, Richtolsheim and Artolsheim, past Bootzheim and Mackenheim to Marckolsheim.

At Marckolsheim is the memorial museum of the Maginot line, in blockhouse 35/3. It opens from mid-June to mid-September, otherwise only on Sundays and public holidays, closed throughout November. There is a steam train to Neuf-Brisach. It is a lively, pretty town with some photogenic buildings.

From Marckolsheim cross the barrage and locks on the Rhine to the wine village of Sasbach, in the volcanic Kaiserstuhl region.

Sasbach, with other Kaiserstuhl wine villages such as Ihringen and Oberrotweil, produces a variety of wines, from Ruländer through late Burgundy, Silvaner, and Riesling, to Gewürztraminer. A large glass of

Sasbacher Gewürztraminer with a fine traditional meal is always worth the effort of getting here.

The Kaiserstuhl is a series of volcanic hills near the Rhine, to the west of the Black Forest. Totenkopf is 557 meters (1,810 feet) high. The Rhine is 183 meters (595 feet) above sea level at this point.

Kiechlinsbergen is another wine village in the hills. Here a white porcelain cat (Mäusefrass) is customarily used to discourage the loss of wine to (two-legged) mice.

From Sasbach return to the east bank of the Rhine, passing below the ruins of Sponeck castle. Cycle alongside the Rhine through the wetland forests to Breisach am Rhein.

[KM 224] The Romans called Breisach Mons Brisiacus for the strange hill that rises on the bank of the river. In the 1930s there was a bridge of boats across the river which nowadays has been replaced by a concrete road bridge. It provides the only harbor on the Rhine between Strasbourg and Basel.

During World War II Breisach suffered more destruction than any town in Germany except for Emmerich. The townsfolk were polled secretly in a referendum of 1950 to test opinion about the creation of a European Union, particularly because they had suffered such destruction during the war. Surprisingly, ninety-five percent came out in favor of the Union.

In 1296 the course of the Rhine shifted, leaving Breisach on the east bank, instead of the west bank as before.

Downstream of the tanker jetty is a gateway designed by Vauban built as a defense and a triumphal arch for the French troops.

Le Forge at Saasenheim, Alsace, France. This building serves as a gîte (rural holiday accommodation).

The Grand Canal d'Alsace going upstream turns away from the Rhine at the Vogelgrün locks. The Canal de Colmar branches off the Rhine at Breisach and continues to the Canal du Rhône au Rhin.

The Stephanmünster (cathedral) on the hill in the Romanesque style has a carved altarpiece (1523–26) by Master H.L. Tradition attributes the carving to Hans Liefrink, who was recommended by Albrecht Dürer. His lover's father challenged him to build an altarpiece higher than the nave of the church with his daughter's hand in marriage as the prize. He carved the piece in lime wood and designed it to curve along the roof. The cathedral was built from about the twelfth century. The cathedral was destroyed in World War II and completely rebuilt in 1945.

November 11 is the festival of the Guild of Fools. The three Guilds are over five hundred years old. The Guild of Gaukler counts tumblers, acrobats, strolling players, and conjurers amongst its members. There is an annual Gauklertag during Lent.

Directions:

Start at Kehl Bahnhof (train station). Exit station building R towards car park

L out of car park, cross road and L along RHS of road

X continue along Hauptstrasse on RHS bike path

R along Friedenstrasse, to Rhine

L alongside Rhine, along Ludwig-Trick-Strasse, river on your RHS

[KM 293]

Continue along Rheindammstrasse

[Pass youth hostel, on your LHS]

Continue along Kronenhofstrasse

Road ends, continue up ramp, continue along asphalt road, dike on your RHS

Exit Kehl

T-R over dike

Cross bridge over canal

Road swings L, dike on your RHS, canal LHS

Cross sluice

X-L-R towards Segel Hafen along hard dirt track, dike on your RHS

Road swings L along bottom of river wall

Continue up ramp to top of river wall

R to top of wall

L along bike path on top of river wall

R down to bottom of wall

R away from river wall along hard dirt track

Cross bridge

Road swings L past small boat harbor, on your RHS

Road swings R towards harbor entrance

Continue between two waterways to Rhine

L alongside river, river on your RHS

Cross sluice

Continue along hard sand road

[KM 287]

Y-R alongside river

[KM 286]; [KM 285]

Y-R across footbridge (steps)

Continue towards river wall

Along asphalt road to top of river wall

X continue along top of river wall on hard sand road

Pass river barrage

Under conveyor (loading point for gravel pit/quarry)

[KM 283]; [KM 282]; [KM 281]; [KM 280]; [KM 279]; [KM 278]

Continue through parking area (L to Ichenheim)

[KM 277]

L through quarry (* Beware loose and deep gravel; better walk through here)

Under conveyor

Exit quarry

Bear R alongside water (on your RHS)

R along dike-top, dike swings R

At Rhine, L along river wall on compacted dirt road, river on your RHS

[KM 276]; [KM 275]; [KM 274]; [KM 273]

Pass quarry loading area, on your RHS (on LHS is road to Ottenheim)

Continue along dike-top

L off dike

Continue, dike on your RHS, canal LHS

X-R towards river, along tar road (L to nearby restaurant/pub)

Continue through dike wall, over canalized stream

Immed. L, to Rhine

L along hard dirt road

Road swings R towards barrage

Pass barrage, on your RHS

Continue alongside river, along hard dirt track

(½)L up bank to roadway

T-R along asphalt road (D426)

* This (6 km/4 miles) section of the route takes you across the Rhine barrage, shipping locks and hydro-electric dam. There are no bike paths nor road verges (shoulders). Motor traffic has a speed limit of 70 km/h (44 mph). At times the traffic can be quite heavy and fast, but on all occasions I have crossed here, I have experienced no problems.

* Beware of drains next to the curb; some are sunk well below the road surface and some have covers missing.

Cross Rhine bridge

Info, in rest areas

Cross lock and hydro-electric bridge

Immed. L towards Gerstheim, along asphalt road (D20), river wall on your LHS

Continue past Erstein turnoff, along D20

[The D20 road alongside and below the river wall has become an extremely busy motor route and is unsuitable for cycling for any length of time]

R towards Gerstheim, along N924

Y-R along main road

Enter Gerstheim on N924

Immed. cross bridge

Continue along Rue de Brigade Alsace-Lorraine

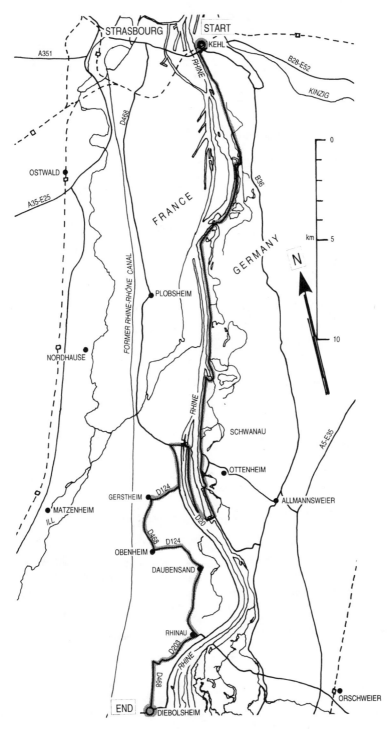

Cross bridge, road swings L

Continue along Rue du Rhin .

Pass Hôtel de Ville (City Hall)

[Public toilets behind Hôtel de Ville]

Info, town map, on LHS

X (circle/roundabout) L along Rue General de Gaulle and D468 towards Obenheim

Exit Gerstheim along D468

Cross bridge

Enter Obenheim on D468, along Rue de Strasbourg

L towards Daubensand, along Rue de Daubensand, on D124

[20 m straight past this turn, Info town map on RHS, opp. church]

Enter Daubensand on D124, along Rue Principale

R towards Rhinau, opposite Mairie (Mayor's office/town hall)

Exit Daubensand

Y-L towards Rhinau

Enter Rhinau

X continue along Rue de Daubensand

T-L along Rue de Boofzheim

Continue along Rue Nouveau Faubourg

Continue along Rue Hôtel de Ville

Info, map of Rhinau at town square and Hôtel de Ville

R towards Friesenheim along Rue du la Dordogne (D203)

Exit Rhinau along D203

Enter Friesenheim on D203

Immed. cross bridge

Road swings L

T-L towards Diebolsheim along Rue Principale (D468)

Pass Mairie, on your RHS

Info, town map

Exit Friesenheim on D468

Cross canal (former Rhine-Rhône canal)

Enter Diebolsheim on D468, along Rue de Strasbourg

Continue along Rue Principale

Info, town map, on LHS

X (circle/roundabout) R towards Saasenheim on D468

Exit Diebolsheim on D468

Enter Saasenheim on D468, along Rue Principale

Pass Mairie

Exit Saasenheim on D468

Enter Richtolsheim on D468

Continue along Rue Principale

Exit Richtolsheim along D468

Enter Artolsheim on D468, along Rue de Strasbourg

Continue along Rue Principale

Pass Mairie

X (circle/roundabout) continue towards Mackenheim/Marckolsheim on D468

Exit Artolsheim along D468

Enter Mackenheim on D468

Exit Mackenheim along D468

X (circle/roundabout) continue towards Marckolsheim on D468

Enter Marckolsheim on D468, along Rue Clemenceau, to Centre Ville

Hôtel de Ville

Info, town map

Immed. L along Rue de la Hôtel de Ville

Cross bridge

X (circle/roundabout) continue along Rue de la Baronne

Pass Centre de Secours

Immed. L along Avenue d'Europe

X (circle/roundabout) R along D424 towards Freiburg, along demarcated (white line) bike lane on RHS of roadway

Cross bridge

Cross rail line

Cross lock and hydro-electric bridge

Info, tourist office in restaurant building (door at side)

Cross Rhine bridge

R towards Limburg/Sasbach

Info, at Limburg car park

Continue along asphalt bike path on RHS of road

Enter Sasbach, bike path ends

L along Marckholheimer Strasse

T-R along Jechtinger Strasse, towards Jechtingen

R towards sports fields and Limburg Halle, along Dorf Insel (street)

Continue along hard dirt track

Continue through gap in dike

Cross bridge

Immed. Y-R, through forest, then fields

T (at line of trees) L

Road swings R towards river

L at Rhine, along compacted dirt road, river on your RHS

[KM 238]

Pass barrage

[KM 237]; [KM 236]; [KM 235]

Through barrier

Continue along asphalt road

R towards river wall

R to top of wall

U-turn L onto top of river wall, at barrage

Continue along compacted dirt road on top of river wall, river on your RHS

Pass small boat harbor

[KM 234]; [KM 233]; [KM 232]; [KM 231]; [KM 230]; [KM 229]

L down bank (steps at KM 228,5) away from river

Cross bridge over canal

Continue along dirt track

Cross sluice

Immed. L along dirt road

T-R along asphalt road (past waterworks)

X-R along roadway

X-R along bike path on LHS of Hafenstrasse

Enter Breisach am Rhein along Hafenstrasse

R at end of Omni Tank factory site, towards Rhine

Bear L through parking lot, to river

L alongside river, river on your RHS

Follow bike path as it swings away from river

T-R along Josef-Boeb-Strasse

Info, on RHS at traffic lights

X (lights) R, continue to Rhine

L along Rheinufer (road)

Under motor bridge

L along road away from river

L over pedestrian bridge

Immed. R along bike path

Y-L along bike path

Through subway under motor road

T-R along bike path

T-L along bike path on LHS of road (Neutorplatz)

Immed. before circle/roundabout, R across road and L along bike path

X (circle/roundabout) R along Bahnhofstrasse

Breisach Bahnhof (train station) on your RHS; route ends here.

Diversion Route 18B: Breisach to Colmar via Neuf-Brisach

Distance: 50 km/31 miles

Terrain: Flat; paved surfaces, compacted dirt roads

Map: IGN Serie Verte (No. 31) St-Dié – Bâle; 1:100,000 (1 cm = 1 km)

Description:

Cross the Rhine from Breisach and cycle through the village of Volgelsheim to Neuf-Brisach.

When Louis XIV lost (Old) Breisach to the Austrians, he no longer had a fortress in the Alsace region. To remedy this he appointed his military engineer Vauban as architect of a new town, Neuf-Brisach, to be built here. This site was formerly a stone-age settlement, later Roman and then Merovingian. Vauban built the octagonal walls with twenty-four defensive towers, moats and four great gates. The streets inside the walls, crossing at right angles, allowed defenders to reach any point quickly. Folk who agreed to live in this new town were given land, and the town was given rights to hold fairs and markets and exemption from taxes.

The Vauban museum is at the Ponte de Belfort and opens every day except Mondays.

Cycle into Neuf-Brisach through the Strasbourg gate to the central square, then out of town through the Colmar gate. On along quiet roads to the village of Wolfganzen, then to Appenwihr and Sundhoffen where you cross the Ill river on its journey to Strasbourg. Continue past fields into the Colmar forest, emerging to reach Colmar.

Colmar is considered the most beautiful town in Alsace. The Old Quarter is situated between the Unterlinden museum and Little Venice on the banks of the canalized Lauch river.

Colmar's name derives from "colles Martis," the hill of Mars, the Roman god of war. Little survives of its history before the thirteenth century and the town has a medieval look.

Musée d'Unterlinden is an ancient monastery building which houses the Issenheim altarpiece painted by Matthias Grünewald in the sixteenth century, as well as pre-historic remains. Schongauer's work is also represented. In the rue des Têtes (road of the heads) there are sculptured heads on a seventeenth century house, Maison des Têtes (house of the heads). In the Grand Rue are historic houses, an old hospital, an ancient customs house and a fountain by Bartholdi.

In the fifteenth century Dominican church (Eglise des Dominicains) are beautiful stained glass windows and The Virgin of the Rose Bush by Martin Schongauer. Schongauer was Albrecht Dürer's master.

Musée Bartholdi is the birthplace of the sculptor Bartholdi, who created the Statue of Liberty. Eiffel (Eiffel Tower, Paris), another Alsatian, planned the structural engineering.

There is a wine festival in mid-August and a choucroute (sauerkraut) festival in September. Colmar Info, Office de Tourisme, 4 rue d'Unterlinden.

Directions:

Start at Breisach Bahnhof. With the Bahnhof on your LHS, cycle along Bahnhofstrasse, past the Info board towards the intersection.

Around circle/roundabout, to L exit (Neutorplatz), along bike path

T-R along bike path immed. before intersection

L under subway

Immed. R along bike path, alongside road (B31), on your RHS

Continue along bike path on LHS of B31

Immed. before bridge, cross to RHS of road

Cross bridge over Rhine along roadway

Continue across bridge over shipping locks and hydro-electric plant

R towards Neuf-Brisach along road D1-iv (bicycle sign)

X-R along D1-iv towards Volgelsheim

Enter Volgelsheim on D1-iv

Over bridge, continue along Rue de la Fôret Noire

STOP, Info on RHS, continue towards Neuf-Brisach (sign across road)

STOP, continue along RHS bike path (sign on RHS)

Info on your RHS

L at wall, along bike path

Bike path swings R

Over bridge

Continue along bike path on LHS of road (Chemin des Ecoliers)

T-R along bike path on LHS of road (bicycle sign)

Bike path ends

Cross rail line

Immed. R across road, immed. L across rail lines

Continue along roadway (D1-x)

Exit Volgelsheim along D1-x

X (circle/roundabout) L along D468 towards Neuf-Brisach

Cross bridge

Enter Neuf-Brisach

Cross rail line

Cross moat, through Strasbourg gate

Continue to town square

R across face of Cathedral

(1st) L, towards Colmar (bicycle sign)

(1st) R, along Rue de Colmar (bicycle sign)

Exit through Colmar gate

Cross bridge over river

Immed. R (immed. before cemetery) along asphalt roadway towards Wolfganzen (bicycle sign)

Continue along asphalt road, cemetery on your LHS, river RHS

Under bridge, rail line on your RHS

X continue, beginning of town buildings

T-L along Rue du Canal, away from rail line

T-L along Rue de la Gare

T-R towards Colmar (bicycle sign at Mairie)

X-L towards Appenwihr and Colmar along Route d'Appenwihr (D1)

Exit Wolfgantzen along D1

Through forest

Enter Appenwihr on D1

X (circle/roundabout) R towards Sundhoffen, along Rue de Sundhoffen

Exit Appenwihr along D13

Continue along roadway (NOT the bike path)

X (circle/roundabout) continue towards Colmar on D13

Cross bridge

L along Rue des Alpes (at traffic island)

(1st) R along asphalt road between fields, towards Colmar

Continue through forest (Bois de Colmar)

T-R alongside freeway (A35-E25) embankment

L through subway under freeway

Immed. L alongside freeway embankment

R away from freeway, through forest, along asphalt road

Cross bridge

X-R towards Colmar, bike lane demarcated (white line) on RHS of road (RN422)

L along Avenue de Fribourg

Continue along Avenue Georges Clemenceau

Continue along Avenue Raymond Poincaré

Cross Rue de la Gare

To Colmar train station (Gare); route ends here

Return by the same route, or choose alternate routes. Other roads will generally be busier than those on the described route.

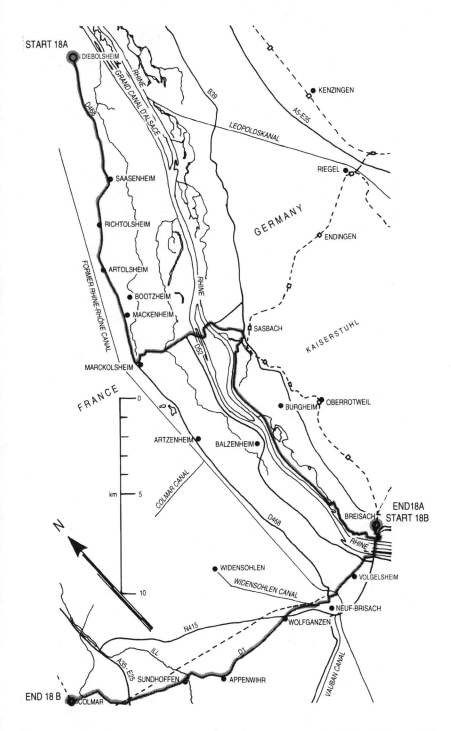

Other Diversion Suggestions

1. The Kaiserstuhl area reaches south and west to Breisach itself. There are over twenty towns, villages and hamlets to explore, all concerned with producing wine. There is a tourist train (Kaiserstuhlbahn) which makes circular tours around the Kaiserstuhl.

2. Freiburg im Breisgau is an old university town some 20 kilometers from Breisach on the edge of the Black Forest (Schwarzwald). You can get there by train or bike. There are numerous cycle and hiking routes in the mountains and forests nearby. The town itself offers countless sights and activities.

3. The Alsace wine route stretches along the edge of the Rhine valley from Obernai in the north to Thann in the south. Any part can be accessed by train from Neuf-Brisach or Colmar. Turckheim near Colmar is a particularly lovely wine town with an interesting history.

18

Switzerland

This last stage of your tour, though partly leadng you over roads in France and Germany, finally brings you to the end of the tour in Basel, Switzerland.

Route 19: Breisach to Basel via Neuenburg am Rhein, Kembs, and Huningue

Distance: 76 km/48 miles

Terrain: Flat; compacted dirt roads, paved roads and bike paths

Maps: IGN Serie Verte (No. 31) St-Dié–Bâle; 1:100,000 (1 cm = 1 km)

ADFC Radtourenkarte Schwarzwald – Oberrhein (No. 24); 1:150,000 (1 cm = 1.5 km)

ADAC Basel Stadtplan; 1:15,000 (1 cm = 150 m)

Description:

Leave Breisach am Rhein on the bike path alongside the Rhine east bank. Cycle southwards in the riverine woodlands and wetlands to the river crossing at Neuenburg am Rhein.

[KM 199] In 1496 the village of Burg was undermined by the Rhine, after which it was moved to the present site and called Neuenburg (New Burg).

During the Thirty Years' War the villagers killed a Swedish patrol. They taunted the Swedes saying, "When we come to Sweden you can do the same to us." The Swedish commander swore he would avenge himself on the town until not a dog remained alive. He repented, but to keep his oath he had all the dogs in the town killed.

In the Franco-Prussian War, Seubert began his deception of the French from here, using one company of soldiers to make the French believe there was a sizeable army in the hills, thereby preventing their invasion of the Black Forest.

Markgräfler wines are produced in the area.

Cross the Rhine bridge to Chalampé. From Chalampé cycle inland to Bantzenheim and on to Ottmarsheim. Ottmarsheim boasts an eleventh century octagonal church, a copy of the chapel founded by Charlemagne at

Aachen (Aix-la-Chapelle). It was consecrated by Pope Leo IX in 1049.

Keep on through the Rhine plain to Hombourg and Niffer, crossing the Rhine junction with the great canals to the Rhône and Saône rivers, as well as the canal to Huningue near Basel.

At Kembs a barrage was constructed after World War I (1914–18) to create a lateral canal and bypass the Istein bar. The Istein bar had become increasingly detrimental to river traffic, often deteriorating into rapids.

The French also wanted to use the potential of the river to produce hydroelectricity and the entire project was completed in 1933. A bypass was cut, using locks to connect both ends with the Rhine waterway and this canal was used by shipping to and from Basel, the upriver section of the Rhine thereafter being neglected for shipping.

From Kembs, cycle alongside the peaceful canal de Huningue. In 1834 this canal had fifty locks to Strasbourg, a drop of 107 meters (350 feet). Continue past Schaeferhof and Rosenau, through the Alsatian Petite Camargue nature reserve, past Village-Neuf to Huningue and the Rhine.

West of Huningue is the Euro-Airport at St. Louis, which serves Basel in Switzerland, Mulhouse in France and Freiburg in Germany. The three countries pylon is at the port of Klein Hüningen.

The tranquil road to Basel, alongside the Huningue Canal.

Weil am Rhein is the German city across the Rhine from Basel.

[KM 170] Basel is the only Rhine city upstream of Köln to lie across the river.

Basel itself dates from 44 BC, when it was a settlement of the Alemanni, a mix of Germanic tribes. Upstream are about forty Roman forts and watch towers and remains of a significant Roman settlement. Since 1529 Basel has been a part of the Helvetic Confederation (Switzerland). It is the second largest city in Switzerland.

The port of Basel is Switzerland's only direct access to the sea. The original port was a wharf (Schifflände) at the foot of a bluff, on top of which stands a cathedral and the old quarter. Supposedly it was the landing place of St. Ursula and the eleven thousand virgins (see Cologne). There is an unpowered (overhead cable) ferry below the cathedral cliff and three other similar sampan-like pedestrian ferries on the Rhine.

At Basel the Rhine is 265 meters (861 feet) wide. There are six bridges; the Dreirosenbrücke (three roses bridge), St. John's bridge. Mittlene Brücke (Central bridge, which has a twentieth-century chapel on it), Wettstein bridge, Schwarzwaldbrücke (Black Forest bridge), and the Railway bridge.

In 1417 two hundred and fifty tuns (302 US/252 Imperial gallons per tun) of wine were loaded at Basel as a present from the Emperor Sigismund to King Henry V of England. The Duke of Brabant confiscated the cargo in Dutch waters. For decades thereafter, Basel confiscated everything Dutch.

An earthquake dropped a bell from the catholic cathedral into the Rhine. This was Lucia, sister bell of Susanna of Schönau. Some Baslers stole Susanna but were caught. Legend says that Lucia will remain in the Rhine until Basel is once more a catholic city.

The Basel carnival is held during Lent. It begins at four in the morning on the Monday after Ash Wednesday, continuing until the Thursday morning. Drummers abound in the festival; there are about thirty drumming schools in Basel. In the January festival a wild man sets off down the Rhine on a raft carrying a small pine tree. When he reaches the Central bridge he is received by Vogel Gryff (Griffin) and Leu (Lion). At noon they dance to the accompaniment of drums in the middle of Central bridge without looking at the city, keeping their eyes on the Black Forest. Their intention is to chase the winter away.

The first powered vessel to reach Basel was the ss Stadt Frankfurt in 1827, powered by a 45 horse power Brunel engine. The Oswald brothers, candlemakers, developed a steamer service to London in 1832, the trip taking four and a half days. The service folded in 1837.

In the 1840s Tulla's engineering (canalization) of the Rhine prevented steamships from reaching Basel. In 1903 the tug Justizia arrived at Basel and in 1904 a cargo of coal was hauled to Basel by a Dutch tug. The harbor was opened in 1924, and by 1925 three million tons of cargo annually was arriving at Basel by boat.

The 1868 Treaty of Mannheim gave all riparian states the right to use the Rhine waterway without fee, from Basel to the North Sea.

The Rhine Shipping museum is in the Basel harbor area. There is a copy of the poem by Johann Fischart about the arrival of the Zürichers at Strasbourg for the arquebus tournament.

Basel sent thirty marksmen to the tourney.

The pharmaceutical industry in Basel is of major economic importance and is strongly represented by CIBA-GEIGY, Sandoz, and Roche. Dr. Paul Müller of GEIGY was awarded the Nobel Prize for creating DDT.

Directions:

Start at Breisach Bahnhof (train station). With the Bahnhof on your LHS, cycle towards the intersection ahead

Info map on your RHS, opposite Bahnhof

X (roundabout/circle) around and L along bike path

R along bike path immed. before intersection

L through subway on bike path

T-R towards pedestrian bridge

L over pedestrian bridge

Immed. R along roadway towards Rhine

L immed. before passing under road bridge over Rhine, to river

L alongside Rhine, on asphalt bike path, river on your RHS

Y-R alongside river

[KM 224]

Asphalt ends, continue along compacted dirt road

[KM 223]; [KM 222]; [KM 221]; [KM 220]

Skirt slipway

Over sluice

L away from river on asphalt road (K4933), skirt campsite

R along compacted dirt road, towards Oberrimsingen (bicycle sign route R2)

Continue along dirt track between boats and caravans

Info on RHS (local fishes)

Y-R towards river

Road swings R towards river

L alongside Rhine, river on your RHS

[KM 218]; [KM 217]; [KM 216]; [KM 215]

Continue past slipway, along asphalt road

Swing R around house (on your RHS), continue along compacted dirt road

Y-R towards river

L alongside Rhine, river on your RHS

[KM 214]; [KM 213]; [KM 212]; [KM 211]

Continue past slipway

[KM 210]; [KM 209]; [KM 208]; [KM 207]

Continue past slipway, towards Basel [bicycle sign Grissheim to LHS]

[KM 206]; [KM 205]; [KM 204]; [KM 203]

[bicycle sign Zienken to LHS]

[KM 202]; [KM 201]; [KM 200]

Continue past slipway, along asphalt road

X-R along concrete bike path, towards river, (bicycle sign Basel 31km)

L alongside Rhine, river on your RHS

[KM 199]

L immed. before passing under road/rail bridge, towards bridge top

R to (Neuenburg–Chalampé) bridge

R along bridge sidewalk, on RHS of roadway

Cross Rhine, cross Grand Canal d'Alsace

* Dismount to get off sidewalk no ramps

Continue along roadway

R along road to Chalampé (follow road signs)

Y (½)L along Avenue de la Gare

X L towards Bantzenheim along Avenue Pierre Emil Lucas (bicycle sign)

X (lights) and continue

Exit Chalampé

X continue along D4-bis (road) towards Bantzenheim

Enter Bantzenheim

X (circle/roundabout) along Rue du General de Gaulle

X (at church) L towards Ottmarsheim (bicycle sign across road)

Continue past Mairie (Town Hall)

X (lights) L towards Ottmarsheim, along Rue de Bâle (bicycle sign across road)

Continue along D468 (road)

Cross rail line

X continue along Rue de Bâle (D468) towards Ottmarsheim

Cross rail lines

Exit Bantzenheim along D468

Enter Ottmarsheim on D468

View from across the Rhine of Basel, Switzerland.

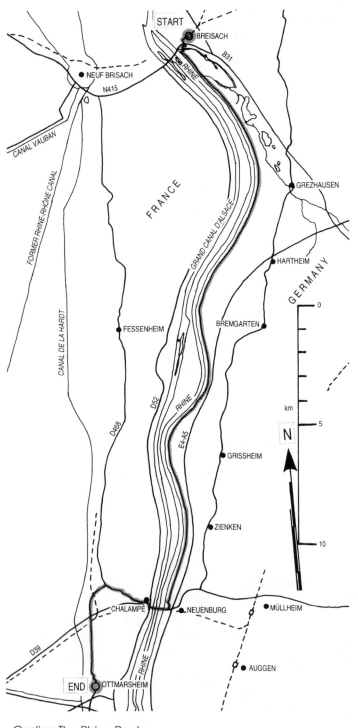

Continue along Rue du General de Gaulle

Info, town map on LHS (before Mairie)

Info at Mairie

X (circle/roundabout) Continue towards Hombourg, along D468

Immed. cross canal

Over bridge across freeway (A36-E54)

Enter Hombourg along D468

Continue along Rue Principale

Info, town map at Mairie

Continue along D468 towards Petit-Landau

[The more easterly road shown on most maps between Hombourg and Petit-Landau, no longer exists.]

Past Chateau de Hombourg (on your RHS)

Pass by Petit-Landau, on your LHS

Enter Niffer on D468

Past Mairie (on your LHS)

Exit Niffer along D468

Swing L along main road (former through road now cut off by freeway)

T-R towards Kembs along D52/D468

Over bridges across Rhine-Saône-Rhône canal

Enter Kembs on D52/D468, along Rue de Mârechal Foch

Info, town map (immed. past church)

Pass Mairie

(1st) L along Rue Paul Bader

R immed. before swing bridge over Canal de Huningue

Continue along asphalt bike path (Chemin du Sipes), canal on your LHS

Continue along compacted dirt road bike path, alongside canal

Continue towards Rosenau (bicycle sign)

Under bridge, continue (Schaeferhof to RHS)

Under bridge, continue (Rosenau to LHS)

L over lock

Immed. R towards Village-Neuf, along hard sand bike path, canal on your RHS

R over lock

Immed. L along bike path (Chemin du Sipes/Chemin du Planetes) towards St. Louis, between waterways

Across small bridge

Continue along hard sand bike path, canal on your LHS

Under motor bridge (St. Louis to RHS)

Under motor bridge, along asphalt bike path

Enter Huningue

Under motor bridge

Under railway bridge, along Quai du Maroc

Under pedestrian bridge

Y-L towards canal bank

Continue along hard sand bike path

Info, at pedestrian bridge

Continue along paved bike path; mind the cross-drains

Y-R

Info

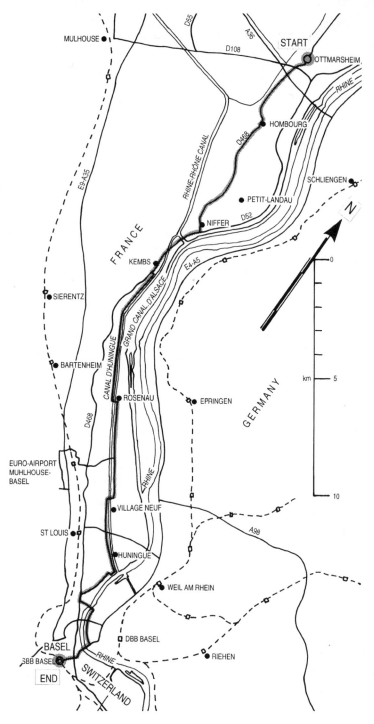

Under subway

L towards lock

R, arrive immed. at Rhine

R along Quai du Rhin, Rhine on your LHS

STOP, R along Rue de l'Anchre

T-L along Avenue de Bâle, on RHS of road

X (* Beware: road ahead gives priority to traffic turning across your path in both directions) continue along D1077/Avenue de Bâle, on demarcated (solid white line) bike lane on RHS of roadway

Cross rail line

Cycle lane ends, cross Swiss border at Customs post

[* Note: cyclists may cycle in both directions along one-way streets in Basel. If this applies, you will see a sign indicating this, so do look for them. If in doubt, don't do it !]

Continue along Hüninger Strasse

Cross rail lines

Bike lane resumes * Note: demarcated by broken yellow lines

Cross tram/rail lines

X (lights) L along Elsässer Strasse

X (lights) L along Voltaplatzstrasse

Continue across Dreirosenbrücke (Three Roses Bridge)

Continue along Dreirosenstrasse

(1st off bridge) R along Klybeckstrasse

(2nd) R along Offenburger Strasse, to end (at Rhine)

(Look for the sampan-like cable ferries crossing the river, one right ahead at this point, St.-Johanns-Fähre)

L along Unterer Rheinweg

Under Johanniterbrücke (motor bridge)

Under Mittlere Rheinbrücke (tram bridge)

Continue along Oberer Rheinweg

[To Badischer Bahnhof, L opposite the Münsterfähre (ferry) landing, along Riehentorstrasse and Riehenstrasse]

Under Wettsteinbrücke (motor bridge)

Immed. L along Theodorsgraben, away from river, alongside bridge

L towards bridge on bike path (opp. Alemannengasse), through park

Cross road (Wettsteinstrasse)

L along bike path on RHS of road crossing Wettstein bridge

Over bridge

* Beware of trams and their tracks

X (lights) (½)L along Dufourstrasse (sign Bahnhof)

X (lights) R along Aeschengraben, on bike path on RHS

X (lights) dismount, walk L across pedestrian crossing

Immed. R across pedestrian crossing

Continue to Basel Centralbahnhof (Basel SBB); route ends here.

Appendix A: Language Help

If you're not familiar with a foreign language, you won't be able to use it effectively by relying on anything as superficial as a glossary. However, having a collection of foreign words and phrases to hand can speed up communication on the basis of "show, point, and mime." It's obviously important, even vital, to be able to decipher wording on road and other signs, although pictograms are mostly used throughout Europe.

Even if you can ask questions with passable pronunciation, you need to understand the response. Fortunately, many people in the Netherlands and in Germany speak English, or understand some. Don't believe that everyone you meet will speak English—it's a common misconception that most Dutchmen and Germans do. Politeness translates well across language barriers and most people are willing to help friendly foreigners.

In Alsace, in general, people of the older generations will speak German as well as French. Younger people and, most often, policemen, will speak French and no German, but they are more likely to speak some English.

Switzerland is multilingual, Basel being where France, Germany, and Switzerland meet. You should have few problems with communication here, as the locals are quite used to dealing with diverse languages.

English/Dutch/German/French Cycling Dictionary

Mechanical

English	Dutch	German	French
Allen key	inbus sleutel	Inbusschlüssel	clé Allen
ball bearing	kogellager	Kugellager	roulement à billes
bell	bel	Klingel	sonnette
bicycle	fiets	Fahrrad	vélo
block (freewheel) remover	tandwielafnemer	Zahnkranzabnehmer	outil pour enlever l les vitesses
bolt	bout	Bolzen	boulon
bottom bracket	trapas huls	Innenlager	boîtier de pédalier
brakes	remmen	Bremsen	freins
brake lever	remgrepen	Bremsgriff	levier de freins
brake shoes/blocks	remblokjes	Bremsklötze	patins de freins
cable	kabel	Kabel	câble
chain	ketting	Kette	chaîne
chain link	schakel	Kettenglied	chaînon
chain wheel	kettingblad	Kettenblatt	plateau

English	Dutch	German	French
cog	kettingkrans	Ritzel	roue dentée
(bearing) cone	konus	Konus	cône
crank	crank	Tretkurbel	manivelle
crank axle	trapas	Kurbelachse	axe de pédalier
derailleur	derailleur	Schaltwerk	derailleur
flat (see puncture)			
freewheel	vrijloop	Freilauf	roue libre
front fork	voorvork	Vorderradgabel	fourche
gear	versnelling	Gang	vitesse
gear shift (lever)	commandeur	Schaltgriff	levier de vitesses
handlebars	stuur	Lenker	cintre
headset	balhoofdstel	Steuersatz	jeu de direction
hub	naaf	Nabe	moyeu
lock	slot	Schloß	serrure
nut	moer	Mutter	écrou
pedal	pedaal	Pedal	pédale
pump	pomp	Pumpe	pompe
puncture	lekke band	Reifenpanne	crevaison
repair kit	reparatie kit	Flickzeug	trousse de secours pour crevaisons
quick-release hub	uitvalnaaf	Schnellspann-Nabe	moyeu quick-release
rim	velg	Felge	jante
screw	schroef	Schraube	vis
screwdriver	schroevedraaier	Schraubenzieher	tournevis
seat (saddle)	zadel	Sattel	selle
seat post	zadelpen	Sattelstütze	tige de selle
spoke	spaak	Speiche	rayon
spoke key (spanner)	spaaksleutel	Nippelspanner	clé des rayons
spring	veer	Feder	ressort
sprocket	kettingwiel	Kettenrad	pignon
tool	gereedschap	Werkzeug	outil
tube (inner tube)	binnenband	Schlauch	tuyau
tyres	banden	Reifen	pneux
valve	ventiel	Ventil	valve /soupape
wheel	wiel	Rad	roue
wrench (spanner)	moersleutel	Schraubschlüssel	clé

English	Dutch	German	French

Lights

battery	batterij	Batterie	pile
dynamo (generator)	dynamo	Dynamo	dynamo
lamp (bulb)	gloeilamp	Birne	ampoule
front lamp	voorlicht	Scheinwerfer	phare
reflector	reflector	Rückstrahler	réflecteur

On the Road

ambulance	ziekenwagen	Krankenwagen	ambulance
bed and breakfast	kamer met ontbijt	Garni	chambre et petit déjeuner
bend (curve)	bocht	Kurve	virage
bridge	brug	Brücke	pont
footbridge	voetbrug	Fußgängerbrücke	passerelle
campground (site)	kampeerterrein	Campingplatz	terrain de camp-
ing	camping	camping	camping
for tent	voor tenten	Zeltplatz	pour les tentes
canal	kanaal	Kanal	canal
caution/prudence	voorzicht	Achtung/Vorsicht	attention /
closed/shut	dicht/gesloten	zu/geschlossen	fermé
road closed	weg gesloten	Strasse gesperrt	fermée a la circul station /barrée
coach (bus) station	bus station	Autobus Bahnhof	gare routiére
crossroads (intersection)	kruising/zijweg	Querstraße /Kreuzung	carrefour
cul-de-sac	doodlopende weg	Sackgasse	rue sans issue
cyclist	fietser	Radfahrer	cycliste
cycle path	fietspad	Radweg	piste cyclable
danger	gevaar	Gefahr	danger
depth	diepte	Tiefe	profondeur
deviation	afwijking	Abweichung	déviation
detour/diversion	omweg	Umleitung	detour
dike (levee)	dijk	Deich	digue
distance	afstand	Entfernung	distance
east	oost	Ost	est
emergency exit	nooduitgang	Notausgang	issue de secours
entrance	ingang/toegang	Eingang	entrée
exit (way out)	uitgang	Ausgang	sortie
ferry	veer	Fähre	bac/ferry
forbidden area	verboden gebied	Sperrgebiet	terrain défendu

English	Dutch	German	French
forbidden to	verboden voor	verboten zu	défense de
full (hotel, etc.)	vol	ausgebucht	compléte
get into lane	file	Einordnen	(mettre) en file
give way to traffic from the right	voorrang van rechts	Vorfahrt beachten	priorité à droite
height	hoogte	Höhe	hauteur
hostel	herberg	Herberge	auberge
youth hostel	jeugdherberg	Jugendherberge	auberge de jeunesse
hotel	hotel	Hotel	hôtel
information	informatie	Auskunft	information
inn	herberg	Gasthof	auberge
keep left	links houden	Links fahren	tenez votre gauche
keep right	rechts houden	Rechts halten	tenez votre droite
keep out	uitbliven	Fernhalten	défense d'entrer
length	lengte	Länge	longueur
level crossing	spoorweg overgang	Bahnübergang	passage à niveau
loose gravel	grind	Rollsplit	gravillons
map	kaart	Landkarte	carte
town map	stadsplan	Stadtplan	plan de ville
(map) scale	schaal	Maßstab	echelle
(map) key (legend)	verklaring	Zeichenerklärung	légende
No Entry (traffic)	verboden doorgang	Keine Zufahrt	entrée interdite
No Entry (people)	verboden toegang	Zutritt verboten	passage interdit
north	noord	Nord	nord
one way (traffic)	eenrichtingsverkeer	Einbahnstrasse	sens unique
pedestrians crossing	voetgangers-oversteekplaats	Fussgänger-Überweg	piétons passage clouté
police	politie	Polizei	police
(police) station	politieburo	Polizeiwache	commissariat
post office	Post	Post	P et T
roadblock	wegcontrole	Straßensperre	barrage routier
railroad (railway)	spoorweg	Eisenbahn	chemin de fer
station	station	Bahnhof	gare
right of way (over traffic from right)	voorrang	Vorfahrt	passage protégé
river	rivier	Fluß	fleuve
river police	rivier politie	Wasserpolizei	agents fluviale

English	Dutch	German	French
road	weg	Straße	route
roadworks	wegenwerken	Straßenbau	attention travaux
rockfall	vallende stenen	Steinschlag	chute de pierres
room to let	kamer (te huur)	Zimmer frei	chambre à louer
slow	langzaam	langsam	lentement
south	zuid	Süd	sud
Stop	Stop	Halt!	Stop
through traffic	doorgaand verkeer	Durchgangsverkehr	toutes directions
to rent (bikes etc)	te huur	zu vermieten	à louer
tourist information center	Inlichtingenburo	Verkehrsamt	syndicat d'initiative
town center	(stad) centrum	Stadtmitte	centre ville
track	pad	Spur	chemin
traffic (vehicles)	verkeer	Verkehr	circulation
circle (roundabout)	circulatieplein	Kreisverkehr	rond-point
lights	verkeerslichten	Verkehrsampeln	feux rouge
police	verkeerspolitie	Verkehrspolizei	police routière
warden (f.)	agente	Politesse	contractuelle
warden (m.)	agent	Hilfspolizist	contractuel
waterfall	waterval	Wasserfall	chute d'eau
width	breedte	Breite	largeur

Useful Phrases

The phonetic translation of the following phrases is based on my perception of how native English speakers could speak and be understood by Dutch, German and French native speakers. The English-speaking world is full of people with different accents and diversely acquired reading and listening skills and, therefore, various translations of words to sounds. I've used my knowledge of languages to create this emergency language.

Speak the sounds as you see and recognize them; the dashes (-) connect sounds making up one word.

Where is the restroom (toilet/WC) please?
D: Waar is het toilet, alstublieft? [V-ar iss hit toy-lit, ull-stoo-bleef-t?]
G: Wo sind die toiletten, bitte? [V-oh zint dee toy-let-tin, beet-uh?]
F: Ou sont les toilettes, s'il vous plait? [Oo sawn lay twah-let, seal voo play?]

Do you speak English?
D: Spreekt U Engels? [Spray-kt oo eng-il-s/]
G: Sprechen Sie Englisch? [Spray-shin zee ing-glish?]
F: Vous parlez anglais? [Voo par-lay-z-ah-n-glay/]

Can you help me, please?
D: Kunt U mij helpen, alstublieft? [Kint oo may hell-pin, ull-stoo-bleef-t?]
G: Können Sie mir bitte helfen? [Cur-nin zee m-ear beet-uh hell-fin?]
F: Vous-pouvez m'aider, s'il vous plait? [Voo poo-vay may-day, seal voo play?]

Are you from here (this town/area)?
D: Komt U van hier? [Corm-t oo fun hee-uh?]
G: Sind Sie von hier? [Zin-t zee f-on hee-uh-r?]
F: Vous êtes d'ici? [Voo-zet dee-see?]

Where is the nearest bicycle shop?
D: Waar is de dichtstbijzijnde fietsenwinkel? [V-ar iss d-uh dix-bay-zyn-der feets-in-v-ink-ill?]
G: Wo ist das nächste Fahrradgeschäft? [V-oh isst d-us next-uh far-art-gis-sheft?]
F: Il y a un magasin des velos près d'ici? [Ill-ear an mag-a-zan day vell-oh pray dee-see?]

The ... is broken/faulty.
D: De/Het ... is stuk/defect. [D-uh/Hit ... iss stick/d-uh-feck-t]
G: Der/Die/Das ... ist kaputt/defekt. [D-er/Dee/D-us ... iss-t cup-oo-t/day-feck-t]
F: Le/La ... est cassé/défecteux. [L-ur/L-ah ... eh cuss-ay/day-feck-ters]

Can you repair it?
D: Kunt U dat herstellen? [Kint oo d-uh-t hair-stell-in?]
G: Können Sie es reparieren? [Cur-nin zee ess rep-air-rear-in?]
F: Vous pouvez le réparer? [Voo poo-vay lur rep-ar-ray?]

How long will it take?
D: Hoe lang zal dat duren? [Hoo lung zull d-uh-t dee-rin?]
G: Wie lange wird es dauern? [Vee lung-uh veer-t ess dow-er-in?]
F: Cela prendra combien de temps? [Sell-ah pron-dr-uh corm-bee-arn d-uh tom-p?]

How much will it cost?
D: Hoe veel zal het kosten? [Hoo feel zull hit k-aw-s-tin?]
G: Wieviel wird es kosten? [Vee-feel veer-t ess k-aw-s-tin?]
F: Combien ça coûtera? [Corm-bee-arn s-ah coo-tare-ah]

It is too expensive
D: Het is te duur [Hit iss t-uh dee-uh-r]
G: Es ist zu teuer [Ess iss-t t-soo toy-uh]
F: C'est trop cher [Say tr-op share]

What is this called (in Dutch; German; French)?
D: Hoe heet dat in het Nederlands? [Hoo hay-it d-uh-t in hit   Nay-d-uh-l-uh-ndz?]
G: Was heißt das auf Deutsch? [Vus high-st d-uh-s ow-f doyt-sh?]
F: Comment dit-on en francais? [Corm-marn dee-torn arn fr-arn-say?]

What does … mean?
D: Wat betekent …? [V-uh-t b-uh-tay-kin-t …?]
G: Was bedeutet …? [V-us b-uh-doy-tit …?]
F: Qu'est-ce que … veut dire? [Kess-k-uh … v-er deer?]

Appendix B: Useful Addresses

Addresses and phone numbers often change. If you experience difficulties, check with your phone company. Note: London dialing codes are due to change in 2000 from 0171+ to 020 7+ and from 0181+ to 020 8+. Auto- operator assistance available during changeover and following six months.

Accommodation: Reservations And Information

Netherlands:

Netherlands Reservation Center (NRC), PO Box 404, NL-2260 AK Leidschendam, Phone (070) 3175456, Fax (070) 3202611, e-mail: info@hotelres.nl

Stichting Vrienden op de fietsen (Friends on bikes: overnight stays including breakfast with private persons, strictly only cyclists and walkers), Brahmsstraat 19, NL-6904 DA Zevenaar, Phone (0316) 524448; Club membership ± US $8 (GB £5), accommodation from U S$13 (GB £8) per night

Bed & Breakfast Holland, 27 Effie Road, London SW6 1EN, Phone (0171) 7315340, Fax (0171) 7367230; booking fee (£10) + accommodation ± US $50 (GB £30) per night.

Holland Tulip Parcs, Camping & Caravanning, Marijke Meustraat 112, NL-4818 LW Breda, Fax (076) 5207305

Germany:

ADZ (computerised reservation service), Corneliusstrasse 69, 60325 Frankfurt am Main, Phone (069) 740767

Hotel Reservation Service (HRS), Heumarkt 14, D-5000 Köln, Phone (0221) 20770

Agrar-Tours (Farm stays), Eschborner Landstrasse 122, D-60489 Frankfurt

UK only: fax on demand (pay line) service for hotels in Köln and Düsseldorf; pick up fax handset, dial 0891 669999; problems call 0990 100410

France (Alsace):

Gîtes de France:

1   Bas-Rhin: Service Loisirs-Accueil, 7 place des Meuniers, F-6700 Strasbourg, Phone (03) 88755650, Fax (03) 88230097

2   Haut-Rhin: Service Loisirs-Accueil, 1 rue Schlumberger, F-68006 Colmar, Phone (03) 89201062, Fax (03) 89233391

Hotel/restaurant Guide:

Tourisme Alsace, BP 357, F-68006 Colmar Cedex

Comité Régional du Tourisme d'Alsace, 6 avenue de la Marseillaise, BP 219, F-67005 Strasbourg Cedex, Phone (03) 88250166, Fax (03) 88521706

Switzerland:

Basel Hotelreservation/Service center, Messeplatz 7, CH-4021 Basel, Phone (061) 6862630, Fax (061) 6862184, e-mail: hotel@messebasel.ch

City-Information und Hotelreservation im Bahnhof SBB, Phone (061) 2713684, Fax (061) 2729342, e-mail: hotel@messebasel.ch

REKA (chalets/apartments), Schweizer Reisekasse, Neuengasse 15, CH-3001 Bern, Phone (031) 3296633, Fax (031) 3296601

Interhome Ltd. (chalets/apartments), 383 Richmond Road, Twickenham TW1 2EF, England, Phone (0181) 8911294, Fax (0181) 8915331

Airports and Airlines

Netherlands:

KLM (information/reservations) 0204 747747 (24 hours)

Schiphol Airport (Information) (06) 35034050

Germany:

Deutsche Lufthansa AG (Head Office, Köln), Phone (0221) 8261

Düsseldorf Airport (Information), Phone (0211) 4211

Frankfurt am Main Airport (Information), Phone (069) 6903051

Köln–Bonn Airport (Information), Phone (02203) 404001/2

France:

Air France, Phone (08) 36681048

Air Inter (domestic service), Phone (01) 45469000

EuroAirport (St. Louis Airport) Basel–Mulhouse, Phone (03) 89903111, Fax (03) 89902657

Strasbourg Airport, Phone (03) 88646767, Fax (03) 88688212

Switzerland

Swissair (Information), Phone (061) 2845522

EuroAirport (St. Louis Airport) Basel–Mulhouse (Information), Phone (061) 3252511

Bike Clubs and Organizations

Netherlands:

ENFB (Eerste Nederlandse Fietsers Bond; cycling advocacy organization) Posbus 2828, 3500GV Utrecht, Phone (030) 2918171; Fax (030) 2918188; www.enfb.org

Vrienden op de fiets (Friends on bikes: overnight stays including breakfast with private persons), Brahmstraat 19, NL-6904 DA Zevenaar, Phone (0316) 524448

Germany

Allgemeiner Deutscher Fahrrad-Club e.V. (ADFC: cycling club, information, maps), Postfach 107747, D-28077 Bremen, Phone (0421) 346290

France

Fédération Française de Cyclotourisme, 8 rue Jean-Marie Jégo, 75013 Paris, Phone (01) 44168888

England

CTC, 69 Meadrow, Godalming, Surrey GU7 3HS, England, Phone (01483) 417217, Fax (01483) 426994, e-mail: cycling@ctc.org.uk, Internet: http://www.ctc.org.uk

Camping Clubs, Organizations

Netherlands:

Netherlands Camping Club, Wolterstraat 99, NL-2871 ZM Schoonhoven, Phone (01823) 2144

Germany:

German Camping Club, Mandlstrasse 28, D-8000 München 40, Phone (089) 334021

France:

Touring Camping Caravanning France, 8 rue Lucien Sampaix, F-75010 Paris, Phone (01) 42407609

Switzerland:

Verband Schweizer Campings, Seestrasse 119, CH-3800 Interlaken, Phone (036) 233523, Fax (036) 232991

Friends of Nature

UK:

The Membership Secretary, Naturefriends Great Britain, Myra Gentle, 19 Parkside Drive, Exmouth, Devon EX8 4LA

Internet: http://www.homeusers.prestel.co.uk/parkside/naturefriends/

Coach and Bus (long distance)

Eurolines, 52 Grosvenor Gardens, London SW1W 0AU, Phone enquiries (01582) 404511, sales 0990 143219

European Bike Express (EBE), 31 Baker Street, Middlesbrough, Cleveland TS1 2LF, England, Phone (01642) 251440, Fax (01642) 232209, e-mail: bolero@jsdesign.demon.co.uk, Internet: http://www.jsdesign.demon.co.uk/bike.html

France:

Gare Routière Internationale, 28 Avenue du Général de Gaulle, 93541 Bagnolet, Phone 1 49725151

Embassies and Consulates

USA:

Netherlands Embassy, 4200 Wisconsin Avenue NW, Washington DC 20016, Phone (202) 2445300

German Embassy, 4645 Reservoir Road NW, Washington DC 20007, Phone (202) 2984000

French Embassy, 4101 Reservoir Road NW, Washington DC 20007, Phone (202) 9446000

Swiss Embassy, 2900 Cathedral Avenue NW, Washington DC 20008, Phone (202) 7457900

UK Embassy, 3100 Massachusetts Avenue NW, Washington DC 20008, Phone (202) 4621340

Canada:

German Embassy, 14th floor, 275 Slater Street, Ottawa, Ontario K1P 5H9, Phone (613) 2321101

French Embassy, 42 Sussex Drive, Ottawa, Ontario K1M 2C9, Phone(613) 7891795

Swiss Embassy, 5 Marlborough Avenue, Ottawa, Ontario K1N 8E6, Phone (613) 2351837

UK Embassy, British High Commission, 80 Elgin Street, Ottawa, Ontario K1P 5K7, Phone (613) 2371530

UK:

USA Embassy, 24 Grosvenor Square, London W1A 1AE, Phone (0171) 4999000, tube station: Bond Street

Canadian Embassy, Macdonald House, 1 Grosvenor Square, London W1X 0AB, Phone (0171) 2586600, tube station: Bond Street

German Embassy, 23 Belgrave Square, London SW1X 8PZ, Phone (0171) 2355033, visa information pay line (0891) 331166

French Embassy, 6a Cromwell Place, London SW7, Phone (0171) 8239555

Swiss Embassy, 16–18 Montagu Place, London W1H 2BQ, Phone (0171) 6166000, Fax (0171) 7247001, visa enquiries (0891) 331313 (Mon–Fri 09h00–12h00)

Eire (Republic of Ireland):

German Embassy, 31 Trimmleston Ave., Booterstown, Blackrock, Co Dublin, Phone 2693011

French Embassy, 36 Ailesbury Road, Dublin 4, Phone 2694777

Swiss Embassy, 6 Aylesbury Road, Ballsbridge, Dublin 4, Phone (1) 692515, Fax (1) 830344

Netherlands:

USA Embassy, Lange Voorhout 102, 2514 EJ Den Haag (The Hague), Phone 70-3109209

Germany:

USA Embassy, Deichmanns Aue 29, 53170 Bonn, Phone (0228) 3391

USA Consulates in Frankfurt am Main, Berlin, Hamburg, Leipzig, München and Stuttgart.

France:

USA Embassy, 2 Avenue Gabriel, 75008 Paris, Phone (1) 42961202

Canadian Embassy, 35 Avenue Montaigne, 75008 Paris, Phone (1) 44432900

Switzerland:

USA Embassy, Jubiläumstrasse 93, 3005 Bern, Phone (031) 3517011

Canadian Embassy, Kirchenfeldstrasse 88, 3000 Bern 6, Phone (031) 3526381

Ferry Bookings

UK:

Hoverspeed, Phone (01304) 240241, Fax (01304) 240088

North Sea Ferries, Phone (01482) 377177, Fax (01482) 706438

P & O European Ferries, Dover, Phone 0990 980980, Fax (01304) 223464

Sea France Ltd, Phone (01304) 212696, Fax (01304) 240033

Sealink UK Limited, Dover, Phone (01304) 203203

Stena Line, Phone 0990 707070, Fax (01233) 202361

Passport Offices/Agencies

USA Passports – Major Post Offices and Federal Offices process passport applications. Usually takes 6 weeks. For information, contact the Washington Passport Agency, Department of State, 1425 K Street, Washington, D.C. 20522, Phone (202) 3266060.

Canadian Passports – Issued by Regional Passport Offices or Passport Office, Department of External Affairs, Ottawa, ONT K1A 0G3.

Railway Operators and Agents

Belgium:

Belgian Railways information service, Phone (02) 5552555

Netherlands:

Holland Rail, Phone (06) 9292

Germany:

Zentrale der Deutschen Bundesbahn Hauptverwaltung (DB Head Office), Friedrich Ebert-Anlage 43–45, D-6000 Frankfurt am Main, Phone (0611) 2656108

British Rail, Phone (069) 232381

Switzerland (Basel):

Swiss Federal Railways (SBB), Phone (061) 2726767, pay info phone line 1572222, Internet: http://www.sbb.ch

German Railways (DB), Phone (061) 6915511

French Railways (SNCF), Phone (061) 2715033

UK:

British Rail (BR), Phone (0171) 8342345

European Rail Travel Centre, PO Box 303, Victoria Station, London SW1V 1JY

Eurostar (Channel tunnel express), Phone 0990 330003 and 0345 881881

Eurotrain/Campus Travel (cheap tickets for travellers under 26 years of age), Phone (0171) 7303402

French Railways, 179 Piccadilly, London W1V 0BA, motorail service bookings Phone (0171) 2037000, brochures Phone (0181) 8808161, group travel Phone (0171) 6339000, also The Rail Shop (French Railways only), Phone 0990 300003 (booking and info), 0990 024000 (24 hours brochure and timetable)

German Railways (DB) agency, 18 Conduit Street, London W1R 9TD, bookings phone (0171) 3170919, fax (0171) 4914689, brochures (01476) 591311, timetable and info pay line (0891) 887755

Le Shuttle (Channel tunnel shuttle vehicle service), P O Box 300, Folkstone, Kent CT19 4QW, Phone 0990 353535

Netherlands Railways, Chase House, Gilbert Street, Ropley, Hampshire SO24 0BY, Phone (01962) 773646, Fax (01962) 773625

Rhine Ship Operators

USA:

KD German Rhine Line, 150 Hamilton Avenue, White Plains, NY 10601, Phone 914-948–3600

Switzerland:

Basler Personenschiffahrtsgesellschaft (BPG) (Passenger ship Information), Blumenrain 2, Basel, Phone (061) 2612400

Student and Youth Travel

Council for International Education Exchange (CIEE– for International Student Identity card + Student Travel

Catalog), 205 East 42nd Street, New York, NY 10017, USA

GO 25 International Youth Travel Cards, FIYTO, Bredgade 25H, 1260 Copenhagen K, Denmark

Student Cards (International)

The International Student Identity Card (ISIC) Association, PO Box 9098, DK 1000 Copenhagen, Denmark, Internet: http://www.istc.org, e-mail: isicinfo@istc.org

Tourist Board Offices

USA:

Netherlands Board of Tourism (NBT):

New York: 21st floor, 355 Lexington Ave., New York, NY 10017, Phone (212) 3707367, Fax (212) 3709507

Chicago: Suite 326, 225 North Michigan Ave., Chicago, IL 60601, Phone (312) 8190300, Fax (312) 8191740

San Francisco: Suite 305, 90 New Montgomery St., San Francisco, CA 94105, Phone (415) 5436772, Fax (415) 4954925

German National Tourist Office (DZT):

New York: 122 East 42nd Street, Chanin Building, 52nd floor, New York, NY 10168–0072, Phone (212) 6617200, Fax (212) 6617174

Chicago: Suite 2525, 401 North Michigan Avenue, Chicago, IL 60611, Phone (312) 6440723, Fax (312) 6440724

Los Angeles: Suite 750, 11766 Wilshire Boulevard, Los Angeles, CA 90025, Phone (310) 5759799, Fax (310) 5751565

French National Tourist Office:

New York: Suite 222, 610 Fifth Avenue, New York, NY 10020–2452, Phone (212) 7571683

Swiss National Tourist Office (SNTO):

New York: Swiss Center, 608 Fifth Avenue, New York, NY 10020, Phone (212) 7575944, Fax (212) 2626116

Chicago: Suite 2930, 150 North Michigan Avenue, Chicago, IL 60601, Phone (312) 6305840, Fax (312) 6305848

San Francisco: 260 Stockton Street, San Francisco, CA 94108, Phone (415) 3622260

Canada:

Netherlands Board of Tourism, Suite 710, 25 Adelaide Street East, Toronto, Ontario M5C 1Y2, Phone (416) 3631577, Fax (416) 3631470

German National Tourist Board, Suite 604, North Tower, 175 Bloor Street East, Toronto, Ontario M4W 3R8, Phone (416) 9681570, Fax (416) 9681986, e-mail: germanto@idirect.com

French National Tourist Office, Suite 490, Tour Esso, 1981 Avenue McGill College, Montreal, Quebec H3A 2W9, Phone (514) 2884264

Swiss National Tourist Office, 926 The East Mall, Etobicoke (Toronto), Ontario M9B 6K1, Phone (416) 6952090, Fax (416) 6952774

UK:

Netherlands Board of Tourism, PO Box 523, GB-London SW1E 6NT, Phone (0171) 6300451, Fax (0171) 8287941, pay info line (0891) 717777

German National Tourist Board, PO Box 2695, GB-London W1A 3TN,

Phone (0171) 3170908, brochure orders pay line (0891) 600100, Fax (0171) 4956129, live operator info line (Mon–Fri, 10h00–12h00 and 14h00–16h00)(0171) 4930080 , e-mail: 106167,3216@compuserve.com, Internet: http://www.germany-tourism.de

French National Tourist Office, 178 Piccadily, GB-London W1V 0AL, Phone (0171) 4917622, pay info line (0891) 244123, e-mail: piccadilly@mdlfdemon.co.uk, Internet: http://www.franceguide.com/.

Swiss National Tourist Office (SNTO), Swiss Centre, Swiss Court, GB-London W1V 8EE, Phone (0171) 7341921, Fax (0171) 4374577, e-mail: stlondon@switzerlandtourism.ch, Internet: http://www.switzerlandtourism.ch

Netherlands:

Netherlands Board of Tourism

Internet: http://www.nbt.nl/holland

Germany:

Deutsche Zentrale für Tourismus e.V. (German Tourist Board), Beethovenstrasse 69, D-60325 Frankfurt am Main, Phone (069) 97464, Fax (069) 751903, Internet: http://www.germany-tourism.de

Deutscher Fremdenverkehrsverband, Niebuhrstrasse 16 b, 53113 Bonn, Phone (0228) 214071/2

Bonn Verkehrsamt, Münsterstrasse 20, Phone (0228) 773466

Düsseldorf Verkehrsverein, Konrad Adenauer-Platz, Phone (0211) 350505

Frankfurt am Main Verkehrsamt, Gutleutstrasse 7, Phone (069) 21201

Köln Verkehrsamt, Am Dom 1, Phone (0221) 2213345

France (Bas-Rhin and Haut-Rhin):

l'Agence de Développement Touristique du Bas-Rhin, 9 rue du Dôme – BP 53, F-67061 Strasbourg, Phone (03) 88154580, Fax (03) 88756764, e-mail: alsace-tourisme@sdv.fr

Association Departmentale du Tourisme du Haut-Rhin, Maison du Tourisme, 1 rue Schlumberger, BP 337, F-68006 Colmar, Phone (03) 89201068, Fax (03) 89233391

Switzerland:

Swiss National Tourist Office (SNTO), Head Office, Bellariastrasse 38, CH-8027 Zürich, Phone (01) 2881111, Fax (01) 2881205, pay info phone line 157120111, pay events phone line 157120101, e-mail: postoffice@switzerlandtourism.ch, Internet: http://www.switzerlandtourism.ch

Basel Tourismus, Schifflände 5, CH-4001, Basel, Information: Phone (061) 2686868, Fax (061) 2686870 (Mon–Fri 08h30–18h00 + Sat 10h00–16h00), e-mail: office@baseltourismus.ch, Internet: www.baseltourismus.ch

Youth Hostels Associations

USA:

Hostelling International, American Youth Hostels, Suite 840, 733 15th Street NW, Washington DC 20005, Phone (202) 7836161, Toll free in USA and Canada only (1) 800 - 4446111, Fax (202) 7836171, Internet: http://

www.taponline.com (go to travel section)

Canada:

Hostelling International, Canada (National Office), 400–205 Catherine Street, Ottawa, Ontario K2P 1C3, Phone (613) 2377884, Fax (613) 2377868

Eire (Republic of Ireland):

Irish Youth Hostel Association, 61 Mountjoy Street, Dublin 7, Phone (01) 8304555, Fax (01) 8305808

England, Wales:

Youth Hostels Association (England & Wales), Trevelyan House, 8 St. Stephen's Hill, St. Albans, Herts AL1 2DY, Phone (01727) 855215, Internet: http://www.yha-england-wales.org.uk

Scotland:

Scottish Youth Hostels Association, 7 Glebe Crescent, Stirling, FK8 2JA, Phone (01786) 451181

Northern Ireland:

Youth Hostel Association of Northern Ireland, 22 Donegal Road, Belfast BT12 5JN, Phone (01232) 315435, Fax (01232) 439699

Australia:

Australian Youth Hostels Association Inc., Level 3, 10 Mallett St., Camperdown, NSW 2050, Phone (02) 5651699, Fax (02) 5651325, Internet: http://www.yha.org.au, e-mail: yha@zeta.org.au

New Zealand:

Youth Hostels Association of New Zealand Inc., PO Box 436, 173 Gloucester St., Christchurch 1, Phone (03) 3799970, Fax (03) 3654476, e-mail hostel.operations@yha.org.nz

South Africa:

Hostels Association of South Africa, 101 Boston House, Strand Street, Cape Town 8001, Phone (021) 4191853, Fax (021) 216937

The Netherlands:

Stichting Nederlandse Jeugdherberg Centrale (NJHC), Prof Tulpplein 4, 1018 GX Amsterdam, Phone (020) 6222859, Fax (020) 6390199

Germany:

Deutsches Jugendherbergswerk (DJH), Postfach 1455, D-32704 Detmold, Phone (05231) 740139, Fax (05231) 740166

France:

Fédération Unie des Auberges de Jeunesse (FUAJ), 27 rue Pajol, 75018 Paris, Phone (01) 44898727, Fax (01) 44898710

FUAJ Alsace, 13 rue des Veaux, 67000 Strasbourg, Phone (03) 88240309, Fax (03) 88240498

Switzerland

Schweizerischer Bund für Jugendherbergen (SBJ), Schaffhauserstrasse 14, PO Box 161, CH-8042 Zürich, Phone (01) 3025503, Fax (01) 3016671

Bibliography

Janet Aldridge et al. *Off the beaten track: Germany*. Moorland Publishing Co Ltd, UK, 1994.

Neil Alexander. *The Swiss: How they live and work*. Praeger Publishers Inc, New York, 1976.

John Ardagh. *Exploring Rural Germany*. Christopher Helm (Publishers) Ltd., UK, 1990.

Babel Translations (transl. and ed.). *Germany*. Phaidon Press Ltd., Oxford 1986.

Bartholomew Road Atlas, Germany. RV Reise- und Verkehrsverlag Gmbh, Berlin, 1991.

James Bentley. *Alsace*. Aurum Press Ltd., London, 1988.

James Bentley. *Blue Guide Germany*. A & C Black, London, 1987.

Douglas Botting (Editor). *Wild France: Traveller's Guide*. Sheldrake Press Ltd, London, 1992.

Philip Bristow. *Through the German Waterways*. Nautical Publishing Co., Lymington, UK, 1975.

Helen Colijn. *The Backroads of Holland*. Bicycle Books Inc., San Francisco, 1992.

Martin Collins et al. *France, Off the Beaten Track*. Moorland Publishing Co. Ltd., Ashbourne, Derbyshire, 1988.

Pat and Hazel Constance. *The Visitor's Guide to Holland*. Moorland Publishing Co. Ltd., Ashbourne, Derbyshire, 1987.

Eberhard Czaya. *Rivers of the World*. Cambridge University Press, Cambridge, 1983.

Dictionary of Biography. Helicon Publishing Ltd., Ware (UK), 1994.

Shirley Eu-Wong. *Culture Shock! Switzerland*. Kuperard (London) Ltd, London, 1996.

H. Constance Hill. *Fielding's Holland 1994*. Fielding Worldwide Inc, California, USA 1994.

Ann Hoffmann. *The Dutch: How they Live and Work*. David & Charles (Holdings) limited, Newton Abbot, UK, 1973.

James Hogarth (transl.). *Baedeker's France*. Jarrold & Sons Ltd., Norwich, 1984..

James Hogarth (transl.). *Baedeker's Germany*. Jarrold & Sons Ltd., Norwich, 1996.

Hostelling International. IYHF, Welwyn Garden City (UK), 1996.

Walter Marsden. *The Rhineland*. B.T. Batsford Ltd., London, 1973.

John Marshall. *Visitor's Guide, Switzerland*. Moorland Publishing Co Ltd, UK, 1995.

F.J. Monkhouse. *A regional geography of Western Europe*, 4th ed.. Longman Group Limited, London, 1974.

Theodor Muller-Alfeld (Editor) et al. *Portrait of a River, The Rhine*. Umschau Verlag, Frankfurt/Main, 1956.

E.A. Pearce and C.G.Smith. *The World Weather Guide*. Hutchinson & Co., London, 1984.

Roger Pilkington. *Small Boat on the Lower Rhine*. Macmillan, London, 1970.

Roger Pilkington. *Small boat on the Moselle*. Macmillan, London, 1968.

Roger Pilkington. *Small boat on the Upper Rhine*. Macmillan, London, 1971.

Goronwy Rees. *The Rhine*. Weidenfeld and Nicholson, London, 1967.

Dr. Ute Gräfin Rothkirch (BMU) and Verena Klinger (BMU) (Editors). *Environmental Policy in Germany*. Federal Ministry for the Environment. Bonn, 1994.

Adam Ruck, ed. Ingrid Morgan. *The Holiday Which? Guide to France*. Hodder and Stoughton, London, 1985.

Lewis Spence. *Myths and Legends of Germany*. Studio Editions Ltd., London, 1993.

John Tomes. *Blue Guide Holland*. A & C Black, London, 1989.

Rick Stone. *Rick Stone's Europe Through the Back Door*. John Muir Publishing, Santa Fe, NM, 2000.

Grant Uden. *A dictionary of Chivalry*. Longmans Young Books Ltd., London, 1968.

Patricia Vance. *Bicycle Touring*. Van der Plas Publications, San Francisco, 2000.

Rob Van der Plas. *The Bicycle Touring Manual*. Bicycle Books, Inc., San Francisco, 1987.

Tim and Glenda Wilhelm. *The Bicycle Touring Book*. Rodale Press, Emmaus, PA, 1980

Index

Other Books from Cycle Publishing / Van der Plas Publications

We publish many different books on the subject of cycling. Our books are available through the book trade in the U.S., the U.K., Canada, and Australia. For a complete listing, or to order directly from us, please visit our web site. You can also contact us directly.

Cycle Publishing / Van der Plas Publications
1282 7th Avenue
San Francisco, CA 94122
U.S.A.
Tel.:   (415) 665-8214
Fax: (415) 753-8572
E-mail: con.tact@cyclepublishing.com
Website: http://www.cyclepublishing.com